War Dance at Fort Marion

Plains Indian War Prisoners

BRAD D. LOOKINGBILL

UNIVERSITY OF OKLAHOMA PRESS : NORMAN

Library of Congress Cataloging-in-Publication Data

Lookingbill, Brad D., 1969—
War dance at Fort Marion Plains Indians war prisoners /
Brad D. Lookingbill.
p. cm.
Includes bibliographical references and index.
ISBN 978-0-8061-3739-1 (cloth)
ISBN 978-0-8061-4467-2 (paper)
1. Indians of North America—Great Plains—History—Sources.
2. Indians of North America—Relocation—Florida—Castillo de San
Marcos National Monument (Saint Augustine) 3. Indian prisoners—
Florida—Castillo de San Marcos National Monument (Saint Augustine)
4. Prisoners of war—Florida—Castillo de San Marcos National Monument
(Saint Augustine) 5. Castillo de San Marcos National Monument
(Saint Augustine, Fla.)—History—Sources. I. Title.
E78.G73L67 2006
978.004'9700922—dc22
2005052900

War Dance at Fort Marion

Contents

Illustrations

Preface and Acknowledgments

THIS BOOK EMERGED FROM MY RESEARCH on Plains Indian war prisoners. During summer breaks and a sabbatical, I visited archives, libraries, and museums from Fort Leavenworth, Kansas, to Carnegie, Oklahoma. For one vacation, I flew to St. Augustine, Florida, to walk the ground that the war prisoners once tread. Other trips took me to Washington, D.C.; Hampton, Virginia; New Haven, Connecticut; and Carlisle, Pennsylvania. With my laptop computer at my side, I traveled many of the roads taken by the main characters of this memorable story.

My version of that story unfolds in the following pages. I attempt to describe a collective historical experience chronologically, however complex or chaotic that experience might have been. I have tried to compose each episode using colorful anecdotes and dramatic motifs. I doubt that I get the story straight at every turn, but narrative history still seems to me worth doing. Regardless of its theoretical shortcomings, narration encourages us to account for facts in a clear and accessible style. It is difficult for an author to explain what happened in the past without artfully telling a story.

The bulk of the evidence for this story derives from primary documents, particularly memoirs, scrapbooks, newspapers, letters, memoranda, and pictographs. To rescue key participants from anonymity, I weave their first-hand accounts into the fabric of the narrative. Because of incorrect or unclear punctuation in some sources, I have edited and polished the quotations without altering their obvious messages. I allow the participants to speak for themselves to a great extent, even when their recorded words might appear offensive, twisted, or antiquated. Likewise, Plains Indian names contain consonants, pronunciations, and configurations that defy easy conversion into English. To compound the confusion, an individual could carry many aliases. For the sake of readability, I have used the simplest English translation of each name as it was originally transcribed and have listed the names in the appendix. I mean no disrespect to anyone whose identity might have been modified by the documentary records, which are carefully referenced in the notes.

Words fail to convey the depth of my gratitude to those who guided me in my study of the records. Roger Bromert suggested that I study the Indian history of Oklahoma and remains a cherished mentor. Gerald Thompson before his passing helped me to rethink my first impressions of the relationship between the Plains Indians and the United States military. Alvin O. Turner pointed me toward Making Medicine, a Cheyenne prisoner who lived a remarkable life. Jim Anquoe, a descendant of one of the Kiowa prisoners, personally shared his insights with me. Also, I have been helped by the work of Parker Mackenzie, a Kiowa scholar distinguished by what he called a "Rainy Mountain Ph.D." He left his research notes in the safekeeping of the Oklahoma Historical Society, which carefully preserved them. John Sipes, a Cheyenne oral historian, preserved a few prisoner reminiscences, some of which have been transcribed and placed online by Barbara Landis. A great deal of ledger art came to my attention through the published collections of Karen Daniels Petersen and other art historians. In one way or another, all of these individuals were crucial to the making of this book.

This book would not have been completed without the generous support of several institutions. As a Frederick W. Beinecke Fellow, I enjoyed every minute of my time at Yale University and the Beinecke Rare Book and Manuscript Library. George Miles, the curator of the Western Americana collection, treated me to a meal and personally aided my search for materials. Professor John Mack Faragher gave me helpful advice on strategies for approaching the subject. Una Belau, the senior administrative assistant, handled the details of my fellowship. To all the archivists and librarians at the Beinecke Library, thank you for facilitating my work. Due to the careful attention of Eleanor Roach, the research administrator at the American Philosophical Society, I received the Phillips Fund Grant for Native American Research. As a faculty member at a school covenanted with the Disciples of Christ, I benefited from the Phillips University Legacy Foundation Award. In addition, Columbia College of Missouri provided me with a Faculty Development Summer Research Grant and a one-semester sabbatical.

Of course, many other good people advanced my work. I wish to thank the staffs of the Western History Collection at the University of Oklahoma; the Oklahoma Historical Society; the Kansas Historical Society; the Missouri Historical Society; the St. Augustine Historical Society; the Cumberland County Historical Society; the Hampton University Museum and Archives; the National Archives and Records Administration; and the Smithsonian Institution. In particular, I appreciate David R. Hunt of the Smithsonian, who unpacked several stored plaster masks for me. I enjoyed the informative conversations I had with Towana Spivey, the Director of the Fort Sill Museum, and Joe E. Mills, park ranger at the Castillo de San Marcos National Monument. Susan Keeter of Grace Church in Syracuse, New York, sent to me a brochure on an event to honor Native Americans. Conferences sponsored by Phi Alpha Theta, the Southwestern Historical Association, the Society for Environmental History, the Council on America's Military Past, and the Society for the History of Education provided scholarly venues for early drafts of chapters. Special thanks to David Wallace Adams for sharing a panel with me and to Lisa M. Miles and Eileen Tamura for giving me written comments.

I am fortunate to work at Columbia College, where numerous colleagues sustain my intellectual curiosity. I am indebted to David Roebuck, Anthony Alioto, Michael Polley, Rebecca Durrer, Kathleen Fitzgerald, Brian Kessel, Mark Price, Larry West, Julie Estabrooks, Jack Barnhouse, Liz Metscher, and Jim Metscher. I received wonderful feedback from Robert Boon and the honors students in the Gilded Age colloquium. Justin Williams helped me to prepare the index. At the College's Stafford Library, Cindy Cole, Allison Ehret, Lucia D'Agostino, Mary Batterson, Vandy Evermon, and Janet Caruthers tracked down monographs, articles, and facts that might have otherwise eluded me. At the First Christian Church in Columbia, Reverend John Yonker, a College board member, allowed me to present my work in evening forums. The College administration, particularly Gerald Brouder and Terry Smith, took a personal interest in the book.

I wish to express my personal appreciation to the University of Oklahoma Press for publishing this book. Alessandra Jacobi and Jo Ann Reece helped to direct me through the process. Their faith in the project moved mountains for me. It was my privilege to have worked with such an honored and distinguished team of editors, including Marian J. Stewart, Julie Shilling, and Jay Allman. Of course, I benefited from the constructive comments of several anonymous reviewers. Even though the result does not reflect every one of their suggestions, I hope that my version of the story will open a door so that others can explore what happened to the Plains Indian war prisoners.

Most of all, my wife Deidra deserves an enormous amount of credit for this book. A gifted writer, she read early drafts and saved me from several mistakes. She created maps, indexed pages, and prepared images for publication. She fixed the computer whenever it crashed and kept our dog, Geronimo, entertained whenever I was absent. She even nudged her brother, Corey, into taking me to Las Vegas to get me away from the tyranny of the blank page. Through it all, she shared with me the love that makes everything seem possible. Whatever in the book is artful must be credited to her and to many others, but its errors are mine alone.

It is often said that the past is a foreign country, but writing this book feels to me much like going home. I am a native of western Oklahoma and grew up in the heart of what once was known as Indian Territory. So I dedicate this book to my mother, Bernita, who never let me forget my roots in the country along the Red River.

War Dance at Fort Marion

Prologue

FOR AMERICAN INDIANS, THE WORD "medicine" denotes mysterious power. Consider the Kiowa, who speak of an energy everywhere called *dwdw*. They venerate its presence in the land, sky, hills, rivers, plants, and animals. It manifests in sacred space as thunder, lightning, whirlwinds, and tornadoes. In times of crisis, eminent visionaries influence others through their capacity to communicate with the Great Spirit.[1] For the Cheyenne, the word *pauwau* signifies a ritual ceremony conducted by a leader to renew and to regenerate a tribe. It derives from an Algonquian term for "medicine maker," but it generally references any gathering in which a tribal headman participates. In the modern era, the term represents pan-Indian events that revolve around dancing, drumming, and singing.[2] As the world turns, Native people continuously make medicine to perpetuate the circle of life.

Medicine represents a special force in the Native universe. It can be used to heal the sick, but it also can be used to chastise with disease or even sudden death. It controls natural events such as drought or flooding. It imparts dreams about the future as well as nightmares from the past. It guides tribal councils in their deliberations. It prepares warrior societies for buffalo hunts and war paths. It fosters diplomacy and inspires alliances. In its broadest sense, it evokes the will to survive. Traditional artistry uses it to convey the richness of collective memories and consciousness. Generations of American Indians have lived by the knowledge that each person makes medicine to empower oneself in the physical realm.[3]

Beginning in 1492, the non-Indian occupants of the Americas forced the Indians to live with a world of new challenges. The essence of "Indianness" withstood pandemics, invasion, and ethnic cleansing. The leadership of the first nations of North America responded to adversity in diverse and ingenious ways. However stressed indigenous cultures became after conquest, they retained an astonishing degree of vitality. Rather than vanishing, they adapted and overcame. Despite relentless assaults upon Native communities, their strategies for survival continued to demonstrate their viability and integrity. They played critical roles in shaping a history replete with triumphs and tragedies.[4] Over the centuries, most fought the good fight in what historian D'Arcy McNickle once described as an "Indian War that never ends."[5]

To facilitate the expansion of the United States, the federal government extended the Indian wars into the West. Beginning in the nineteenth century, Congress appropriated money for the "civilization fund" used by missionaries to enter the "Indian frontier." Driven by an ideology of "manifest destiny," officials in Washington, D.C., presumed that Indians represented an inferior race to Europeans and their descendents. The policy makers encouraged schooling on reservations, where religious, academic, and practical instruction would "uplift" the unfortunate ones. For instance, academies founded at Fort Leavenworth and at Fort Coffee offered training in manual labor to indigenous populations. After the American Civil War, day and parochial schools spread across the trans-Mississippi region. By the early 1870s, Howard University in the nation's capital undertook an experiment to educate three Indians, including a Cheyenne and an Arapaho. Designed almost exclusively by non-Indians, the educational programming of the Bureau of Indian Affairs began to proliferate.[6]

Historians consider the incarceration of Plains Indian war prisoners a turning point for the educational programming. James L. Haley closed his narrative about the "Buffalo War" with the exile of resistance leaders from Indian Territory to Florida's Fort Marion (the present-day Castillo de San Marcos), where they remained as "tourist attractions" from 1875 to 1878. Karen Daniels Petersen called them the "first exponents of the Contemporary school of Indian art." With a host of patrons circulating through St. Augustine, they became an "artist colony" in the resort community. In an award-winning study of Indian education, David Wallace Adams wrote that the prison school at the old Spanish castle constituted a "bold experiment." He found that it served as a model for the programs educating children at off-reservation boarding schools in later years. In fact, Adams called it "education for extinction," an allusion to cultural genocide. Generally, historians view the education of the "Florida boys" as either the twilight of one era or the dawn of another.[7]

Richard Henry Pratt, a U.S. Army officer deployed to Fort Marion, supervised the "Florida boys." That officer observed first-hand what he called "Indianism," denouncing it whenever he saw it. On his watch, he later insisted, "those hardened leaders became, in some measure, reconstructed to an industrious producing basis of thought and action, and they are today reported to be about the only exceptions to savage life and superstition among their tribes."[8] Writing to President Rutherford B. Hayes, he recalled that General of the Army William T. Sherman had "endorsed my course at St. Augustine." His division commander, Lieutenant General Philip H.

Sheridan, saluted him as well.[9] Speaking to the National Convention of Charities and Correction, Pratt celebrated the education of chiefs and warriors:

A great General has said that the only good Indian is a dead one, and that high sanction of his destruction has been an enormous factor in promoting Indian massacres. In a sense I agree with the sentiment, but only in this; that all the Indian there is in a race should be dead. Kill the Indian in him and save the man.[10]

Inspired by the treatment of the war prisoners, Pratt's words became a mantra for federal Indian policy in America's Gilded Age.

The story of the war prisoners begins with the struggles in Indian Territory for American Indian unity. The resistance leaders conducted insurgencies against the occupation of their homeland, but their militant uprising failed. Once the U.S. Army defeated the buffalo-hunting nations, they detained the headmen and their loyalists. Totaling seventy-two in number, the detainees included Southern Cheyenne, Kiowa, Comanche, and Arapaho Indians. A Caddo was added to their lot. Two women and one child joined with the men, though only one woman was counted as a prisoner. The war prisoners experienced an arduous passage overland from the guardhouse at Fort Sill to the casemates at Fort Marion. Bound by chains and guarded by soldiers, they endured a journey into the unknown. Within the prison cells, they began a path to recovery from the trauma of exile. Showing no fear, the chiefs and the warriors seemed willing to learn something from those who had fought them on the battlefield. Eager to gain access to the power of their wartime adversaries, they lived through the agony of defeat.

The war prisoners showed great strength while overcoming many obstacles. They repaired and remodeled the old Spanish castle. They donned uniforms and performed guard duty. They mastered drill and inspections. They honed skills for reading, writing, and arithmetic. They studied behind the enemy's lines and used the knowledge imposed from the outside-in to sustain traditions from the inside-out. They looked ahead to a moment when they could return to their families and their friends with honors. Meanwhile, they met curious strangers in the ancient city of St. Augustine. They traded with the non-Indians and profited from the tourist industry. They practiced their traditional ceremonies in performances for visitors to the fort. Women and clergy in town volunteered to instruct the rank and file, who distinguished themselves as students. The day to day routine facilitated their movement from battlefields to classrooms. Officials in Washington, D.C., doubted the efficacy of schooling adults and preferred to hand out rations to them instead. The U.S. Army treated them otherwise, and recruited a few good soldiers in the process. Without a doubt, the art of survival illustrated their finest accomplishment at Fort Marion.

During their last days at Fort Marion, the survivors punctuated their desires to save both the Indian and the man. Beyond the military outpost, a number of them chose to study in places such as the Hampton Institute in Virginia. One group trained in New York to become Episcopalian missionaries. A few labored at the army barracks in Carlisle, Pennsylvania, which became the first off-reservation Indian boarding school. They followed long and winding roads that eventually resulted in their repatriation. Even though some died in captivity, many of the returning students emerged as leaders on their native grounds. However, the Indian Bureau expressed little interest in a program of continuing education for them. Instead, federal policymakers launched a campaign targeting Indian children for enrollment in educational institutions.

By concentrating on the bleakness of the educational institutions, historians have told only part of the story. The painful parts, which inform a tragic view of American Indians, include tales of terror, abuse, shame, futility, and death. Unfortunately, they perpetuate a misleading impression of the students at Fort Marion. Labels such as the "Florida boys" insinuate a pejorative based upon the language of paternalism. The "white man's Indian" appears to be nothing if not a "ward" of the federal government, thus reinforcing the myth of a "savage." Depicted in a state of arrested development, the "children of nature" seem "pacified" by the overwhelming forces arrayed against them.[11] However, the men who waged war against the armed forces of the U.S. were not dependent, school-age children. In the prison house of education, adult learners remained calculating, savvy, and agile. Even if incarceration controlled the bodies of the condemned, it did not break their spirits. Under the gaze of military authorities, they found a way out of its iron cages. What did not kill the Indians made them stronger.[12]

This book describes the capture, incarceration, and return of the Plains Indian war prisoners at Fort Marion. In doing so, it asks an essential question: How did they survive the ordeal? It features mysterious figures called such names as Sky Walker, Roman Nose, and Pile of Rocks. A kind of collective biography, it unveils the lives of the warriors and the chiefs behind the walls. It shows the unintended consequences of their confinement, including the meeting of individuals from different cultures. Going inside the fortress, it highlights the flexible responses of the mature thinkers to a coercive regime. They borrowed tools, gained insight, and gathered intelligence in exile. Recognizing the constraints, they discerned ways to dance in the stronghold without forgetting who they were. They were determined to pass on what they knew to the next generation. Their strategic adaptations made their experiences multifaceted, helping to turn Fort Marion into a camp, a shop, a theater, a school, and a shrine. Their actions spoke volumes about the power of Indian leadership. They lived a decidedly human tale of emergence in America's Gilded Age. Though they went their separate ways, they made medicine with those who tried to change their world.

Chapter 1
Spirited Resistance
War on the Southern Plains

SOUTHERN PLAINS INDIANS LIVED in the heart of the North American grasslands, situated between the 98th and 103rd meridians and ranging from the Platte River southward to the Rio Grande. The federal government endeavored to dispossess them of their homeland, creating the conditions for the seizure of Indian country by non-Indians. The Buffalo War, which formally began in 1874, originated in the preceding decades of sporadic combat and escalating violence. Forces of the U.S. Army were deployed against the people of the Kiowa, Comanche, Southern Cheyenne, and Arapaho nations. Even though Native leaders disagreed about their strategic and tactical responses, they shared a sense of power flowing from the vast bison herds. Ultimately, they watched in horror as their primary source of food, clothing, and shelter was virtually annihilated.[1] The annihilation constituted what the Kiowa author N. Scott Momaday once termed "deicide," that is, the murder of a sacred being. Determined to fight using any means necessary, the tribal councils of the buffalo-hunting nations called for spirited resistance.[2]

One buffalo-hunting nation, the Cheyenne, maintained a balance of power in the Southern Plains before the war erupted. Calling themselves "The People," these Algonquian speakers believed that they were made from the "sacred red earth mother" to walk "the road of life." They migrated to the mid-latitude prairies during the eighteenth century, practicing small-scale agriculture in the river valleys. They developed their political economy by hunting the plentiful game and by monopolizing the trading corridors between the Missouri River and the Rocky Mountains. The Northern and Southern Cheyenne, though geographically separated by the Platte River, shared a linguistic and cultural system. The latter concluded an alliance with the Arapaho, a smaller group whose name meant "traders." In fact, the acquisition of the horse enabled the Cheyenne to expand their hunting grounds. In addition, they exchanged buffalo hides for finished goods, particularly firearms. By the mid-nineteenth century, they numbered more than two thousand in population. The Cheyenne were revered not only for their strength but also for their affluence.[3]

Consider Nockkoist, whose Cheyenne name meant "Bear's Heart." Using pictographic drawings, he recorded his own exploits on tipis, clothing, hides, and shields. His earliest and most vivid memories included buffalo hunts with his father and kin. Whereas the Cheyenne subsisted by following the mobile herds, he cherished his semi-sedentary existence. He remembered fashioning lodges and moving encampments with the change of the seasons. Much of his world centered upon the family circle and their camp sites. He enjoyed grand feasts and annual gatherings such as the sun dance, a sacred ceremony that his people believed regenerated life. Instead of suffering toil and routine, he mused, the Cheyenne "played all the time." After his father acquired firearms for him, he used them on hunts against prey and in warfare against the Ute. He joined parties to steal horses and to battle rivals, recalling that he was "a bad man" in search of "a big fight." At a young age, he amassed an impressive record of war deeds and hunting kills in the service of his people. After earning a reputation for bravery, he became a member of the Lance society.[4]

Another young Cheyenne, Wouhhunnih, or Roman Nose, earned a reputation for bravery as well. "When I was ten years old in Indian Territory," he later reminisced, "I commenced to kill buffalo calves, shooting them with bow and arrows." His family camped along the North Canadian River. Thanks to his father's training, the youth once led a hunt that "killed about seven buffaloes." He was praised for his ability to shoot birds and to catch turtles, with which he supplemented family meals. From his vantage point, the hunting grounds seemed abundant with game and adventure. His first direct action in warfare occurred at the age of thirteen against the Pawnee. Though a skilled warrior, he recalled being "anxious to go back home in Indian camp" to parade his trophies. War honors, or coups, were counted to verify his courage under fire. While counting coups, he obtained a variety of enemy scalps—one red, one blond, and seven brunette. Individual achievement on the war path fostered an eagerness on the part of the brave to defend the homeland from enemies.[5]

During the mid-nineteenth century, the geopolitics of the Cheyenne and Arapaho homeland began to change. Although the Fort Laramie Treaty of 1851 recognized their extensive territorial claims, they could not arrest the colonization of Kansas and Nebraska. Railroad surveys, gold rushes, and overland trails increased the flow of traffic across the wide, open spaces. The Indian Office of the U.S. Interior Department dispatched commissioners to negotiate new treaties in deference to the claims of non-Indians. They intended to concentrate the Plains Indians on reservations, which would limit their mobility and degrade their strength. Accommodating federal government demands, pacifist Cheyenne leaders such as Moketavoto, or Black Kettle, signed the Treaty of Fort Wise in 1861. In exchange for accepting what came to be known as "the white man's road," they expected to receive land allotments, annuities, and protection. In effect, the peace accords concentrated the Cheyenne and Arapaho on reservation lands along the upper Arkansas River.[6]

Militant Cheyenne dubbed "dog soldiers" rejected the peace accords. Originally a military police society known as Hotamitaneo, this band of brothers eschewed commerce, agriculture, and pacifism. Forsaking the comforts of camp life, they worked to protect the village. They lived off the booty captured from overland trails, trading posts, and wagon trains. They terrorized farmers, plundered freighters, sacked ranches, and seized captives. Lacking a single headman, their parties included belligerents from various factions and societies.[7] Each member carried "war medicines" consisting of charms, songs, and tricks for combat. One of the youngest warriors to participate in the sacred ceremonies was Okuhhatuh, or Sun Dancer, who became an officer of the Bowstring society. By the age of thirty, this emerging leader of the resistance had assumed the alias Making Medicine. He and his older brother, dubbed Little Medicine, embodied the potency of the dog soldiers.[8]

Most of all, dog soldiers were outraged by the atrocities committed against Indians by non-Indians. On November 29, 1864, John Chivington led volunteers sworn into federal service against Black Kettle's peaceful camp along Sand Creek in Colorado. At least 163 men, women, and children were massacred. As more and more Natives suffered losses from violent confrontations, they came to terms with the Treaty of Medicine Lodge in 1867. It assigned the Cheyenne to a five million acre reservation between the Cimarron and Arkansas Rivers in Indian Territory. When Colonel George A. Custer led the Seventh Cavalry in a winter campaign during 1868, Black Kettle, who had escaped Sand Creek, was slain at the Washita River. Because the U.S. Army destroyed their winter supplies of meat, Cheyenne and Arapaho survivors were forced to camp near military posts. At Fort Cobb, Lieutenant General Philip Sheridan, the division commander, gazed upon the starving bands and allegedly remarked, "The only good Indians I ever saw were dead."[9]

The plight of their Cheyenne and Arapaho rivals was observed by the Kiowa living near the fort. The Kiowa, whose name meant "Coming Out," derived their identity from a belief that their ancestors emerged from a hollow cottonwood log through a hole made by an owl. A Tanoan-speaking population, they originally occupied the prairies near the Yellowstone River and the headwaters of the Missouri. Driven out by the Sioux in the mid-eighteenth century, they moved southward along the front-range of the Rockies and settled near the Wichita Mountains. Before acquiring horses, they had used domesticated dogs to transport their wares. Their precarious existence improved dramatically following their first encounters with the grazing bison near the Red River. Their expanding traffic in captives enabled lower-status raiders to accumulate greater influence and prestige in the tribal councils. Acquiring horses enhanced their range and their capabilities. Profiting from their location within the borderlands, they grew in population to approximately 1,300 people. Before the onset of a deadly smallpox epidemic, the early nineteenth century represented a "golden age" for the Kiowa.[10]

Etahdleuh, a mixed-blood Kiowa warrior, came of age as the Kiowa faced gathering threats. Born in 1856, his name literally meant "we are seeking boys." It probably denoted the fact that his mother was a Mexican captive seized by his father during a raid. Boy Hunting, as he was commonly known, embraced the Kiowa as his people and adapted their customs as his own. They moved camp to keep near the buffalo and lived on a rich diet of meat and berries. He bragged that Kiowa males "like to hunt and fight," joining in raids to obtain prizes and acclaim. He recalled seasonal hunts as well as clashes with the Ute, Navajo, and Pawnee. He remembered bringing back "scalps of white men and women," which were displayed as trophies during "a big dance." Clad in a buffalo robe, he grew his hair long and painted his face for the ritual cere-monies. As badges of courage, he kept decorative rings in his ears. Boy Hunting aspired to be a "big chief" among the Kiowa, who selected him to lead raiding parties despite his youth.[11]

Boy Hunting followed a Kiowa chieftain, Guipahko, or Lone Wolf, who gradually became an advocate of warfare against the U.S. A member of the Onde aristocratic caste and the Tsetanma warrior society, he had traveled to Washington, D.C., as early as 1863. "A long time ago when I was little I began to study medicine," he once stated in reference to his leadership. Along with other chiefs, he signed the Little Ar-kansas Treaty on October 18, 1865. He attended the Medicine Lodge Council in Kansas but refused to make his mark on the treaty. When hostilities erupted in Indian Territory during 1868, Lone Wolf agreed to remain on the reservation. During the fall of 1872, he was selected as a delegate to accompany special commissioner Henry Alford to Washington for a peace conference. Though a principal chief, he shared leadership with Tsetainte, or White Bear; Setankia, or Sitting Bear; Ado-etta, or Big Tree; and Teneangopte, or Kicking Bird. However, he ended his negotiations after soldiers of the Fourth Cavalry killed his son near Kickapoo Springs in Texas on December 10, 1873. A grieving Lone Wolf plotted revenge upon those responsible.[12]

Within the councils of the Kiowa, he aligned himself with a mysterious figure called the Swan. A tall, slim man with straight, shiny black hair and a slender face, the Swan cultivated an elegant gait and subtle charms. He married the sister of Tsentainte, or White Horse, a member of the Sheep society and a fearsome warlord. Known as a "buffalo medicine man," the Swan may have been one of the first members of Pauewey, a society noted for healing wounded fighters. Although many Kiowa claimed to make medicine, this particular cult communicated with buffalo bulls to understand the cosmos. They emulated the behavior and attributes of the great beasts in their ceremonies. They considered themselves "children of the buffalo," using the tail as a ceremonial switch and building altars out of the animal's excrement. They would leave the camps and journey to an isolated place—a grove, a thicket, a river, a mountain, or a canyon—where, in solitude, they would quest for visions.[13]

During a long, hot day in 1869, the Swan received a vision at a creek, where he heard the sounds of a screech owl. He, like other Kiowa, believed that the bird embodied the spirit of deceased relatives. Its messages to the living constituted a death omen. Becoming ill with a fever, he fell into a trance for four days. He later recalled: "I lost most of the meat from my bones, and my face was so poor that I looked like a dead man. Finally one evening I died, and my breath went out of my mouth and right on up." After his revival, he sat in front of his lodge with an owl wrapped in a red shroud. Declared the Dohate, or Owl Prophet, the holy man exhibited the creature on his arm and received gifts from those who sought to understand the great mysteries. According to legend, his curative powers quieted the stormy weather and removed sickness and pain from the body. On the hide of his tipi, he painted a blue buffalo bull on one side and a domesticated cattle bull on the other. The mural included his emblem of a bird perched upon each of them. It foretold of a clash between two worlds, marking the last days of the Kiowa. The Kiowa renamed him Ma-manti, a special alias meaning Sky Walker.[14] His prophecies resonated with the defiant chiefs and warriors:

I saw the dead man's road, which I followed from afar off to the top of a smooth ridge. From the summit I could see a clear, sparkling stream in the valley beyond. Beside the timber along the stream was a very big village. The lodges were as numerous as the blades of grass in the field. Many people were moving about in the village, while off to the side were grazing thousands of horses. . . . We are worse off than they are. Their country is better. They live better than we do. I now am homesick for that land. I do not want to live here. I want to go back to the land of the dead men![15]

An inspiration to Kiowa militants, the Owl Prophet rebuked the passive leadership of the peace factions.

The Kiowa militants allied with the Comanche, who were beset with factional disputes of their own. They numbered approximately 1,500 members and dwelt upon the Llano Estacado of the Texas Panhandle, but they were divided into several groups. The Penatekas, or the Wasps, accepted the presence of non-Indians as well as the provisions of the Medicine Lodge Treaty of 1867. The Quahadas, or the Antelopes, refused to cooperate with the federal government at all. The latter attracted renegades from other bands into their rank and file and became notorious for frequent raiding in Texas and Mexico. A Comanche medicine man named Isatai, or Wolf Dung, and a young mixed-blood named Quanah, or Fragrance, participated in sun dances organized by the Kiowa and Cheyenne. Fierce war leaders such as Pokadoah, or Black Horse, "talked defiantly" to pacifists. Among the eager recruits for the war parties, Taawayte, or Telling Something, earned a title of distinction as a "buffalo scout." Wherever they rode, the Plains Indian militants adapted the Comanche language for intertribal communication.[16]

As Plains Indian militants formed strategic alliances, clashes with the U.S. Army intensified. Troops fresh from service in Civil War battlefields provided surveillance over scattered Indian communities. Among the companies of uniformed regulars were African Americans labeled "buffalo soldiers." Lacking the manpower, weaponry, and supplies of their blueclad adversaries, Native insurgents used surprise attacks and sudden withdrawals to undermine the occupation. Avoiding direct combat, they preferred guerrilla tactics to battlefield campaigns. The loss of anyone on a raid represented a high price, and, whenever possible, they avoided casualties and operated undercover. Since sustained or symmetrical engagements rarely occurred, skirmishes often seemed nasty, brutish, and short. Non-Indians would interpret an elusive enemy's reluctance to fight to the last as a form of cowardice, a mistake that on occasion would cost them their own lives. The armed forces endeavored to keep the peace in Indian Territory, even though they seemed ill-prepared for their mission.[17]

To sustain the peacekeeping mission, the U.S. War Department maintained a significant presence in Indian Territory. Lieutenant General Philip Sheridan ordered the erection of cantonments, outposts, and garrisons. Fort Sill was established on January 8, 1869, near the Wichita Mountains. Likewise, Fort Reno appeared along the Canadian River five years later. During the 1870s, the regiments at the fortified strongholds received orders from General Christopher C. Augur of the Department of Texas and General John Pope of the Department of Missouri. However, they failed to enforce provisions of the Medicine Lodge Treaty prohibiting non-Indian entry onto tribal lands. As the federal government defaulted

on its obligations to the Indians, conditions on the reservations worsened. Liquor, guns, and ammo flowed throughout
Indian Territory. Moreover, local outlaws rustled Native stock.
With the sentinels of the U.S. Army watching, rations disappeared or ran short. Whatever the intentions of the military,
the buffalo-hunting nations found few reasons to trust them.[18]

In fact, the military became entangled with the contradic-
tions of what was labeled the "Peace Policy." In 1869, President Ulysses S. Grant declared that the reservations were part
and parcel of a policy to move Indians toward "civilization and
ultimate citizenship." Encouraging churchmen to serve as Indian agents, Grant pledged to expand the "white man's road"
through humanitarian patience, moral suasion, and paternalis-
tic authority. On the Indian's part, this policy required the
abandonment of traditional hunting and the adoption of farming and stock-raising. Members of the Society of Friends, or
the Quakers, soon dominated the administration of Indian Affairs for the Interior Department. For instance, Quaker missionaries headed the separate agencies to the Kiowa and Comanche and to the Cheyenne and Arapaho. Disputes between
the War Department and the Interior Department undermined the efficacy of the "Great Father" in Washington, as
did corruption and scandal. In 1871, Congress ended the practice of conducting relations with Indian nations through treaties. Threatening to use force against resistance leaders, the
policy-makers stirred another series of outbreaks in the Great
Plains.[19]

One such outbreak, the Jacksboro raid, happened in
1871. Near the north Texas settlement of Jacksboro, William T.
Sherman, the General of the Army, was journeying with a military caravan to Fort Richardson. On May 18, a party of Kiowa
and Comanche struck one of his freighters, killing the teamsters and destroying the wagons. Afterward, Sherman arrested

three of the "ringleaders" at Fort Sill and transported them to Texas for trial. Sitting Bear attempted to escape and was killed, but White Bear and Big Tree were convicted and sentenced to hang. Pressure from Quaker agents led Texas Governor Edmund J. Davis to commute their sentences to life imprisonment in the state penitentiary at Huntsville. They received parole in 1873, although White Bear violated it and was arrested and sent back a year later to serve out his sentence. Even if the capture of chieftains constrained the resistance movement, incursions into Texas continued.[20]

Colonel Ranald Mackenzie campaigned in the Panhandle with the intention of driving all the Comanche out of Texas. During 1872, his Fourth Cavalry captured 120 Comanche women and children and placed them in the Fort Concho corral under heavy guard. Soon, husbands and relatives of the corralled Comanche ceased their raiding. They attempted to negotiate with military authorities, agreeing to surrender, to cooperate, and to disarm. In effect, the military detained the families as a bond for the good behavior of their kinsmen. Perhaps the Comanche feigned compliance in response to the power of blackmail. Perhaps the Comanche feared a mass lynching by the Texans. The depredations in Texas stopped, and the Quaker agents intervened again and arranged for their release from the corral. Promising to remain on the reservation, the Comanche returned to Indian Territory the following year.[21]

To secure the borders of Indian Territory, the federal government authorized a "hard war" in 1874. With full support from President Grant, officials in the War Department agreed to a robust plan of action.[22] For its implementation, General of the Army Sherman mobilized cavalry, infantry, and artillery units and granted wide latitude to his subordinates. Because raiders often found sanctuary under the watch of Quaker

agents, Lieutenant General Sheridan's divisions were authorized to "pursue and punish" Indians wherever they fled. According to orders, five separate expeditions would converge
upon them during the late summer, trapping them near the
caprock of the arid grasslands in western Texas. Meanwhile,
the various agencies registered "pacified" Natives who camped
on the reservation. Tribal members at large, then, would have
nowhere to hide. Once the so-called "hostiles" were found and
captured, military guards would escort them to confinement at
the outposts. Their weapons, supplies, and horses would be
taken from them by the U.S. Army. With the headmen and
their loyalists in shackles, their raiding parties would end.[23]

As anticipated, the Native raiding parties sparked several
firefights during the intense heat of the summer. One party
beheaded a Texas Ranger in the Lost Valley fight on July 12,
1874, giving Lone Wolf his revenge for his dead son. Between
June 27 and July 1, a band of 700 warriors attacked a buffalo
hunters' camp at Adobe Walls on the Canadian River. As many
as seventy Indians died in the futile charges, prompting the
hunters to behead several corpses and spike the trophies on
the corral gateposts. Meanwhile, Colonel Nelson A. Miles
departed with the Fifth Infantry and Sixth Cavalry from
Fort Dodge on August 11. During a miserable drought, Miles
clashed with a Cheyenne band along the Red River. On August 22, a Kiowa band killed at least five laborers at the agency
store in Anadarko. In a separate incident, a Caddo named Huwahnee shot farmer E. B. Osborn, son-in-law of a Delaware
scout, Black Beaver. Lieutenant Colonel John Davidson, com-
mandant at Fort Sill, ordered the Tenth Cavalry to give the
Plains Indians in the vicinity "a thrashing." Non-Indians attributed a host of crimes to dog soldiers, including a bloody
attack on a surveyor party in late August. Off the reservations,
rumors of war spread like prairie fire.[24]

On the morning of September 11, 1874, the family of John and Lydia German camped along the Smoky Hill River of western Kansas. They were moving from Georgia to Colorado in a covered wagon with their seven children: Rebecca, Catherine, Sophia, Stephen, Joanna, Adelaide, and Julia. After breakfast at sunrise, they watched a wild antelope dart over the dew-covered landscape. Eager for the day ahead, they completed their chores, herded their cattle, and prepared for the trail. On the horizon, they spied a party of nineteen mounted Cheyenne riding toward them. At the head rode the Bowstring leader Mihuhheuimup, or Medicine Water, who was accompanied by his wife, Mochi, or Buffalo Calf. Behind them rode Bear's Heart and a host of dog soldiers: Nohhunahwih, or Chief Killer; Otoastuhhos, or Rising Bull; Owussait, or Hail Stone; Cohoe, or Limpy, and several others. The Indians scrutinized the movements of the non-Indians, who were armed with only two muzzle-loaded weapons.[25]

Gunshots exploded, hitting John in the back and knocking him to the ground. Suddenly, a hatchet plunged deep into his skull. Scalped and mutilated, Lydia and three of her children died next. Four daughters survived but, according to one account, "were stripped naked and bound on the backs of ponies." Medicine Water's party left behind five scalped corpses, a looted and charred wagon, and the German family Bible. Being on the verge of starvation, the party also seized the cattle and roasted the meat. They plundered the provisions and claimed trophies. Buffalo Calf, whose bitter memories of the Sand Creek massacre moved her to become a "warrior woman," tortured the captives. Catherine, age seventeen, and Sophia, age thirteen, suffered gang rape and remained in concubinage to the dog soldiers. Julia, age seven, and Adelaide, age five, were ravished, abused, traded, and abandoned. Avoiding the columns of bluecoats, the party left Kansas for

Texas. Across the country, newspapers recounted the lurid details of the attack on September 11 and called for swift and severe retribution against the perpetrators.[26]

Meanwhile, Sky Walker told a gathering of militants at Elk Creek to head for Palo Duro Canyon, which the Kiowa called Agotapa. Carved by the Prairie Dog Town Fork of the Red River, the canyon contained game, waterfalls, grass, trees, and caves. In early September, an advance party of Kiowa militants crossed the path of a supply wagon train commanded by Captain Wyllys Lyman of Colonel Miles's Fifth Infantry. They raided the convoy as it reached the upper Washita River, killing a sergeant and a civilian teamster. In addition, a firefight occurred at a nearby buffalo wallow. Major William Price of the Eighth Cavalry arrived on September 12 with three companies and a howitzer. Captain Lyman eventually delivered his supplies, but the raiders scattered into the fog of war. Because of thunderstorms, severe weather, and flash flooding, the Indians dubbed their frantic flight to Palo Duro the "Wrinkled Hand Chase."[27]

Wherever the Indians fled, Colonel Mackenzie doggedly pursued. He led a column of eight companies from the Fourth Cavalry, five companies from the Tenth and Eleventh Infantry, and host of Seminole, Lipan Apache, and Tonkawa scouts. After a skirmish in Tulé Canyon on September 26, he lost the mounted warriors but found the hidden camps of women and children. At dawn on September 28, Mackenzie's troops descended the steep traces of Palo Duro. They killed at least three Indians and torched several encampments located within the walls. They slaughtered over a thousand Indian ponies. Most of the refugees fled southward on foot, suffering near-starvation during blizzards and ice storms. The warriors on foot began drifting back to the reservations. Without distinguishing refugees from combatants, newspapers following the events called for internment of the "prisoners of war." In fact, the military operation at Palo Duro Canyon broke the spirited resistance.[28]

Armed forces continued to patrol Indian Territory throughout the late autumn and early winter of 1874. On October 28, Cheyenne and Arapaho agent John D. Miles at Darlington requested rapid troop deployments in order to provide "proper control of all interests at this Agency." General Pope, headquartered at Fort Leavenworth, detailed a detachment of the Sixth Cavalry under Lieutenant Colonel Thomas Neill to police the agency. On November 8, Lieutenant Frank Baldwin marched a detachment from Colonel Miles's Fifth Infantry to McClellan Creek. Flanking and dispersing the encampment of a Cheyenne dog soldier known as Gray Beard, they discovered Julia and Adelaide German in an abandoned lodge. For finding them, Lieutenant Baldwin later received the Congressional Medal of Honor. After talking to the two little girls, Colonel Miles reported, "Their story of woe and suffering is simply too horrible to describe." With the two older sisters still missing, searchers crisscrossed the short-grass prairies during one of the coldest winters on record.[29]

While the search ensued, military authorities contemplated the fate of their own captives. As early as October 5, Lieutenant General Sheridan had telegraphed President Grant with his opinion about handling the prisoners of war. He asserted that "all who have committed murder or stolen cattle within the last two years should be tried by a military commission" and face punishment for their crimes. Even if they were determined "exempt" from legal proceedings, he desired to confine the "ringleaders" from each tribe "at Fort Snelling" in Minnesota. A month later, he announced his intention to order "a military commission for the trial of the Indian prisoners held at Fort Sill and the Cheyenne agency." Citing a previous legal opinion of the Justice Department concerning the Modoc War of 1873, he argued for commissioners to adjudicate the cases of murder, depredation, and theft. On December 9, he proposed banishing the guilty to the "Florida coast." E. D. Townsend, the Adjutant General, agreed with his proposal and suggested St. Augustine for their incarceration.[30]

At Fort Sill, Kiowa and Comanche agent James M. Haworth on December 5 wrote to the Commissioner of Indian Affairs, Edwin P. Smith, regarding the possible incarceration. With the close of "the present troubles," he opined that confinement of the warriors and the chiefs in Indian Territory remained "wholly impracticable unless a strong military guard was kept over them." Instead, he preferred transporting whole tribes "to some new location far removed from this frontier where there [sic] troubles have been."[31] The Quaker suggested a scheme whereby

> some may be taken and confined at some point as a matter of punishment, which I believe could be done to a good effect on the tribes. Say five or ten from each tribe who have taken part in the present troubles, be taken to Fort Leavenworth, which is not a state institution, and there be subjected to such confinement as would be necessary to secure their presence. It would not cost the Government much more, if any, to support them there than with their tribes—transportation considered, no more. A teacher might be employed for them. Most of them should be young men, and when the time for their release would come, they would be prepared to benefit their people. Thus two ends be reached—punishment by separation, and improvement by the punishment. So great a number absent would exert a restraining influence upon those left behind.[32]

By separating resistance leaders from their homeland, Haworth's scheme for regime change ostensibly would end the hostilities.

By 1875, military authorities openly endorsed Haworth's scheme. Irritated by "refractory and troublesome Indians" in Texas, General Augur on January 12, 1875, called for their exile to a garrison at "Ship Island or Dry Tortugas." Under the supervision of armed guards, the exiles could reside "in the open air with their families, and to a certain extent support themselves by fishing." On that point, Lieutenant Colonel Davidson concurred with General Augur. He claimed that "one half of the prisoners of war" expressed a desire to "do anything the Government required of them." On February 23, General Pope proposed "to remove them entirely from the country in which they have lived," and to march them closer to his headquarters at Fort Leavenworth. Promising to "dispose" of the tribes effectively, he recommended their "deportation" to the Missouri River. A massive removal "towards the East" would place all of the Plains Indians closer to cheap supplies and to railroad traffic. With their homelands "vacated," they would accept "civilization and Christianity" at a military outpost. They would live securely under martial law. They would cease depredations and capitulate to a more coercive regime. "The Indian question," wrote Pope, "will be finally settled."[33]

Clearly, the press wanted a final answer to the Indian question. The *Leavenworth Daily Commercial* declared: "On the score of humanity it would be vastly better to make war on the Indian to the death than to capture him." To end the raiding of the "hostile Indians," all of the tribes deserved to "be stationed somewhere within bounds of real civilization." Left in their homelands, military authorities eventually would be forced "to exterminate them outright." Reporters in the battlefield called for a more "civilized" approach to controlling the population, that is, a form of ethnic cleansing. They preferred to "march the captives, including men, women, and children," out of Indian Territory to Fort Leavenworth. They expected to uproot "about six thousand," belonging "chiefly to the Arapaho, Comanche, Kiowa, and Cheyenne tribes." They declared it "the most sensible thing that could be done with the red devils of the frontier." They considered wholesale relocation a humane policy, which promised to make peace along the borders and to save taxpayers millions of dollars each year. Whatever their underlying motives, a number of voices conspired on behalf of a removal policy for the Plains Indians.[34]

In fact, the Grant Administration agreed to the general proposition for Indian removal. Even Commissioner of Indian Affairs Smith offered his support for it, albeit with one stipulation. "But as far as relates to the women and children," he surmised, "it would not be advisable to have them accompany the men to their place of confinement." Indian women in the vicinity of uniformed soldiers "are quite certain to be debauched." He preferred placing the children "in a boarding school," while giving their mothers "rations sufficient for a comfortable living" at a government agency. Secretary of the Interior Columbus Delano suggested relocating them "to some other portion of the Indian Territory—and if possible, East of the 96th meridian—at as early a day as practicable." He considered such discretionary authority "a war measure," thus abrogating the claims of the "captive Indians" to their homeland. The Indian Office named C. F. Larrabee a "special agent" and General J. P. C. Shanks, a former congressman from Indiana, a "special commissioner." In conjunction with Superintendent Enoch Hoag, they procured 40,000 acres from the Quapaw near Baxter Springs, Kansas.[35] To break the resistance once and for all, officials planned to dispose of its instigators by confining them to a military reservation.

At first, General of the Army Sherman appeared reluctant to accept such a disposition. Although he authorized "the sale of their ponies and arms" to fund their subsistence, he delayed provisioning the prisoners until their number could be determined. Also, he wanted them interrogated and sorted. With so many "hostile Indians" under arrest, he insisted that all the prisoners receive fair treatment. He remained unwilling to say "how many Indians should be construed as ringleaders," though he wished to make "the number as small as possible." He ordered all of the tribes "to remain close to Fort Sill under the immediate guard and control of the garrison." On March 1, he wrote to the Secretary of War that he doubted "the fitness" of Fort Marion in Florida and suggested sending "the worst" to Lake Superior, to Fort Leavenworth, or even to the Texas State Prison. Wherever they served their time, he wanted "no end to this imprisonment, except by death." In particular, he was open to "any scheme" that proposed to "make these rascals work for their food." He left the Indian question open with the arrival of spring because ending the insurgency represented his first priority.[36]

The most wanted of the insurgents, those holding the elder German sisters, demanded a ransom from the "Great Father." Medicine Water traded Catherine and Sophia to members of Stone Calf's peaceful band, who camped along the Pecos River that winter. Colonel Miles sent Kiowa informants to warn them that peace depended upon the safe return of the captives to the Darlington agency. Heeding the warning, Stone Calf's band trekked eastward over 400 miles to return the young girls. A few dog soldiers joined the great trek, surrendering under Stone Calf's flag of truce. Nearing the agency on February 28, one of the subchiefs, Chaseyunnuh, or Long Back, relinquished the captives to an ambulance driver dispatched by Lieutenant Colonel Neill. Finally, the sisters' ordeal was over. More than 800 destitute Cheyenne settled into a prison camp two miles from the agency to await their fate.[37]

On the road to the agency, the German sisters were greeted by crowds celebrating their return. On March 12, Lieutenant Colonel Neill paraded a number of captive Indians for inspection. Colonel Miles recalled that "the two elder German girls went along down the line pointing out to the officers the different men who had been engaged in the murder of their family." In total, they helped to identify Medicine Water, Buffalo Calf, and "sixteen Indian bucks." The officers dispatched the accused straight to the guardhouse, although the sisters exonerated Stone Calf from any charges. Catherine and Sophia were subsequently reunited with Julia and Adelaide at Fort Leavenworth, where Colonel Miles became their guardian. Eventually, Congress set aside $10,000 from Cheyenne annuities as an endowment for the "maintenance, education, and support" of the girls. Upon reaching the age of twenty-one, each sister received payment from the fund. A reporter from the *Kansas City Times* interviewed General Sherman on April 9 about their rescue and asked: "What will be done with Medicine Water and the others of the party that committed the murder?" He replied: "I can hardly tell as yet . . . but they will probably be sent to a reservation in Florida, where they will be held as prisoners of war."[38]

The military dealt harshly with all of the prisoners, not just the raiders and the renegades. Agent Haworth estimated "about two-thirds of the Kiowas" and "one-half of the Comanches" remained loyal during the outbreak, choosing "the side of peace." Because they had fled Fort Sill in fright, however, they were obliged to surrender along with the "hostiles." He claimed that they had lost more than "two thousand head of stock," including horses, ponies, and mules. White Horse, for instance, enrolled with the agency during the summer. Taken into custody on December 21, 1874, the Kiowa considered his arrest another example of the government's broken

promises. Agent Haworth believed that he was seized "on account of his previous bad character, and not because of any
recent depredations." On February 26, 1875, Lone Wolf and
Sky Walker arrived with a cohort of more than 250 followers.
Because the last holdouts, the Quahadi Comanches under
Wolf Dung and Fragrance, delayed arrival until June 2, they
escaped the round-up of their kinsmen. Disarmament and arrest for approximately fifty of the "really bad Indians" among
the Kiowa and Comanche culminated that spring. Individuals
not detained were enrolled, receiving orders to muster for roll
call each morning.[39]

One journalist described the detainment for the *Catholic
World*. When he entered the guardhouse, the prisoners acted
as though "their hour was nearly come" and appeared as desperate as "drowning men." He met White Horse, calling him
"a murderer, ravisher, and as great a general scoundrel as could
be found in any tribe." With his double-iron chains clanking,
White Horse put out his manacled arms and eagerly shook
hands with the stranger. A large, powerful man, the Kiowa
wore a dark-colored blanket that covered his entire body. The
journalist watched as White Horse's mother and aunt entered
the cell and embraced their beloved, standing silently as tears
rolled down their faces. They sat together on a rough wooden
bench, each holding one of his fettered hands in both of theirs.
Over 120 more detainees languished in a small, unfinished
icehouse, where guards tossed chunks of raw meat to them
over a wall once each day. Touring the icehouse, the curious
guest noted canvas tents ranging along the walls and fires burning down the center aisle. The crowded occupants "were
mostly engaged in gambling with Monte cards," seemingly
content with their pastime. Though uncomfortable in the
cramped quarters, they warmly acknowledged the non-Indian.
An additional number of Kiowa and Comanche camped near

the outpost, although their circumstances appeared little better.[40]

Meanwhile, Agent Miles observed the encampments of detainees near Darlington. As the rank and file swelled to hundreds of Cheyenne and Arapaho, the prison camps represented a shocking spectacle. "A more wretched and poverty-stricken community than these people," he wrote in one report, "would be difficult to imagine." Sickness spread among them, owing to the heavy rainfall, the rank vegetation, and the squalid conditions. Without adequate shelter, clothing, supplies, water, or food, they appeared on the brink of catastrophe. With no ponies or other means of transportation, they became docile. For the first time, they "seemed to realize the power of the government and their own inability to cope successfully therewith." They expressed gratitude for the "white man's medicine," indicating to the agent that the "superstitious rites over the sick and disabled are fast becoming things of the past." He complained about the selection of "the leading spirits" for rougher treatment, which "was not made in strict accordance with justice." Military officers confiscated guns, saddles, bows, arrows, and other possessions, placing sixty-two prisoners in the guardhouse. With the military occupation extended, the Indians held under guard at the agency seemed utterly dispirited.[41]

Guards supervised the chaining of several Cheyenne prisoners, who were fitted by the agency's blacksmith. On April 6, a lone brave kicked the blacksmith and ran away. Although he was not charged with any crimes or wielding any weapons, the troops began firing at him. Later, he would die from his wounds. However, the shots generated greater consternation, which spread throughout the prison camp. Fearing that the blueclad soldiers intended to massacre their families, warriors quickly produced a number of arrows and retaliated against a guard. Lieutenant Colonel Neill ordered a company from the Sixth Cavalry to stop the potential riot. The frightened Cheyenne escaped to a nearby sand-hill, where they had previously concealed arms, munitions, and knives. They entrenched themselves in the pits and held off the troopers in a massive firefight. Even though a Gatling gun sprayed rounds onto the trenches from four hundred yards away, the defenders held the line. Before the cavalry finally stormed the sand hill, the Cheyenne fled their position. Newspapers sensationalized the events, declaring that "the Indian prisoners at the agency had massacred the garrison and escaped." They crudely warned non-Indians to watch out for the "amiable dog cookers" and to shield young women from the "dusky warrior preferences."[42]

A small number of Cheyenne briefly camped at Sappa Creek, though most fled beyond it. On the morning of April 23, Lieutenant Austin Heneley, who commanded H Company of the Sixth Cavalry, conducted a surprise attack on those at the creek. Trapping them in the dark and shallow waters, they killed at least nineteen men and eight women and children, though one account placed the total number of dead at seventy. The company invoked the memory of Indian ambushes as they charged the Cheyenne with the battle cry, "Remember the German Family!" Afterward, Lieutenant Heneley alleged that his men had found "in the camp of the Indians a memorandum book containing rude though expressive sketches." One depicted the unforgettable tragedy at the Smoky Hill River, which the officer used to justify the rage of the bluecoats. Running for their lives, a handful of Cheyenne headed northward to join their kinsman beyond the Platte River. Most of them, though, returned to their confinement in the prison camps under amnesty terms promised by General Pope. Eight medals of honor were awarded to the servicemen responsible for the Sappa Creek massacre. The Cheyenne regarded it as one of the worst killing fields of the war.[43]

As the war came to a close, the ecology of the buffalo-hunting nations collapsed. Between 1874 and 1875, they had experienced a dreadful summer drought and a terrible winter freeze. Plagues of grasshoppers flew in darkening clouds, eating all the vegetation in their path and leaving the forage severely degraded. Likewise, scouts, sharpshooters, runners, and skinners ferociously attacked the bison herds, leaving on the ground millions of skeletons as the carcasses rotted under an open sky. The great beasts that had once thundered through the hunting grounds quickly dwindled in number. Disease spread by range cattle, furthermore, increased mortality among the bulls and heifers and undermined reproduction of the buffalo calves.[44] Old Lady Horse, a Kiowa storyteller, mourned the horrors of the "war between the buffalo and the white men." She lamented:

The white men built forts in the Kiowa Country, and the woolly-headed buffalo soldiers shot the buffalo as fast as they could, but the buffalo kept coming on, coming on, even into the post cemetery at Fort Sill. Soldiers were not enough to hold them back. Then the white men hired hunters to do nothing but kill the buffalo. Up and down the plains those men ranged, shooting sometimes as many as a hundred buffalo a day. Behind them came the skinners with their wagons. They piled the hides and bones into the wagons until they were full, and then took their loads to the new railroad stations that were being built, to be shipped east to the market. Sometimes there would be a pile of bones as high as a man, stretching a mile along the railroad track. The buffalo saw that their day was over. They could protect their people no longer.[45]

In full effect, the losses of the Plains Indians reached cataclysmic proportions.

The Buffalo War brought an end to the world as the Plains Indians knew it. It caused the near-annihilation of once-plentiful game as well as the eventual opening of the Texas Panhandle and Indian Territory to non-Indian settlement. The massive destruction to the homeland of the Native people extended from the Arkansas River southward to the Pecos River and swept far and wide across the continent. Because of their concentration into camps on the reservations, epidemics and malnourishment spread rapidly and decimated their population. Famine threatened to starve their children to death. To be sure, chiefs and warriors mounted insurgencies against the invaders. They refused to die without a fight. Atrocities occurred on all sides. Innocent victims suffered from the violence. Vigorous and bold campaigning by armed forces, however, devastated the spirited resistance. In a smashing and sweeping blow, the U.S. Army tried to decapitate the leadership of the buffalo-hunting nations. At fortified outposts and prison camps, the headmen and their loyalists endured the scourge in silence.

Chapter 2
Iron Road
From Fort Sill to Fort Marion

A BAND OF KIOWA surrendered to the U.S. Army in February of 1875. Zepkoetta, or Big Bow, who had negotiated the surrender in exchange for his own amnesty, orchestrated a ceremony to mark the occasion. He met with military authorities and pledged to walk "the white man's road." Camping in the Wichita Mountains forty miles west of Fort Sill, the Kiowa gave their guns, pistols, bows, arrows, spears, and shields to a scout company of the Tenth Cavalry. They, in turn, issued sugar, coffee, and hardtack to the war prisoners. After dusk, Big Bow invited the uniformed soldiers to sit in the midst of a great circle around a campfire. One of the seated officers, Lieutenant Richard Henry Pratt, called it a "strange scene," which he found both "weird and impressive." As he stared into the flickering flames, he sensed the chill of the night air. He saw a red blanket spread on the ground to one side of the blaze and a small open space to the other. He heard tomtoms, singing, and conversations, all of which were incomprehensible to him. He anxiously anticipated a grand entrance by a troupe of Kiowa dancers. Music commenced, but nobody danced.[1]

A powerful man sitting near Pratt rose and stood before him. Known as Podaladalte, or Snake Head, he took his name from a personal charm, a rattlesnake tail that he wore in his scalp lock. They also called him Zotom, or Biter, a nickname derivative of the nasalized root word for "tooth." He took a large butcher knife from his belt, stuck it in the ground, threw off his blanket, and began to move around the campfire. Pratt became nervous, observing that the dancer was "almost nude" and that his face and body appeared "hideously painted." He shook "wildly with grotesque crouching, swaying, and posturing" in perfect rhythm to the music. In the midst of his animated performance, he gestured toward Pratt and seized the knife from the ground. Suddenly, a brief struggle erupted between the dancer and another painted brave. Finally, the dancer grabbed a blanket and used the knife to cut it into several pieces. As if on cue, the men, women, and children rose up to dance enthusiastically. Unable to grasp the nuances of the ceremony, Pratt assumed that the encounter was a "test" of his courage. The dance continued throughout the night, while Pratt quietly retired to his tent to rest. The next morning, he conducted the Kiowa band to Fort Sill for confinement.[2]

Born at Rushford, New York, on December 6, 1840, Richard Henry Pratt was the oldest of three sons reared by Richard and Mary Pratt. In 1846, his family resettled in Logansport, Indiana. His father, who joined the California gold rush of 1849, died at the hands of a fellow prospector on his journey home. At the age of thirteen, young Pratt left school and toiled as a printer's devil, a rail splitter, and a tinsmith's apprentice in order to support his widowed mother and younger brothers. He grew to a height of six feet and developed handsome features, although his face remained scarred from a bout with smallpox as a child. When the American Civil War erupted in 1861, he volunteered for the Union army and campaigned in Kentucky, Tennessee, and Georgia. On a recruiting detail to Indiana during the winter of 1863–64, he met Anna Laura Mason, a New Yorker visiting relatives in the Hoosier state. They were married on April 12, 1864, though he was soon back in the field as a first lieutenant. On May 29, 1865, he was mustered out of service. After briefly operating a hardware store in Logansport, he returned to active duty two years later.[3]

Appointed second lieutenant in the Tenth Cavalry, Pratt received the brevet rank of captain for his meritorious war service. Promotion to first lieutenant soon followed his deployment to Indian Territory, where subordinates often addressed him as "Captain" out of respect.[4] During his tour of duty, he commanded a regiment of African American "buffalo soldiers" and led Indian scouts, who were often called "wolves" in sign language. He believed that they acquired "intelligence, civilization, and common sense" through the agency schools and military regimentation. From cultures accustomed to ascribing significance to naming, perhaps the scouts found his surname both humorous and appropriate. It was English slang for "buttocks." Pratt attended tribal councils around Fort Sill, where he smoked a "peace pipe" with Native leaders. Kicking Bird, a leader of the Kiowa peace faction, once dressed him for an affair in paint, leggings, moccasins, beads, and bonnet as "one of their chiefs." When the Plains Indians resisted government policy from 1874 to 1875, Pratt campaigned in the war to subdue them.[5]

As that campaign unfolded, Pratt received orders to conduct a confidential investigation of the various and sundry crimes. He gathered evidence about the murders, atrocities, and depredations. He attempted to determine "the personal character of every Indian" held in irons at the agencies and at the posts. His inquiry yielded testimony that incriminated chiefs and warriors, including about 150 already under arrest. His informants included scouts and "fort Indians," fellow officers and enlisted men, and former captives and victims. Though he understood elements of native sign language, he relied upon translators to communicate directly with them. After interrogating the accused, he identified individuals liable for possible trial before a military commission. He recorded his information in ledgerbooks, even though it represented mostly hearsay. Reluctantly, he respected "pledges of immunity from punishment" made by his superior officers to certain leaders, including Big Bow. Although the Tenth Cavalry under Lieutenant Colonel John W. Davidson redeployed to Fort Concho in the spring of 1875, Pratt remained at Fort Sill to complete his investigation.[6]

Pratt collaborated with Major C. D. Emory, Judge Advocate for the Army's Department of Texas. In March of 1875, the judge visited Fort Sill with orders to indict the prisoners liable for trial. Even though Pratt's evidence pertained to crimes that had been committed over a span of almost eight years, Emory's orders covered the active war record only. He confessed to the new post commander, Colonel Ranald Mackenzie, that "it will be difficult to establish that the state of war necessary in my opinion to gain vitality to a trial by military commission then existed." With regrets, he surmised that only "four Indians can be convicted by evidence already obtained." In particular, he concluded that "Lone Wolf, White Horse, and others of the more prominent and influential of the malefactors can not be secured." Though he considered Lone Wolf "one of the biggest scoundrels" in the guardhouse, he doubted the credibility of the evidence against him. He predicted that commissioners would have little faith in "Indian testimony for what it is worth," adding that "I can hardly say how reliable it is after it is gotten." Before returning to Texas, he encouraged Pratt to collect more non-Indian testimony about their wartime activities before pursuing convictions. The judge left the matter in Pratt's hands but anticipated "escape from trial of some of the most persistent of the raiders." Clearly, the War

Department's plans for swift adjudication and severe punishment were in jeopardy.[7]

The War Department awaited final instructions from President Ulysses S. Grant, who submitted the matter to the Attorney General's office. The lawyers in the office informed the President "that a state of war could not exist between a nation and its wards." Because the law required a state of war to warrant a military trial, appointed commissioners could not legally convict the Indian prisoners for their actions. Nevertheless, they could face trial in courts of limited jurisdiction where innocent noncombatants had suffered specific crimes. The cries for vengeance in Texas and Kansas remained intense, making it unlikely that any case presented to a jury of non-Indians could be conducted fairly. On March 13, the President decided that "the ringleaders and such as have been guilty of crimes are to be selected to be sent for confinement" to a military outpost in Florida. The War Department's Adjutant General, E. D. Townsend, turned the selection process over to General of the Army William T. Sherman, who then placed the matter in the hands of Lieutenant General Philip Sheridan. Sheridan, in turn, passed it down the chain of command until Pratt became a "de facto military commission" charged with selecting prisoners to be banished without trial.[8]

During April, a cohort of Southern Cheyenne and Arapaho were selected. Though most of the Arapaho had refused to join the Cheyenne during the fighting, authorities charged two of them, Nunnetiyuh, or Packer, and Huhnohuhcoaj, or White Bear, with violations at the agency. They also selected Cheyenne dog soldiers implicated in the attack on the German family and the captivity of the girls. They rounded up prominent leaders such as Moeyauhayist, or Heap of Birds; Minimic, or Eagle's Head; Ouachita, or Lean Bear, and Nockoyouh, or Bear Shield. To meet his quota of "desperadoes" for extradition, Lieutenant Colonel Thomas Neill organized a line-up. Apparently he was drunk when he ordered eighteen struck-off from the right irrespective of charges or culpability. He promised to correct the matter at a later date but glossed over it in his records instead. According to one account, Making Medicine volunteered to join his older brother, Little Medicine, out of sibling loyalty. A total of thirty-three Cheyenne and two Arapaho prisoners were conveyed under military guard from Fort Reno to Fort Sill.[9]

At Fort Sill, they joined a group of Kiowa and Comanche prisoners selected for extradition. Kicking Bird, who had been anointed as the principal Kiowa chieftain by military authorities, helped to select a number of the Kiowa in the group. The chief maneuvered to parole allies and to undermine rivals, fingering such adversaries as Lone Wolf, Sky Walker, and White Horse. He also incriminated such headmen as Mányiten, or Woman's Heart; Tanati, or Bird Chief; Tozance, or Double Vision; and Coaboteta, or Wolf Stomach. He included in their number a handful of notorious raiders, obscure braves, and Mexican captives. Boy Hunting, for instance, was ironed with shackles around the ankles and herded into the group to "go to Florida." With several prominent Comanche yet to arrive at Fort Sill, an aging Nokona chief called Horseback selected Black Horse to bear the punishment for the Quahada division. Eight of his warriors bore it as well, including Telling Something. Even though a greater proportion of Comanche than Kiowa had participated in the insurgency, the prisoners selected from the latter tribe outnumbered the former by twenty-seven to nine.[10]

Meanwhile, Pratt volunteered to assume responsibility for the prisoners of war. On April 26, he wrote to the division commander, Lieutenant General Sheridan: "If, in the care of these Indians east, the government requires an officer of my rank, I want to go, because I have been down here eight years and am hungry for a change." He opined that "some of them ought to be tried and executed here in the presence of their people," although he admitted that most were "not so culpable as at first seems." He asserted his belief that "much can and should be done for them while under this banishment." Hence, he was detailed by Colonel Mackenzie to accompany the exiles during their transfer from Fort Sill to Fort Leavenworth. Shortly before leaving, the post commander informed Pratt's wife that her husband would likely inherit permanent charge of the prisoners.[11]

At midnight on April 28, the prisoners left the confines of Fort Sill. Each stepped forward with a small bundle of clothes, a few personal items, and heavy iron shackles. Companies D and L, Fourth Cavalry, and Companies C and I, Eleventh Cavalry, escorted them to a column of eight wagons. Despite the arbitrary proceedings, Pratt classified them into categories. First, he listed those charged with committing murder, stealing stock, and assaulting troopers. He specified offenses with dates, places, and testimony. Second, he listed chiefs and warriors who were reportedly engaged in criminal activities. He obscured the fact that he lacked substantive evidence against them. Finally, he listed those against whom no crime was charged but who were considered "turbulent, disobedient, agitators, stirrers up of bad feelings, and otherwise troublesome." Clearly, this represented a category sufficiently elastic to catch all of the strong and cunning men. In haste, he produced a final roster with fifteen pages of information scribbled onto foolscap paper.[12]

One at a time, the prisoners shuffled into the wagons as Pratt checked their names against his roster. There was Huhnahnee, a forty-five-year-old Caddo man held in the guardhouse for murder charges. One of the Kiowa was inscribed as Onkoeht or, more accurately, Auncauit. The name meant "about the ankle," possibly an alias given to him when he was shackled. Black Horse's wife, Peahin, and seven-year-old daughter, Ahkah, clung desperately to the Comanche chief as he boarded. Although Pratt relented and placed them into the wagons together, he considered them "squaws" rather than prisoners. He also loaded a man named Dick, an African American previously considered Lone Wolf's captive. A former soldier and possibly a deserter, he was not listed as a prisoner but apparently preferred to accompany his captors. In all, Pratt's roster listed thirty-three Cheyenne, two Arapaho, twenty-seven Kiowa, nine Comanche, and one Caddo. He scrawled information about the three "non-prisoners" in the margins. Whatever its inaccuracies, misnomers, and errors, the list of exiles was final.[13]

The exiles sat ten to a wagon on scattered hay. They were secured by lacing their shackles with a chain extending the length of the wagon. One end of the chain was padlocked at the tailgate and the other was carefully bolted in the front at the bottom of the bed. It bound them together, alternating first on one side then the other. It passed between their legs, above their shackles, and around their ankles. Additional chains linked them to a beam affixed to the bottom of each wagon bed. Word of a planned rescue attempt reached Colonel Mackenzie, who invited their kinsmen to observe them chained into the vehicles. Armed guards supervised the crowds and thwarted any attempt at rescue. With their families broken apart, mothers, wives, and children shed tears of mourning that night. They stood upon a nearby hillside and watched the solemn embarkation.[14]

As the wagon train set out, Kicking Bird rode past the hillside on a handsome gray steed, a gift from one of the officers at the post. The Kiowa chief allegedly proclaimed:

Brothers! The time has come to say goodbye. I am sorry for you. But because of your stubbornness, I have failed to keep you out of trouble. You will have to be punished by the government. Take your medicine. It will not be for long. I love you and will work for your release. I have done my best to keep you in the right road, and I hope that the time will come soon when you will return to us happy, at peace, and of a different mind.[15]

Sky Walker responded by scowling at the rider and declaring, "You will not live long." The wagon masters then took the reins, cracked their whips, and steered their caravan overland.[16]

Under cover of darkness, the caravan conveyed the exiles toward the town of Caddo, 165 miles east of Fort Sill. Captain T. J. Wint held general command over the blueclad regulars in the caravan. The infantry rode in the wagons with the prisoners while the cavalry on horseback trekked along each side. At night, the men in irons remained chained together and to the wagons. One end of the chain was securely padlocked to one wagon, and the other end was securely locked to another wagon some distance away. In addition, sentries marched on each side of the line. Another set of guards patrolled a line about the camp. One evening, after hearing word of another planned rescue attempt, the guards became alarmed. A shadowy form moved near the camp and refused to halt at their challenge. They fired a few shots at the phantom but missed their target. It was a stray ox grazing in the brush. Otherwise, the transfer to Caddo was made without incident.[17]

The road trip took six days to complete, with the caravan arriving at Caddo on May 4. There they received word that Kicking Bird had died at Fort Sill the previous day. Agent James Haworth, his close friend and advocate, reported that he had suffered from a "disease of the heart." The post surgeon somehow diagnosed poisoning by strychnia, although he performed no autopsy. There followed speculation about assassination plots ordered by the deposed chieftains, who arranged for a strange brew of his coffee. One newspaper called his death a "revenge" killing, concluding that "there is no doubt but that he died of poison." According to Kiowa lore, the peace chief was cursed by Sky Walker, the Owl Prophet. Two nights after leaving Fort Sill, he had reportedly hosted a council under the watch of the guards. With fettered hands, they had passed a pipe back and forth. Eagle Chief had turned to the Owl Prophet, asking him to pray that "Kicking Bird may die right away." The medicine maker had agreed, but warned that using his power against a fellow Kiowa would demand the eventual forfeiture of his own life. For the prisoners, Kicking Bird's sudden death resulted from the curse.[18]

Meanwhile, the prisoners prepared to board the M. K. and T. Railroad at Caddo station. Guards were posted at each end of the railcar and on the platform adjacent to the tracks. Two regular companies, sixty troopers in all, herded the passengers to the line. Pratt, Lieutenant W. J. Kyle, and Lieutenant W. H. Wheeler barked instructions. The prisoners, who were dressed in their traditional garb, crowded into one car like cattle. They spoke only to Rafael Romero, a Cheyenne-Mexican interpreter fluent in several dialects. With all aboard, Pratt tried to calm their fears about the locomotive. Bear's Heart, the Cheyenne warrior, expressed great fear about dying on the train. Aside from Lone Wolf, none of the prisoners had ever traveled by rail. Indeed, few of them had even seen the ominous "iron horse" before that day. As it began rolling down the tracks, they drew their blankets over their heads. The lonesome whistle blew, and the train moved full speed ahead down the iron road.[19]

The train passed through Sedalia, Missouri, where a correspondent from the *Kansas City Times* came aboard. He mingled with the prisoners in their car, as frightened of them as they were of him. He tried to speak with the "noted Indian chiefs," whom he considered responsible for "the late border outrages." They seemed uninterested in his queries while gripped by severe motion sickness. Some fainted from nausea and others from hunger. Soot and cinders covered their dormant bodies. Calling them "A Nice Batch of Copper Colored Rascals," the reporter joked that "spelling schools" would wrestle with their names. His dispatch exaggerated their criminal records and dirty deeds. Calling them "blood-thirsty," he expected them to "be convicted and hung." He wanted them terminated at once so that "they should not be held at the expense they daily cause."[20]

The sensational press coverage of the transfer drew a crowd of approximately twenty thousand men, women, and children to the Union Depot at Kansas City on May 5. They waited for days in long and weary expectation, but many missed the passage of the celebrated "Indian captives." Their enthusiasm to see "the savages" waned once the train was delayed. The train finally arrived about 4:00 P.M. on May 8 but stopped only briefly. To the disappointment of the remaining crowd, the locomotive and its five coaches quickly proceeded to the next stop.[21]

At Fort Leavenworth, the uniformed troopers filed out and drew up in line upon the platform. They placed the manacled Indians ten to a wagon. With troops escorting them to their left, right, front, and rear, the prisoners were conveyed to the guardhouse for temporary confinement. Two sick prisoners were lifted separately into an uncovered ambulance. The town buzzed with excitement about the ones charged with "arson, murder, rape, and robbery." Eager to witness a public execution, they anticipated watching them "stretch hemp." A flood of correspondents from across the country entered the

stockade to glimpse those kept under lock and key. The prisoners, however, remained reticent and unwilling to converse.
Families of alleged victims were paraded before them. On one
occasion, Buffalo Calf reportedly "rose up and looked at them
eagerly, almost wildly, as though some chord in her heart had
been touched, but said nothing, and after a little time sat
down in silence." The press, which held a strong bias against
the accused, wanted them "hung or shot" at the outpost. "If
ever crimes deserved punishment," wrote one reporter, "their
bloody deeds merit the fullest demands of justice."[22]

In contrast, one reporter for the *St. Louis Republican*
pleaded for leniency. "As prisoners of war," he wrote, "these
Indians are entitled to those rights and privileges usually ac-
corded to such persons by all civilized nations." However, it
"appears they are not to receive such treatment." He observed
that the "most prominent warriors" were unfairly separated
from their families and banished for life. They were treated as
if they "have no rights that a white man should regard, and
certainly no rights that belong to civilized natives." He added
that their "expatriation might not be so terrible were it not that
they are to be torn from their families, their wives, and children." He called it "a species of cruelty" unworthy of "a great
nation like ours." He preferred that their punishment by the
federal government be "tempered with humanity and justice."
He called for resettling them to an "interior state, where
they cannot return to the prairies" but will become "self-
sustaining." Even the friends of the Indians did not want to see
them incarcerated at the fort and hoped that they would not
remain there for long.[23]

Fort Leavenworth remained their prison for nine days as
Pratt awaited further orders. On May 9, he scribbled a note to
the Cheyenne agent, John D. Miles, stating that chiefs Gray
Beard and Eagle's Head "want me to write to you to tell their

people to settle down at their agency and do all that the Government requires of them." The chiefs desired them "to plant corn, to send their children to school, and to not get into any trouble" on the reservation. They expected to "travel on the white man's road," or so wrote Pratt. Prepared to sacrifice themselves on behalf of their people, they would go "a long ways off and may never return."[24] Indeed, Gray Beard unsuccessfully attempted suicide in his cell at Fort Leavenworth. Late one evening, he cut a strip from his blanket and tethered one end of it to an iron bar in the cell window. After tying the other end around his neck, he stood on a support to hang himself. When Eagle's Head heard the commotion, he and his inmates rescued Gray Beard before strangulation occurred. Afterward, Pratt tried to assure the despondent chief that the post commander would work for his release.[25]

Colonel Nelson Miles, the post commander, heard the pleas from the chiefs under his watch. Though he had once attacked Gray Beard's camps in war, he now interceded on his behalf and tried to secure the freedom of the principal Cheyenne chief. However, his superiors rejected his entreaties and kept Gray Beard captive. Eagle's Head, meanwhile, asked the guardian of the German girls to adopt his own captive son, Honanistto, or Howling Wolf. Colonel Miles described him as "one of the handsomest Indians I have ever seen, a stalwart young man of about twenty-two years." He appreciated the sentiment of a father concerned about his son. Nevertheless, the officer doubted "any good results with but one Indian" and refused the request. In his official report about the military campaigns that year, he called for the education of "the Indian youth." Nevertheless, Miles did nothing on behalf of Howling Wolf while exiled from Indian Territory.[26]

During the stay at Fort Leavenworth, Pratt complained about the problems in Indian Territory. In reports to superiors, he described the beef rations distributed at their former agencies as "not one half of the meager allowance fixed by the table of Indian supplies." They were "entirely unfit for issue." He lamented that he had never seen "poorer cattle than those issued from these two agencies this winter," which had left his charges emaciated and unhealthy. Because of the rotted flour, the Indians he saw at the agencies generally "kept only the sacks." He called for "a strong and honest investigation by parties familiar with frontier work" in order to unveil the cause of the adulteration. Although he often praised Agent Miles at Darlington, Pratt vented about Agent Haworth at Fort Sill. Whatever Pratt's motives, he confided to a friend that Haworth "lied officially and otherwise." He opined that the Quaker agent "was not clean in beef transactions."[27]

At Fort Leavenworth, Pratt received word that Lieutenant General Sheridan had recommended him to conduct the prisoners to Florida. On May 11, the War Department issued Special Orders No. 88, placing them in Pratt's "immediate charge" until further notice. He was ordered to "attend to the supply of their proper wants" and to provide supervision. Curiously, his orders were marked "keep from the press." Four days later, the Army's Department of the Missouri issued Special Orders No. 76. It authorized a commissioned officer, an interpreter, and twenty enlisted men to maintain security during the transfer. The small detachment was expected to return to their duty station upon completion of the journey. To ship them to their final destination, the Chief Quartermaster of the Department contracted with interested corporations.[28] Pratt observed "lively competition among the railroads for the business of transporting the prisoners because of the notoriety of the movement." The transportation costs amounted to $10,272.95, which was expensed to the federal government. The expense included the fees paid to the railroad companies for the Indian passengers as well as for the military escorts. Returning to the iron road, Pratt and his entourage prepared to leave Kansas behind.[29]

At 3:00 P.M. on May 17, the train left the station. A reporter for the *Leavenworth Daily Commercial* announced that "the captive Indians" were headed east, where they would experience "confinement for the remainder of their lives." He gleefully bade them farewell:

No more will these dusky sons of the forests be allowed the sacred privilege of murdering women and children. So many of them have gone and the frontiersmen need stand in fear of these seventy-five no longer. We hope they will become accustomed to the climate and settle down with a fitting resignation to their daily toil. Goodbye . . . We should have been much more pleased to have filled this space with a fitting obituary for you all, but as it cannot be so, we humbly submit and grant you godspeed on your journey South and may you never return.[30]

Thus, the prisoners journeyed by rail to a destination far and away from their homeland.

On their journey eastward, the prisoners experienced a long, strange trip. Peering out the windows of their car, they looked upon an exotic countryside filled with abundant woodlands and vibrant rivers. They observed the towering architecture of urban realms. They saw strange people gathering at every railway station. The passage overland inspired them with vivid impressions of vistas they had never imagined. Biter, one of the most gifted prisoners, later sketched such sights and wonders as the St. Charles Bridge, the first railroad span over the Missouri River to link with St. Louis. From the moving train, his mind's eye captured details of the trestle bridge with the accuracy of a stereographic image. Along with the other passengers, he gained perspective on America's Gilded Age.[31]

When the passengers arrived at Indianapolis, Indiana, at 4:30 P.M. on May 18, the Union Depot was crowded with so great a throng that the railroad tracks were completely obstructed. The obstruction forced the train to divert to the Jeffersonville stockyards until the crowds abated. Because Pratt refused to allow the prisoners out of their cars, "a murmur of dissatisfaction" emanated from the sightseers on hand. Major Robert Emmet and W. D. Wetherell, passenger agents of the Vandalia Railroad, offered to conduct tours. When gentle ladies passed through the cars, they were received "with great urbanity by the inmates." A few chiefs obliged visitors by shaking hands, providing autographs, and making gestures. The sight of the prisoners, who were wearing random pieces of army uniforms accessorized with ear rings, brass chains, red paint, and knick-knacks, entranced the guests. They were also shocked by the exiles' long, braided hair, which caused much ado about "the difficulty of distinguishing the sexes." Taken altogether, it was remarked, the prisoners presented "a curious spectacle" and a "puzzling problem for the government." From outside the train, spectators could only obtain a dimmer view through the doors and windows. The exhausted passengers closed their windows and screens, reserving only a small aperture through which they could be seen by onlookers.[32]

The onlookers turned to their newspapers to learn about "Lo, the poor Indian." One wag, who claimed to have met "the condemned redskins," described "a fine looking body of men" in his column. However, he also complained about transporting them "at so much expense when scalping is so cheap." With impunity, the press invented lurid stories, bogus dialogue, and fanciful caricatures for the satisfaction of their readers. One reporter incorrectly described Big Tree as "one of the most sociable" of the prisoners, even though Big Tree was not even among the exiles. It was also falsely reported that a prisoner had "slipped his feet from the shackles," "crawled through a window," and been shot in the leg and recaptured at the station in Indianapolis. The newspapers correctly reported that Pratt re-boarded with several new passengers. They included his wife, Anna, and three children, Nana, Mason, and Marion. He also brought along an interpreter, George L. Fox, who was skilled at speaking the Comanche language. The newspapers reported that the train continued to the next line, the J. M. and I. Railroad, which took them to Louisville, Kentucky.[33]

Huge crowds gathered in Louisville, where the train stopped next. It arrived at midnight, carrying what one newspaper labeled "the hardest lot of red faces that have ever plundered and murdered Western settlers on the frontier." The coverage insinuated the "humbug" of a carnival or circus. The storylines repeated crude details of bloody mayhem and axe-murders, claiming that Indians "cut the heads off the women and girls after they had been killed."[34] One Louisville journalist, offering typical coverage, wrote:

Our reporter passed by Lone Wolf and shook hands with him. The Indian smiled, and, at the request of the reporter, Mr. Fox asked him to stand up and show his height. He stood up proudly, but with the most treacherous look ever seen in a mortal face. A rough, jagged face, with two keen, subtle black eyes, full of deceit, a form erect and about five feet eleven inches in height, broad shoulders, head thrown backwards and chest forwards clad in an old soldier's jacket-all this constitutes Lone Wolf. Bird Medicine, perhaps next to Lone Wolf the most famous of the Indian chiefs, is dying of consumption, and was cooped up in a corner of the car.[35]

They passed through the city quickly, though, and took the midnight train for Nashville, Tennessee.

In Nashville, the press stirred the public to frenzy. One journalist tried satiating the public craving with news about "the gang of Indians which passed through this place going southward last week, prisoners in charge of a military guard." He recounted their "horrible murder and outrage," which surpassed "the Newgate Calendar" as a record of their "devilish" crimes against humanity. He wished to disabuse readers of "their idea of Indians from reading the *Last of the Mohicans*." Instead, he wrote, they deserved deportation "far from their breezy homes" and to suffer "in fetters under the burning sun of Florida." In addition, he opined, the convicts "in our State's prisons" were "a dozen times more worthy of help and sympathy" and "a dozen times as likely to become a decent human" than the "best of the gang who have just gone by us on their way to their Florida prison." The report expressed concern that if they "escape into the Everglades," the country would face "another Seminole war" or worse. Hence, a penal institution with maximum security represented an appropriate place for the dangerous "rattlesnakes."[36]

In fact, security on the train broke down about five miles outside of Nashville. On the morning of May 19, Lean Bear, a Cheyenne chieftain labeled a "bad character" by Pratt, secured a seat alone. He was monitored by guards from the Fifth Infantry, who stood at either end of the car. As the locomotive paused briefly at the Madison, Tennessee, station, Private Hennesey of Company F became suspicious of the Cheyenne's behavior. He summoned Corporal Allen of Company K, and, drawing back the blanket from Lean Bear's head, the soldiers discovered blood on his face and neck. He had cut his own throat and punctured his chest with a small pocketknife. In a swift stroke, Lean Bear stabbed both of the men in uniform. Then he struggled with the soldiers for possession of a rifle. Though very small and with his strength reduced from the loss of blood, he almost succeeded in getting the weapon away from them. When finally overpowered, he immediately collapsed to the floor of the car. Pratt, who sat in the car next in rear, rushed to the scene and called for a physician to attend the wounded. After feeling for a pulse, the doctor turned back the eyelids of the chief and pronounced him dead.[37]

In Nashville, Pratt arranged to leave an officer and three men with the dead Indian, ordering them to carry the corpse out on a blanket. When dropped on the platform, though, the dead man suddenly revived and would have slipped away had it not been for the shackles. However, two soldiers chased Lean Bear, grabbed him, and wrestled him to the ground. Once again, his body appeared lifeless. "Well he is dead now anyhow," the doctor again concluded after examining him for a second time. The body was placed onto an express wagon and carried off for burial at a military post, where he again revived and asked to be shot or have his throat cut. One newspaper account incorrectly claimed that "some wicked miscreant must have furnished the savage with a knife." Actually, his fellow travelers on the train had been allowed to retain their knives. For the remainder of the trip, though, Pratt ordered sharp objects taken from them.[38]

As their thousand-mile trip continued, they passed into the Deep South. They traveled through Chattanooga, Tennessee, and Atlanta, Georgia. They paused briefly at Macon, Georgia, resting for an hour. One of the Cheyenne voiced concern over Gray Beard, who appeared particularly morose, and asked Pratt to tie the chief's hands and fasten him to a seat. Pratt declined, confident that Gray Beard was already as restrained as a "Roman slave." As Pratt passed through the cars with his six-year-old daughter, Nana, he stopped briefly at Gray Beard's seat. He introduced the chief to his daughter as "a man of great physical and native intellectual power." Misty-eyed, the weary elder said that he had only one child, a girl, about the same age as Nana. With his voice trembling, he asked in his own language: "How would you like to have chains on your legs and be taken far away from your home, your wife, and your daughter?" Pratt offered no answer, admitting that it was a "hard question." He proceeded to sleep on it.[39]

About 2:00 A.M. on May 21, the train entered the pine woods and dense palmetto growth along the Florida border. The locomotive slowed to twenty-five miles an hour between Live Oak and Lake City. As Gray Beard sat by himself, he discreetly opened his window. With the car still moving, he crawled out of the opening still in chains. The guard saw his escape, but was not quick enough to prevent it. Pratt, awakened at once, swiftly stopped the train. The conductor immediately backtracked the locomotive to the spot where Gray Beard had struck the ground. There they discovered his blanket by the side of the track. By lantern light, the guards undertook a diligent search to no avail. After a considerable delay, the engineer reported that the water supply for the steam engine was nearing exhaustion and that they would not be able to make the next tank unless they moved on at once.[40]

Pratt reluctantly agreed but left a sergeant and three soldiers to continue the search until the next train passed their way. As Pratt took his seat, though, the sergeant directing the search party hallooed from the rear of the train. He had heard the clanking of shackles in the darkness. The soldiers advanced nearly a hundred yards to a dense growth of bushes. Suddenly, the Cheyenne chief broke from the cover and dashed toward the "iron road." "Here he is," the sergeant shouted, and instantly fired. From his window seat, Biter witnessed the scene and later sketched it, showing the close range of the deadly shooting. Pratt arrived at the spot too late to intervene and found Gray Beard lying in a pool of blood on the tracks. The shot had entered in the lower part of his chest at one side and exited the other just above the waist. The guards lifted the gravely wounded man into the rear car. With Eagle's Head at his side, he whispered in his native tongue that he had "wanted to die ever since being chained and taken from home." He gave a personal message for his lifelong friend to pass along to his family. He expired two hours later as the train neared the next station. His body was left for burial at Baldwin, Florida.[41]

Later that day, the passengers disembarked at Jacksonville, Florida, and boarded a steamer to Tocoi. They walked a gangplank to board the boat, which carried them up the St. Johns River to another train station. Appearing weathered and ill from their harrowing ride, they taxied on the St. Johns Railway for the final twenty miles. Crossing the St. Sebastian River, the prisoners saw porpoises leaping out of the water. Around 5:00 P.M. they arrived in St. Augustine, where they were approached by a columnist from the *Tri-Weekly Florida Union*. He met "the haughty Black Horse," who answered his barrage of questions in pidgin-English: "Me no talk to white man, he mean no good." Lone Wolf reportedly offered a similar remark: "No like the Pale Face . . . Give no good medicine." In contrast, the inquirer found the Cheyenne "talkative and jovial," but warned his readers to not "laugh at them, or say anything to make them mad." Still in irons, the new arrivals waded through the throng of townspeople anxious to see, hear, or touch the so-called "savages." They were escorted to several horse-drawn conveyances, which carted them through the plaza. The prisoners drew their blankets over their faces to hide from the bystanders gawking at the procession.[42]

The procession passed through the narrow streets of St. Augustine, the oldest continuously inhabited European settlement in North America. Founded in 1565 as a strategic sea and land base for the Spanish Empire, it was located on the edge of an inlet. In 1672, Spanish authorities had ordered the construction of the massive Castillo de San Marcos on the north end of the settlement. It was built with approximately 500,000 coquina blocks, a kind of shell conglomerate hardened into stone. To erect the medieval-type fortress, the Spanish had mustered Native people in the area into a labor force. They had built it complete with ramparts, parapets, bastions, turrets, garitas, ravelin, moat, drawbridge, and watchtower. In places the walls were sixteen feet thick and thirty feet high. The courtyard was a hundred feet on each side. After acquiring Florida in 1821, the Americans renamed the castle in honor of the revolutionary war hero General Francis Marion. The oldest masonry stronghold in the country, Fort Marion provided a military base during the Second Seminole War and a dungeon for two famous chiefs, Coacoochee and Osceola.[43]

Earlier in 1875, the War Department had begun refitting Fort Marion as a prison house for the Plains Indians. E. D. Townsend, the Adjutant General, requested "repairs to be put on the fort as will make it secure enough to keep them." Captain James C. Post and the Corps of Engineers visited the site in April and observed signs of deferred maintenance. The facility had fallen into disrepair after the Civil War, and the casemates and the courtyard were only being used to store munitions for the garrison at the St. Francis Barracks almost a mile away. Post had a barricade built across the ramp heading to the terreplein so as to prevent entry into the casemates except at the discretion of guards. He closed the thirty-seven windows with two-inch plank flush against the wall so as to prevent any prisoner from climbing upward through the openings to reach the terreplein. He ordered heavy doors of two-inch plank to cover a number of the fifteen doorways within the coquina walls. He also authorized the flooring of the casemate adjoining the sally port, which he allocated as a guard room. The cost of these repairs reached $1,500, with the work continuing until May 10.[44] Eleven days after the repairs had been completed, the prisoners of war reached the castle.

The prisoners were astonished by the castle, finding it unlike any structure they had ever seen. Before entering it, they conducted a general survey of the facade. The cannons at the fort excited both distrust and admiration, and they inspected the big guns from cascabel to face. With their ankles still bound, they crossed the grounds into the courtyard. Moving like a chain gang, they folded their blankets about them with a majestic sweep. Once inside the walls, their escorts shut the two massive pitch-pine doors behind them. Puzzled by the coquina, they scraped the porous stone and scrutinized its tiny shells. They scaled the ramparts to reach the upper deck. In what signified one of Biter's most haunting portraits, he depicted the chiefs and the warriors emerging from the terreplein. It featured the blanketed men as they gazed upon Matanzas Bay and Anastasia Island. Still shackled and guarded, they stared intently beyond the shore. Only a steamboat and two lighthouses appeared on the horizon. The Atlantic Ocean rolled in the distance. They stood dejected and forlorn, reconciling themselves to imprisonment in a fortress of solitude. The warrior artist called it their "melancholy prospect."[45] After twenty-four days of hard traveling and years of relentless struggle, the iron-bound leaders had arrived at the end of their road.

Chapter 3
Basic Training
The Fort Marion Regimen

THE PLAINS INDIANS IMPRISONED AT Fort Marion were a motley crew. They came from five distinct nations and spoke at least six different languages. Their median age was about twenty-six. The youngest prisoner, a Kiowa named Tounkeuh, or Good Talk, was approximately sixteen. The oldest, Double Vision, was nearly sixty. As a consequence of their plight in Indian Territory and their deportation to Florida, they appeared lean, frail, and ill. Long Back, a Cheyenne, stood the tallest, reaching almost six feet two inches in height. He towered over Zopehe, or Toothless, a Kiowa who measured a diminutive five feet, one inch. The Comanche warrior, Quoiyouh, or Pile of Rocks, weighed a robust 186 pounds, in contrast to the 126-pound Arapaho White Bear. Thirteen prisoners were listed as tribal headmen. Thirty-seven were implicated in various murders around their reservations. The rest were accused of armed robbery and seditious acts.[1] Whatever the charges against them, they now belonged to the U.S. Army.

At first, the prisoners remained shackled and lodged in the castle casemates. The Comanche, Kiowa, and Caddo occupied the west side while the Arapaho and Cheyenne shared the north side. The married couples stayed apart from their fellow inmates and occupied two small tents. In addition, four larger hospital tents were pitched in the parade area. During the first week, armed guards of the First Artillery from St. Francis Barracks directed all of their movements. At the point of loaded weapons, the prisoners marched from their cell blocks for daily exercise sessions in the high-walled courtyard adjacent to the casemates. They moved the shot and the shell scattered about the grounds and stored them in one of the cells. During the day watch, they were allowed to circulate about the interior of the fortress. Under the night watch, they slept upon the dirty floors. Even if Fort Marion housed them, their homes and hearts remained elsewhere.[2]

Fort Marion contained a kitchen and mess area, which was located to the right side of the main entry. Regular army rations were prepared for the prisoners three times a day, with the armed guards supervising their meals. Private Robert Jones from Company C of the First Artillery served as their cook, earning the sobriquet "Big Chuckaway." He was assisted by Dick, Lone Wolf's former captive. The Cheyenne Hoitoich, or Star, began to bake bread under their direction, producing wholesome brown loaves. In the chow line, the diners received a substantial mess of bacon, beef, tripe, potatoes, beans, molasses, rice, and soup. They developed a fondness for tropical fruits as well as for fresh oysters. They enjoyed the fresh and exotic cuisine, which gave them a well-balanced diet. Other victuals issued to them included a soldier's luxury items— coffee, sugar, vinegar, salt, and pepper. They appreciated the commissary at the military post, which contrasted favorably with the agencies and their paltry rations.[3]

Issued soap by the post commissary, the prisoners were escorted in small groups to the beach just outside the coquina walls to bathe. They plunged into the murky waters, tasting its saltiness with great surprise. They delighted in the sensations generated by the thundering ocean waves. They pointed at a shark swimming within a few feet of them, but, because of the shallowness of the water, it threatened no harm. They laughed at the fiddler crabs scrambling along the shore. One bit the foot of a bather, who hopped about with astonishment and pain. A large alligator's tooth, which they found on the beach, further confounded them. They expressed doubt about such a sizeable fang. Without a term to identify the exotic beast, a waving motion of the hand and arm was offered to denote "snake." Soon, the prisoners were the talk of the town, prompting residents to join them when they appeared for their morning ablutions and face painting. A curious reporter from the *Florida Press* approached Eagle's Head, the Cheyenne chief, on the beach. The headman surprised the reporter with his wit and congeniality. Strangers in a strange land, the exiles from Indian Territory began to recover from the disorientation of their exile.[4]

Rather than reside with the exiles at Fort Marion, Lieutenant Pratt rented a comfortable house nearby. As he began to associate weary faces with the strange names on his roster, the officer worried about their morale. "The severe circumstances of their imprisonment and their being taken so far away from their homes," he wrote, "made these special prisoners almost lose hope." One day in the courtyard, he approached the Kiowa, who were sitting together and conversing in a low tone among themselves. Hoping to cheer them and to offer a diversion from their sorrow, he told them tales about "his Indian adventures." As the other tribesmen joined the attentive Kiowa, they began listening with great interest. With the help of George Fox, the interpreter of Comanche, Pratt reminisced about visiting their camps, giving them provisions, and attending their dances. He related anecdotes to illustrate his "most dangerous" experiences. He told of the dancing warrior who, during a "test" of his courage, had stood over him in a threatening manner and wielded a knife in his hand. He spared no detail to make it graphic, remarking that he "almost felt that knife enter my body." Suddenly, a great roar of laughter arose from the Kiowa. They pointed to one of the young men, declaring that he was the knife-wielding brave. There stood Biter, next to Aulih, or Wise, who also recalled the dance.[5]

To Pratt's great surprise, the captive audience began to retell his story. On the evening of the surrender in the Wichita Mountains, they said, Wise had been scheduled to perform first in the ceremony. When the time came for his performance, he refused to move. The chiefs tried to persuade him, but he disobeyed their orders. In retaliation, they directed Biter to take his counterpart's blanket and to cut it into pieces. In other words, the incident had been a dispute between the two at the ceremony and not a "test" of the officer at all. By filling in the missing details of the story, they made it clear to Pratt that he had assumed too much. Standing at ease among them, he listened to their version of events and chuckled at himself. They laughed at the misunderstanding with him. Pratt admitted to them that non-Indians frequently "misapprehended" Native people. Whether or not he fully appreciated it at the time, the captives had taught Pratt a valuable lesson.[6]

Pratt came to believe that his experiences with the captives gave him great insight into their tragic circumstances. While gaining respect for the martial spirit of the Plains Indians, the officer expressed disdain for their culture on the whole. He presumed that they were inferior to non-Indians in many respects. Their inferiority stemmed from their environment, he posited, but not from their race. Thus, a chief or a warrior could be reformed if exposed to the proper training. "He is born a blank like the rest of us," Pratt once said of the "savages" he encountered. Left to the darkness of their homeland, they could not possibly advance to the enlightenment of civilization. The reservation, which permitted aspects of com-

munal hunting and gathering, reproduced the conditions for
"uncivilized" tribalism. However, their incarceration offered
an ideal institutional setting for "individualizing" them. A strict
regimen in captivity would engage their minds in a disciplined
way and infuse them with the "Great Father's" notions of manhood. Pratt determined that his objective at Fort Marion was
to encourage the rapid assimilation of the Indians—that is, to
remake them in his own image.[7]

Pratt was fond of calling them "his Indians"; they began
referring to him as their "white chief." He embraced his authority with enthusiasm, voicing a desire to keep "these prisoners under the control of a single, well defined head." Of
course, Fort Marion and the guards were administered by
Major John Hamilton, the post commander. However, Pratt
assumed command over virtually every detail of their incarceration. It was his responsibility to see that "they not escape
into the swamps of Florida," where, General of the Army Sherman warned, they "would be a dangerous and formidable enemy."[8] Fox, the interpreter, joined the army payroll at $100 per
month. Though Raphael Romero remained on the payroll of
the Cheyenne and Arapaho agency, Pratt requested that he
continue his service with him. Pratt complained about the soldiers at the post, who intimidated the prisoners. Also, he pro-
tested "the injustice" of appropriating the supplies for the Indians "to the uses of the Post Guard of St. Francis Barracks."
He insisted that the surplus should go to the "benefit of the
prisoners." Even if prickly toward his superiors, he was generous with army provisions for the inmates.[9]

The War Department allocated the provisions, but the
Office of Indian Affairs in the Interior Department received
the bill. The Commissioner of Indian Affairs, Edwin P. Smith,
and the Secretary of the Interior, Columbus Delano, pledged
to the Secretary of War, Alfonso Taft, that the military stores

would be compensated. Thereafter, they diverted funds to the army from a $300,000 congressional appropriation designated for the support of "captive Cheyenne, Arapaho, Kiowa and Comanche Indians." For their first year in Fort Marion, Taft budgeted the amount of $4,319.04 for their care and support. Food alone constituted more than half of the expenditure, and the Quartermaster General enumerated expenses inclusive of $2,568.65 during the fiscal year. According to the commissary records, the promised reimbursements were delayed and the stores at the St. Francis Barracks became deficient. On at least one occasion, officials complained about the amount of medicine charged to them. In fact, the Indian Office took exception to what it considered excessive expenses.[10]

As the federal government wrangled over the budget, the captives struggled to survive. Struck by an illness during the arduous journey to Fort Marion, Wolf Stomach, a Kiowa also called the Sun Chief, was carried to the post hospital. His brother, Zopehe, or Toothless, visited him daily. Convinced that his time was short, Wolf Stomach tried to persuade Toothless to accompany him into death by cutting both their throats. However, Toothless refused and instead dressed his dying sibling in full regalia, painting him and preparing him for his final journey. Wolf Stomach died on the evening of May 24, 1875. The next day, White Horse, Woman's Heart, Double Vision, and Lone Wolf attended to the deceased. Major Hamilton asked if they objected to a non-Indian burial service, to which they consented after its significance was explained to them. After a short speech from Toothless, they placed his body into a pine coffin. It was borne by four privates to the southeast corner of the post cemetery. The small congregation stood in respectful silence at the gravesite and stated their satisfaction with the interment of the deceased. His clothing, a tin cup, and his personal effects were placed in the grave. They covered his body with sand. Even if buried along side honored servicemen, his bones rested in a place far from those of his ancestors.[11]

Alarmed by the death, Pratt complained to his superiors that the dreary facilities caused an outbreak of sickness. He wrote that "a short time in such confinement will destroy the general health of the prisoners under my charge." The humidity and heat coupled with their concentration inside the casements and behind the walls intensified their misery. He reported that most of them suffered with gastro-intestinal ailments and from heat exhaustion. The debilitating effects of living in chains and under constant guard exacerbated their physical disorders. "The roofs and walls of every casement are dripping with water," Pratt observed, "and in places covered with a green scum, while all the cells have a musty, sickening odor." He requested tar for the roofing and canvas for tents. On a work schedule, the prisoners began cleaning the walls by means of ladders and ropes. Even though a few continued to loiter, the physical exertion relieved a great deal of tension. One visiting journalist found them "perfectly contented and quiet" after work, lounging in "sunny corners of the bastions, sleeping or dreaming of other scenes and other days." Demanding hard work by the "prison labor," Pratt directed them to sanitize and to whitewash the place.[12]

One afternoon, Pratt received a notice about another ailing prisoner. By June 10, Lean Bear had recovered sufficiently from his wounds to be sent under guard from Nashville to Fort Marion. After his arrival, Dr. John H. Janeway, the post surgeon, tended to him. The chief declined to eat, though every effort was made to overcome his hunger strike. Because he exhibited an "unsound mind," Janeway recommended "solitary confinement with a view as much to the removal of all causes apt to disturb the emotions of the individual, as to the restraint of any impulse likely to compromise the security of a community." Considering the patient "unfit" for the hospital, the surgeon dispatched him back to the casemates. Pratt kept him confined in a cell separate from his inmates. In fact, he wanted him transferred "to the Insane Asylum." Experiencing delirium, Lean Bear confessed that he "stabbed himself and the soldiers" on the train and requested execution for his crimes. Pratt called him one of the "agitating elements" among his people, adding that "the damp foul casemate in my opinion aids Lean Bear in reaching his death." Alas, the once-invincible chief finally expired on July 24.[13]

More than anything else, the prisoners were homesick. The loss of their wives, children, relatives, and friends reinforced their despondency. Ironically, the bad feelings united the divided tribesmen, sparking an extraordinary intertribal council on June 9. Once they achieved consensus, they petitioned the federal government to bring their families to live with them. They desired to lead their people off the reservations and receive training to make a living. They selected Sky Walker, the Kiowa Owl Prophet, as their spokesman. Perhaps his deadly curse upon the deceased chieftain, Kicking Bird, frightened potential rivals at the council. Perhaps they admired his clairvoyance. A few days later, Pratt sent an account of his "Indian talk" to Edward Townsend, the Adjutant General. Major Hamilton endorsed the request, saying that such words "excite my sympathies." Lieutenant General Sheridan, however, dismissed it as "mere Indian twaddle."[14] On behalf of their common cause, Sky Walker had said:

We want to learn the ways of the white man. First we want our wives and children, and then we will go any place and settle down and learn to support ourselves as the white men do. If you go with us and Washington says so, we will go across the big water. We want to learn how to make corn and work the ground so we can make our own

living, and we want to live in a house just as a white man. Take us to
any part of the country and we will go like a man that is blindfolded
knowing that you are ahead and no harm will come to us. We do not
want to go back to our country to live. It is a bad country and bad
people live there. There has been dark work done there, the people
are crazy, and now we want to go to another place where the people
are not bad and crazy, where we can settle down and live in peace. . . .
We have thrown our road away.[15]

Yearning for new hope, Sky Walker's words struck a harmo-
nious chord among the disparate ensemble at Fort Marion.

As the days passed, Sky Walker suffered declining physical health from the onset of dysentery. "My friends, I am sick,"
he declared from the post hospital, adding that "about three
hours after sunrise tomorrow I am going to die." Unable to
"live well here," he determined to "go back to that land above,
where I was before." Early the next day, his fellow prisoners
entered his room and found him sitting upon an army cot. "I
am going above this morning," he reiterated. He rose up and
mingled with the tearful audience, shaking hands with each of
them. Then he went back to his bed, laid down, and pulled the
blanket over his head as if he were going to sleep. As the room
fell silent, he did not move again. Soon, one of the attendants
pulled the blanket off his face. "He isn't breathing," he whispered, and felt that his body was "getting cold." The Kiowa
told the physician at the hospital that Sky Walker had departed
for "the dead men's village," this time to stay. At 8:00 A.M. on
July 29, his death became official. Later that day, they placed
him in a black box and buried him in the post cemetery. The
sad news caused "considerable mourning" over the passing of
the Kiowa and inspired one eulogist to remember him as "the
greatest medicine man" he had ever known.[16]

Meanwhile, Lieutenant General Sheridan relented and

issued a call to the War and the Interior Departments to send the wives and children of the prisoners to Fort Marion. On July 22, the Secretary of War agreed, albeit with the stipulation "not exceeding one wife to one Indian, and send the children under twelve years of age." The prisoners, who claimed ninety-two dependents, were elated by the news. Quickly, President Grant directed action. Agent James Haworth furnished Colonel Ranald Mackenzie, the commanding officer at Fort Sill, with a list of sixteen Kiowa women and eleven children and two Comanche women and two children who had consented to go. While preparing for departure, they reportedly asked that two or more chiefs accompany them eastward. Likewise, the Cheyenne and Arapaho relatives at Darlington expressed anxiety about heading east without Indian escorts. After three days' consultation with friends and family, chiefs Whirlwind of the Cheyenne and Powder Face of the Arapaho announced their opposition. They opposed the removal of any more tribal members from their homeland and cited fear of the locomotives, suspicions about the military, and rumors about early parole.[17]

Undeterred by this opposition, the War Department decided that Pratt, one imprisoned chieftain, and one interpreter would travel to Indian Territory to collect the prisoners' next of kin. Pratt wanted to bring "a prominent Cheyenne and a Kiowa" on the mission, saying that their presence would make the travel "far safer for them than an escort of soldiers." Because Fort Marion's capacity could not safely exceed 100, they planned to house the families in tents on the grounds surrounding the fortress. Additional repairs upon the facility began in earnest. However, President Grant on August 9 revoked the order to send the families.[18] Outraged at the Indian Office for changing Grant's mind, Pratt believed that "narrow minded and unvisioned" agents provided "false information" to the federal government. As a conciliatory gesture, the Kiowa sent moccasins to all of their tribesmen in captivity. Indeed, Lone Wolf's wife sent him two pairs, a calico sack, a deer leg pipe, and family trinkets. Pratt replied to the agencies: "Tell the wives and other relatives of all of them that their friends receive the best of care, and are just as happy and contented as they can be under the circumstances." Nevertheless, the officer confided to his superiors that they appeared "much depressed" about their prolonged separation.[19]

Concerned about their worsening depression, Pratt received permission from Major Hamilton to undertake an experiment that summer. "The duty of the government to these Indians," he reasoned, "seems to me to be the teaching of them something that will be permanently useful to them." Ever since leaving Indian Territory, they had repeated "many talks" about "the white man's road" and their desire to walk it. In response, Pratt promised to instruct them to build, to cobble, to blacksmith, and to farm. He hoped to inculcate "manliness" through hard work. He expected to "push them patiently along." He claimed that they demonstrated "the greatest willingness and industry" under his direction. They embraced "any means offered for their future self-support with a will strong enough to overcome its difficulties." He wanted to run the prison along lines similar to "some of our northeastern penitentiaries," where the facilities for industrial trades existed. Much as "state prisons" demanded hard work of criminals, his "proper management" promised to make them productive members of society. He asked: "Why not do the same for these people, when they want it?" If he failed to rehabilitate them, then he pledged to resign his commission.[20]

Even though his superiors expressed apprehension about the experiment, Pratt went to work. Confident of the security of the coquina walls, he unlocked the shackles and removed the irons. He turned to Lone Wolf, the Kiowa chief, to take the lead in several new activities. Under Pratt's coordination, they built a large shed exactly 41 feet wide and 113 feet long upon the north side deck. Serving as their quarters, it exposed them to open air but sheltered them from direct sunlight. They fashioned wooden bunks and stuffed mattresses with dried grass to add to their sleeping comfort.[21] He trained them to maintain their quarters, clothing, and bodies according to army regulations. Reluctantly, they trimmed their hair. They were held accountable for regular sanitation, and the dining, kitchen and bakery were subject to inspections. They began daily drilling, which greatly improved their condition and carriage. Pile of Rocks, a Comanche, mocked the military exercises, though. Upon finding a dead alligator's carcass nearby, he manipulated its flaccid limbs and quipped: "Heap Good Soldier!"[22]

Despite such creative responses, Pratt imposed a coercive regime. He replaced their blankets with uniforms that were expensed to the Indian Office. During their first year, he issued forage caps, blouses, trousers, knit shirts, stockings, and shoes at a cost to the department of $615.98.[23] In daily drills, four Native buglers summoned them into formation on the ramparts. The officer called the cadence for the "setting up" process and for parade marching. He used "double quick" time, in which they were made to run all around the courtyard, up the ramp, all over the terreplein and even along the beach. He wrote to the War Department about enlisting "a force of not less than twenty-five to include two sergeants and three corporals," using them in "guarding themselves." He intended to use "a picked fifty to sixty of these men" for auxiliary service. Eventually, they would become "the best corps for operating in conjunction with troops in the staked plains and in the country about the heads of the Red River, the Brazos, Concho, Colorado, and Pecos that could be sent there." Through basic training, Pratt expected to turn them into "wolves" for the U.S. Army.[24]

Of course, elements of their training sparked ordinary resistance. According to one account, the uniformed tribesmen proceeded to demolish "the oppressive suit of blue" after receiving the first issue. They cut off the legs of the trousers at the hip, laying aside the upper part and using the lower part as leggings in their traditional style. Unimpressed by this fashion statement, Pratt formed them into a line in the courtyard. Showing them a pair of mutilated trousers, he barked that "the clothing belonged to the United States Government." He corrected them and issued more pants. As a number of ladies about the town gathered at the gate to see them exercise, he anticipated that their uniformed appearance would be a revelation. When he ushered in his guests to view the rank and file, the objects of their interest engendered quite a shock. Some wore their standard trousers, to be sure, but some wore nothing more than a gee-string. The impropriety gave the officer a "heavy heart." Quickly, he ended the public display in frustration. When later visitors walked across the drawbridge to watch a drill hour, the trainees wore the artillery attire in full. They shined their brass buttons, creased their trousers, polished their shoes, and donned their coats and caps. Maintaining their soldierly appearance became a matter of honor, much as they once maintained the ornaments of native dress.[25]

Furthermore, Pratt organized a chain of command among them. He mustered nearly fifty of the able-bodied into special service, assigning them guard duty alongside the First Artillery. They even carried guns on post. He designated Making Medicine, a Cheyenne dog soldier, as the first sergeant of the guard to call roll and to keep a roster. He picked Boy Hunting, a Kiowa raider, as quartermaster sergeant, making him responsible for drawing stores from supply and keeping memoranda on government issues. Pratt gave to them colored pencils and ledger books, instructing them to make pictures in "serial order." Blending their task as record keepers with their traditions for winter counts, they began in their own way to document the incidents of army life. Instead of buffalo hides, however, they inscribed their memories upon their ledgers. They sketched compelling images of their drilling, marching, and saluting. They depicted facing and flanking maneuvers. They accounted for a range of militia activities. At the same time, they revivified their warrior tradition under the guise of militarism. Thus, the non-commissioned officers, or N.C.O.'s, served as intermediaries as well as recorders.[26]

The intermediaries would regularly select a well-ordered trainee to be excused from duties in order to run errands about town. With Pratt's guidance, the sergeants sponsored contests to secure the orderly for the day. While standing by a bunk, each contestant was examined from head to foot. The inspectors looked over their bodies, even their ears, to see whether they were clean. They checked their hair to see whether it was nicely brushed and noted whether their shirts and stockings were fresh. They scrutinized their belongings and equipment. In fact, the orderly competition accentuated their ambition, precision, diligence, and pride. On one occasion, Pratt helped to make the determination of the orderly by comparing the fingernails of two finalists. He held their hands side by side to enable the first sergeant to see the contrast. Making Medicine at once formed a native sign with his forefinger extended, raised his hand and brought it down quickly, which meant "I understand."[27] The new order of things resonated with their martial spirit, or so it seemed.

Of course, a few of the trainees despised the routine of the new order. Just before one inspection, Biter reportedly became "heap sick" from eating a big piece of meat. Unable to stand at attention, he stayed in his bunk. Suspicious of the sick call, Pratt turned to Palo, a Kiowa warrior commonly referred to as Pedro. Pedro crafted a poultice of mustard and muslin and placed his medicine upon Biter's midsection. Moments later, Pratt gathered the trainees to watch as the feigned illness ended. Leaping up, Biter paced the room, ranting in the native tongue. Although the officer could not decipher his language, the Kiowa assured him with a smirk that "Indians have no swear words." Later, Pratt wrote that the brave was "so perverse and insubordinate" that he "almost determined to shoot him" as an example to his companions. Although Biter sulked during the next inspection, Pratt considered his public humiliation "a good lesson."[28] Peer pressure effectively served as a deterrent to dereliction of duty.

In addition to using peer pressure, Pratt demanded that the trainees police themselves. For instance, he inaugurated a penal system for court-martial cases. Once charges were made, a court composed of sworn peers convened. The accused heard the charges and was allowed to object to any person serving on the court. After pleas were made and testimony heard on both sides, the court determined the verdict and penalty. Pratt presided, reviewing each case of delinquency based upon the proceedings. When a local resident complained that "some chickens were stolen by an Indian," the culprit appeared in the court for a "trial by jury." They found him guilty and sentenced him to eight days of confinement in the dungeon without bread or water. After a day and a half, Pratt interceded and asked for a retrial. The jury met again and moderated the terms, allowing him bread and water. Nevertheless, they insisted that he serve the time. They wanted to make him an example to the townspeople. Later, the court tried "a Comanche for stealing a dollar" and for "threatening one of his fellows." Finding him guilty, they sentenced him to ten days in the dungeon. Though the sentence was harsher than Pratt believed necessary, the "Indian court" insisted upon swift and severe justice in such cases.[29]

Back in Indian Territory, the families of the exiles pleaded their cases to government agents, who called for an official inquiry. On September 30, 1875, Agent Haworth filed a complaint about "the lack of care" evinced by the military during the selection process. He had "never received anything more than the charges," and wanted to know "what evidence caused their banishment." In particular, he noted that White Horse had been arrested despite promises to the contrary made by officers at Fort Sill. Jonathan Richards, an agent at Anadarko, wrote on behalf of the Caddo, Huwahnee, whom he described as "a peaceable and loyal Indian." Black Beaver, a famous Delaware scout and father-in-law of Huwahnee's murder victim, requested his "release and restoration to his family." He believed that "Lone Wolf and the Kiowas" were to blame for the homicide, not the accused. Even Pratt wrote letters recommending the release of the Caddo. However, the *National Republican* issued a scathing editorial about the "premature sentimentalists," which squelched the pleas. The War Department claimed "discretion and good judgment" in each case, even if the Indian Office had its doubts.[30]

Even as officials discussed their cases via written communication, the Indians in exile gained an appreciation for mail call. With each letter passing between Pratt and the agencies, "glad faces" gathered to hear the welcomed words. "The Cheyenne and Arapaho are delighted to hear of the good health and spirits of the absent braves," stated one letter from the Darlington agency. Their people accepted the "corn road" and that "war is a bad thing," or so one of them reported. Left Hand, an Arapaho chieftain at the agency, informed his imprisoned brother, Packer, that he intended to "make corn" in his absence. Thus, he was anxious for his brother to learn everything possible while imprisoned "so that when he returns the tribe may receive the benefit of the knowledge." In a posting to the agency, Pratt wrote about the absent chief, Eagle's Head: "I have found Minimic one of the most sensible Indians I have ever met." The Cheyenne wanted the agency chiefs to know "that their boys are well and most of them grown fat from good local meat and living." He described "all the benefits of view and sea breeze, vessels coming and going, the bay, and ocean in the distance." The correspondence elicited joy and relief and enabled the Indians to keep in touch across the long distance of their separation.[31]

Frequently, the correspondence flowed with good news. For instance, Pratt wrote that his trainees "are generally in good health, and I have no doubt far better off than their friends think." He noted that they had ceased wearing scalp locks and breech cloths, cut their hair to a short length, wore uniforms, kept clean, and attended church. Though dressed in blue, the Cheyenne retained their moccasins for off-duty use. Pratt observed that they were "rapidly learning to read and talk English," and that he expected to return to Indian Territory with "thirty odd fair interpreters." He predicted that "the young able bodied fellows" would become respectable soldiers, informing the families about the promotions of Heap of Birds and Howling Wolf. Among the Kiowa, he promoted White Horse to the rank of sergeant as well. For the benefit of the Arapaho, he added that "White Bear and Packer are among the best I have." The officer characterized "his boys" as "loyal to the core." According to the letters home, the blue-clad tribesmen embraced the most rigorous elements of their training.[32]

In order to demonstrate the efficacy of the training, Pratt organized scouting expeditions. Between October 1 and 25,

1875, they bivouacked near Jack Mound at Anastasia Island, about five miles from St. Augustine. The officer and his sergeants pitched their white canvas tents on a high bluff overlooking the beach, while the rest of the men occupied a long row of smaller tents a little further down the coast. The Stars and Stripes waved overhead. They camped with the necessary equipment and organization, performing the duties of a company in the field. They conducted intertribal contests. They raced long distances on foot. They fished and hunted. They collected seashells. They sat in boats at low tide and ate oysters with great relish. Calling the retreat their "sanitarium," Pratt took them to the island for their recuperation. In addition, the officer wanted to test their fidelity to the corps.[33]

Overall, Pratt asserted, they were "vigilant" and "efficient" to a remarkable degree. In fact, they received "the greatest liberty to roam in directions not occupied by citizens within five miles of camp." On October 21, Pratt ordered Fox to take a party of twenty southward down the coast as far as Matanzas Inlet. They completed an eighteen-mile road march and returned the next day. Based upon their sterling behavior, he requested permission "to use them as guards at Fort Marion after their return on Monday next to the relief of troops." However, one prisoner misbehaved. The Cheyenne Paeyis, or Big Nose, left camp and disappeared with a non-Indian party of boaters. One of them was "a lassie," who Pratt called the brave's "special friend." He was absent without leave for about four hours. After his return, he was forced as chastisement to carry a heavy log in the presence of his peers for two hours, and he remained under their charge until morning. The squad leaders asked to punish him more severely, but Pratt refused. Aside from watching the elusive Big Nose, the guards of the camp passed their time by chasing wild razorback hogs.[34]

Limpy, a Cheyenne noted for good conduct, sketched

scenes of their camp life in a ledger book. He included in
the background the two lighthouses—one an ancient Spanish
structure and the other an American tower built the previous
year. They loomed so large on the island that he brought them
together into a single frame. In the foreground, he depicted
the sea wall, the beach, the underbrush, and the palmetto
growth. He featured his companions on duty in sky-blue pan-
taloons, dark blouses, and fatigue caps. Despite the change
from their traditional garb, he portrayed them using their old
and familiar squatting positions by the pup tents. In a departure from the ground-level vignettes common among Plains
Indian artists, he imagined a "bird's eye" view of their operations in the field. He achieved a kind of panoptic perspective
that illustrated his companions eating their army rations, tend-
ing their campfires, and patrolling their bivouac areas. His
attention to detail indicated their reconnaissance of the island. His mapping technique insinuated a linkage between the
towering sentinels of the coast and their own campground
sentries. Most of all, it signified an awareness of constant
surveillance.[35]

Because of their general rectitude while under surveillance, Pratt deemed their training nearly complete by the end
of autumn in 1875. Typically, he offered them affirmative
marks in his monthly ledger: "Conduct, excellent; Health, fair;
clothing, fair; Progress, good." The system of guard duty continued to develop and "all the details of company service and
police kept up" without "any exceptional cases of bad conduct"
or "want of cheerful obedience." He praised another company
outing in November, when two parties, one of ten and the
other of twelve, ventured to Matanzas Inlet for a week each.
He tracked the issuance of military clothing and equipment, as
well as the number who voluntarily attended church services
each Sunday. He remarked upon the planting of a winter gar-

den, which Eagle's Head superintended. He also recorded another death, the Kiowa Ihpayah, or Straightening an Arrow, who expired on October 5 from "consumption." In fact, the corpse was "hid away" on Anastasia Island at the request of his kinsmen. Despite the officer's upbeat assessments of their basic training, the body count continued to grow.[36]

The demise of Big Moccasin, a Cheyenne prisoner, represented one of the more painful cases to assess. According to the attending surgeon, James Laird, he suffered for eight days with "bilious fever." Nonetheless, he improved under treatment and eventually appeared bright and well. The surgeon supposed that he "would be fit for duty within a few days." On the morning of November 4, however, Laird found him cold with a weak pulse and laboring respiration. Examining him further, the surgeon "found the penis tied up, and the whole organ as well as the scrotum much swelled and infiltrated with urine." Laird inquired about the "incontinence of urine," but detected "reticence" to say anything about it. However it had happened, Big Moccasin evinced "the symptoms of uremic poisoning." In spite of a strong stimulant, he "could not be aroused from the lethargic state" that morning. Later that night, at 10:30 P.M., he died in great agony. In reporting the death, Pratt admitted that he had "killed himself." Glossing over the matter, he claimed that "there seemed to be little sympathy for him with the others."[37] Though unable to discern their hearts and minds fully, he sensed the depth of their emotional angst.

On January 3, 1876, Pratt encouraged the Cheyenne to express their feelings in a letter to their former agent, John D. Miles. "Tell my family I am well," Heap of Birds spoke, saying that "they must not cry or mourn for me, but have strong hearts." He believed that "the President will turn me back some day, and will leave me to live in peace." He added: "I

want my children to go to school." Bear Shield echoed his
sentiments, promising that "my ears are very large now" and
asking the agent to "tell my wife I am well and get well fed
here." He admonished her to "not think hard," but to trust that
he would return "to plant corn."[38] Likewise, Eagle's Head
voiced their positive outlook for the new year:

*I have had a good time since I came here. Tell the agent to tell all my
friends I have good clothes and plenty to eat. I am learning the white
man's road very fast. I am picking it up everyday. Tell Agent Miles I
want him to hurry up and have me a house built by the time I learn to
be a white man that I may have my family about me and have cows
and chickens like a white man. I like to hear the chickens holler in the
morning to wake me up. Tell Agent Miles to tell all my friends I have
thrown away leggings, breech cloth, and blanket and dress like a
white man. I have my hair cut, and feel like a white man. I feel a great
deal better. I want the Agent to tell Whirlwind and all my friends to
hold their hearts hard that I shall see them some day. Tell the Agent to
keep my children at school. Tell my wife and daughters not to feel bad
that when I come back I can learn them what I have learned. All I
want is a house and to live in one little place . . . . Tell the agent to take
all them hard-headed Cheyennes and put them on the Corn road,
and make them work. If he don't know them, I can point them out
when I come. If Capt. Pratt ever goes back with me, I can show him
the ones who done the mischief. We are soldiers now, and we can go
right along and jerk them out.*[39]

Of course, the nuances of the chief's speech were lost in translation. Through Pratt, though, the Indian leaders at Fort Marion sent messages articulating good will.

Meanwhile, non-Indian leadership at the post changed
hands in 1876, when Lieutenant Colonel Frederick T. Dent,
President Grant's brother-in-law, replaced Major Hamilton.
Dent suggested that Pratt take his trainees "out in the piney

woods" and "make them build some log houses." Pratt obtained a whip saw, axes, and other tools, which they used in several construction projects. He taught them to rive the clapboards, to erect stick chimneys, and to chink and to daub the wood. He paid fifty cents per tree and estimated the total expense of their building at less than $200 worth of timber. Also, he drilled them in English terminology, suggesting that "one of our greatest hindrances in dealing with the Indians is the difficulty of language, which renders us dependent on interpreters who are generally not the men we desire." If "forty or fifty of these men could speak our tongue," he wrote, then it "would facilitate matters in civilizing them very much." Lieutenant Colonel Dent, in fact, declared that the final solution to "the Indian problem" would be achieved by "making soldiers of them." His confidence prompted Pratt to ask an awkward question of one Indian agent: "Why would not a company of active young Cheyennes and Arapahoes at your Agency under the command of Lt. Pratt be the best part of a police force for you?"[40]

Pushing the question further, Pratt wrote directly to Lieutenant General Sheridan in early 1876. He declared that "the behavior of the prisoners has been so good that I would recommend their release and return to their people at an early day." He contended that "all have been cured." The officer compared them favorably to the regulars of the First Artillery stationed at St. Augustine, where incidents of drunkenness and sleeping on post seemed common. He boasted that "there has not been a single case of breach of discipline," even though his ledger noted "two cases of bad conduct" occurring in January. He wanted to take them to a "good agricultural district," where they would practice "raising corn and other products." Thereafter, he anticipated, they would be enlisted "as soldiers at their agencies." In another letter to the division com-

mander, he pledged that "not one of these men will ever take
up arms against the government unless driven by the gross-
est bad treatment." They had experienced "enlightenment"
through army life, or so he believed.[41]

Irrespective of Pratt's beliefs, officials in Washington
seemed indifferent. To maintain fiscal balance, the War Department and the Interior Department curbed expenditures.
When Romero was discharged from agency service, Pratt re-
employed him as a full-time cook. He squabbled with his superiors about funding, and they rejected his requests for a school
teacher and for advanced training for the men in uniform.
During the spring, Fox was discharged because no appropriation had been made to cover his salary. The Indian Office
complained that his monthly salary of $100 represented an
unnecessary expense. Pratt convinced Fox to stay in St. Augustine for another year and continued his pay under "inciden-
tal expenses." Unfortunately, his services became subject to
the "caprice of politics." Decrying the lack of support for the
"elevation" of Native people, the officer woefully concluded
that "my efforts to that end only meet with base toleration."
He pleaded with the Indian Office to help the prisoners, asking that they "recommend their release very soon." He fore-
cast that "they would act promptly against the lawless of their
own tribes and make the best police force that could be used
among their own people." Although he expressed interest in
Pratt's experiment, General of the Army Sherman remained
skeptical: "I fear these Indians will betray his confidence."[42]

To be sure, basic training at Fort Marion forged a tenta-
tive alliance between the war prisoners and the U.S. Army.
Despite their subtle forms of dissent, the training worked to
the extent it resonated with native zeal for militarism. The
trained Indians excelled in their duties by operating as a cohe-
sive unit. Locked into a relationship that required interaction

and uniformity, they maneuvered in concert to remove their fetters. They were invigorated by drilling and scouting, which improved their physical fitness and collective morale. They strove to gain favors and to secure positions to distinguish themselves. They dressed in fatigues and stood at attention, making gestures toward the power of strong leadership. Beneath the bluecoats, they sustained a sense of mission to serve and to protect their people. They respected the mastery of their new commander and became guardians of the outpost, but the training did not alter their goal. Under the banner of martial law, the goal of the warriors and the chiefs remained to march home one way or another.

Chapter 4
Curio Class
The St. Augustine Experience

CALLED THE "CURIO CLASS" BY Lieutenant Pratt, the Plains Indians at Fort Marion were a sight to behold. Although the officer attempted to eliminate a great deal of what distinguished them, they exhibited an uncanny ability to keep their culture alive. By manufacturing souvenirs and producing entertainment, they began to conduct business with the populace near the government's oceanfront property. Aroused by the exaggerated imagery of the "Indian frontier" given by dime novels and lowbrow theater, visitors wanted to see the notorious men of the Great Plains. Public curiosity reinforced the popular assumption that the Indian, much like the frontier itself, represented something wild and fleeting. Strangers came to St. Augustine for a brief encounter with the "vanishing race." Ironically, the prisoners' confinement behind the coquina walls of the military outpost opened a lucrative market for the enterprising men. By engaging in the nascent industry of tourism, the chiefs and the warriors became more than mere pawns in the hands of Pratt.[1]

The Indians held by Pratt responded constructively to the non-Indians they encountered. They were experienced with trading commodities and offering gifts to strangers in their midst. For centuries, their ancestors participated in a network of exchange relationships with their indigenous neighbors as well as with the Spanish, French, and Americans. They had functioned as middle men in the far-flung commerce that de-

veloped across the North American grasslands. The flow of
goods, ideas, and services represented a means to strengthen
alliances and to balance power. With a rich and dynamic mate-
rial culture, Native people displayed tact and innovation in
their negotiations with clients. In some sense, the marketing
strategies at St. Augustine underscored the resilience of their
conventions and customs. Cunning men whose worlds re-
volved around hunting and warfare also understood elements
of nineteenth-century capitalism.[2] Even as exiles on a foreign
and distant shore, they knew how to treat the tourists as potential customers.

Before the exiles had arrived there, St. Augustine had developed into an alluring tourist destination. One of the Cheyenne prisoners, Roman Nose, believed that people flocked to
the area annually because of the fine weather. Unlike his land-
locked home, the Florida coast did not turn cold with the
coming of winter, and it was not a place of extreme tempera-
tures. Roman Nose also praised the local hospitality, noting
that he was able "to find good friends" among the residents.[3]
Folks from surrounding locales came to the beach for weekends and holidays, thanks to the availability of the steamers
and the railroad. In fact, the low cost of travel made the
trip accessible to virtually anyone. It was fast becoming one
of America's sentimental dreamscapes, a place where guests
sought recovery and respite. It provided asylum and physical
health for the ill. It attracted "Yankee" sojourners who preferred "wintering" in the American South. Hotels, boarding-
houses, and shopkeepers grew to depend upon the increased
flow of traffic through the plaza. The resort community thrived
thanks to the frequent pilgrimages of sightseers, who sought
amusement, relaxation, and recreation.[4]

For the sightseers, "Captain Pratt's Indians" were no
ordinary attraction. Posters and handbills advertised guided

excursions to the dungeons of Fort Marion. For four dollars, travelers to St. Augustine could purchase round-trip tickets on steamers and railroads from Jacksonville, Florida. The Great Atlantic Coast Line requested permission to photograph "the prominent Indians now incarcerated in the Old Fort" for inclusion in brochures about Florida. Even General of the Army William T. Sherman encouraged his cousin to stay in the ancient city for a winter so that he and his family could see the Indians. Soon after arriving in the summer of 1875, Pratt began admitting anyone who had obtained permission from the post commander. To regulate the crowds, he issued General Order No. 51, which prohibited visiting on Sundays. To the annoyance of the officers, the gawkers expected the army to display the "caged tigers" seven days a week. "This is not a good place to advance them," complained Pratt, because "they are simply objects of curiosity here." In voyeuristic fashion, thousands of people asked to see them during their captivity.[5]

Sidney Lanier, a nineteenth-century writer, documented his sighting of the captives while staying in St. Augustine. In 1875, he included scenes of local color in *Florida*, which was essentially a guidebook for tourists. Reflecting the popular genre of travel literature, the author drew particular attention to the presence of the Indians in the castle. He imagined them "rapidly degenerating" behind the coquina walls where the government kept them "locked-up." Privately, he complained about their confinement "by some ass who is in authority." Describing their "strange tongues and barbaric gestures," he evoked pity about "the unspeakable maddening wrongs" perpetrated against them. He noted that they were men of consequence in their tribes, some of whom were known to have been guilty of atrocious crimes.[6] His guidebook highlighted the eccentricity of the prisoners:

And so here they are—Medicine Water, a ringleader, along with White Man, Rising Bull, Hailstone, Sharp Bully, and others, in the terrible murder of the Germain [sic] family, and in the more terrible fate of the two Germain [sic] girls who were recently recaptured from the Cheyennes; Come See Him, who was in the murder of the Short surveying party; Soaring Eagle, supposed to have killed the hunter Brown, near Fort Wallace; Big Moccasin and Making Medicine, horse thieves and raiders; Packer, the murderer of Williams; Mochi, the squaw identified by the Germain [sic] girls as having chopped the head of their murdered mother with an axe. Besides these, who constitute most of the criminals, are a lot against whom there is not a particular charge, but who are confined on the principle that prevention is better than cure.[7]

Lanier accentuated the alien features of the Indians, even including one of their drawings in the guide book to the Sunshine State.

Once Pratt had removed the fetters from their hands, the warrior artists began filling their ledger books with a rich variety of original drawings. These drawings compelled many visitors to open their pocketbooks and make the Indians generous offers. Sold for around two dollars per book, the art ledgers were often broken up and the pages separated. Observers noted that the Indians shared a passion for illustration and seemed to delight in demonstrating their skill. They even left murals upon the interior of Fort Marion. Of course, they adapted their traditional artistry to virtually any paper product. They decorated hand fans for respectable ladies. Upon seeing a few sketches, one journalist pronounced its creator "an expert with his pencil." Another discerned "a caustic humor" pervading their work. The vivid and imitative renderings constituted quaint mementoes of a trip to the fortress.[8]

In fact, visitors were drawn to the prisoners through these mementoes. Eva Scott, a New York artist who later took the name Fényes, gave blank drawing books to Biter and Howling Wolf. Fascinated by their sketches, she later became a noted watercolorist of landscapes and an avid student of prisons. During a tour of the facilities, General Sherman received a book of Plains Indian drawings, which he later gave to his children. He called their work "curious and ingenious" and suggested that it might prove "a device of profit." He sent a five-dollar bill to Pratt, who passed it along to the artist. Ledger books were sent to the Commissioner of Indian Affairs, John Q. Smith. Pratt also sent them to senators and to prominent philanthropists. He even contacted a friend about publishing "a small book" with sketches and a history of the tribes. Although it was never published, he estimated that such a book could be sold to tourists for about a dollar apiece. A number of the artists began crafting their imagery to suit the requests of patrons.[9]

A local jeweler named Ballard wanted to employ the artists to manufacture curios. He asked them to comb the beaches, which were full of hard fiber bean-like seeds that washed up on the shores. After collecting the "sea beans," the prisoners polished and ornamented them with insignias or initials. The curios sold quickly, prompting Ballard to contract with Pratt for the work of polishing six thousand "sea beans" at ten cents apiece. The Indians finished the chocolate-colored trinkets and returned them to the jeweler, who then offered to pay them to polish ten thousand. Because the Indians were able to do the work almost perfectly, another dealer in Jacksonville contracted with them for six thousand more curios. Recognizing the quality of their work and its novelty appeal, the dealers used the fact that the souvenirs were crafted by Indians to enhance their allure.[10] Bear's Heart, a Cheyenne, recalled the deal: "Capt. Pratt see boys have no money. He got sea beans. He give every Indians two sea beans. He say make sea bean shine. He told us how, and when we make sea bean good, we take to him. He give us money." Over time, they made more than $1,600 off their efforts, which represented an unexpected windfall from their prison industries.[11]

After polished "sea beans" glutted the souvenir market, the prisoners diversified and began manufacturing other curios. They combed the beaches for unique shells and polished them for sale, keeping the profits for themselves. Alligators' teeth were another popular souvenir. They made canes, palm hats, and beads. Tourists wanted to buy keepsakes directly from the so-called "Florida boys." Roman Nose recalled that they sold most items for twenty-five cents, with the most popular ones—bows and arrows—going for a dollar and a half. Their best quality bows and arrows went for a premium, as high as five dollars. When the price was right, they traded their moccasins as well.[12] They asked Pratt to obtain raw materials from the Darlington agency in Indian Territory for use in making more items for profit. In exchange, Pratt sent some examples of the Indian crafts made in St. Augustine to the agents.[13]

Pratt encouraged the prisoners to send part of their earnings home. In keeping an account for Pratt, Agent John Miles sent him a receipt: "Matches-mother-$5.00; Manimic [sic] -wife-$10.00 and daughter-$2.00; Heap of Birds-wife-$4.00; Howling Wolf-wife-$4.00 and friend-$2.00; Making Medicine-mother-$6.00; total $33.00." The Cheyenne also sent home unique gifts obtained locally, though money was more useful. When Romero returned to the Darlington agency, Medicine Water gave him five dollars to forward to his daughter. Hail Stone sent along four dollars for his wife. When the Kiowa White Horse mailed a letter to his mother, he included a five-dollar bill. On one occasion, the prisoners gathered their spare change and sent a post office order for $2.65 to a fund in Chicago for orphaned children. Working for themselves, they created an impressive revenue stream from curio sales.[14]

To market their curios, the Indians produced cultural exhibitions. About twice each week, they held grand powwows, conducted war dances, and sang traditional songs for audiences. The performers seemed to entertain guests with relish, though at times observers discerned that they were merely acting for public amusement. They were paid as much as two dollars each to participate in the performances. On one occasion, Pratt gave a dancing group sixty dollars. Nevertheless, he expressed mixed feelings about what he saw. On the one hand, he realized that the interaction with the crowds indirectly aided the efforts to instruct the Indians in English. On the other hand, the spectacles "were not calculated to promote any advantage to the interracial respect." He was forced to watch as "they carried out their home methods of dress and adornment, stripping to the skin, wearing only the gee-string and the breech clout which it supported, and painting their bodies most impressively." Reluctantly, the officer tolerated the exhibitions, which helped them to earn more money.[15]

During their first summer in St. Augustine, the exiles joined in Independence Day celebrations. The warm weather, admirable preparations, and extraordinary amusements created a fortuitous combination of events. Among the featured attractions, the prisoners presented a mock demonstration of a buffalo-chase. Emerging from the fortress, four horsemen appeared dressed and painted in all the splendor of their tribes. Pile of Rocks, a Comanche; Bear Killer, a Cheyenne; White Bear, an Arapaho; and White Horse, a Kiowa, rode together. While their display insinuated a high level of intertribal cooperation, each tribal cohort cheered for its own regal rider. Observers compared the riders to fabled centaurs in the way they blended their strength and grace with that of their steeds. Armed with bows and arrows, they let loose four projectiles into a bull playing the role of the buffalo. The leader of the entourage, White Horse, delivered the fatal blow. After the bull was dispatched, the rest of the prisoners dressed the carcass. Tired of beans and salt pork, they were excited by the prospect of fresh beef. Although they typically cooked their food before eating it, they considered the raw heart and liver to be good medicine.[16]

According to one tale, the townspeople were initially unimpressed with the hunting prowess of the horsemen from the Great Plains. Critics opined that the Spanish tradition of bullfighting was more skillful and manly. They pointed out that the European matador stood inside an arena with a raging bull and was armed only with a cape and sword. Responding to the challenge, Pratt offered to put on a bullfight, wherein "his Indians" would kill—without the aid of a gun, a bow, or an arrow—any bull that the critics could supply. The principal thoroughfare in St. Augustine was roped off to form an arena. On the appointed day, citizens rushed to the plaza to sit in improvised grandstands. They crowded the grilled balconies above both sides of the narrow street. After a fanfare of speeches and trumpets, White Horse stepped forward for the fight. The Kiowa warlord dressed for the occasion by stripping himself to a gee-string and brandishing for a weapon only a sharp butcher knife. One Cheyenne brave, sharply dressed in turkey feathers and gaily colored flannel, also accepted the challenge. The two contestants mounted nags from the local livery stable and dashed out of a side alley at the end of the arena. They waited for the entrance of a huge bull named Toro, who seemingly possessed an unpleasant disposition.[17]

Once released, the great beast charged ferociously into the arena. He first pursued the Cheyenne, who received applause from his admiring fellow tribesmen but then fled to the other end of the enclosure. Undaunted, White Horse drove his steed after the bull until his right knee touched the animal's rump. His knife flashed high in the air and then downward in a terrific thrust. It caught the bull above the loin, severing its spinal column. The animal gave an agonized bellow and dropped to its belly. In an instant, the experienced buffalo hunter jumped to the ground, slashed a great hole in the bull's side, and pulled out a kidney. He devoured it raw. The blood from the organ ran down his chin and chest, prompting the spectators to roar. To be sure, White Horse had engaged in a bit of theatrics. However, he seemed willing to give the crowd what it wanted—a show.[18]

The Indians, in fact, refined their sense of show business to tease the curiosity of the audience. They gave equestrian exhibitions in full war costume, riding impressively through the moat and over the grounds. After scheduled mock hunts, they transported their captured game into the open courtyard, where they served beef stew with coffee. Pedro, a captive of the Kiowa since age five, built grand bonfires for the evening programs. As he stoked the flames, the eager guests scaled the sea wall. On the road leading up to the fortress, they congregated in a single dark mass. On either side of the entrance sat the patrons in reserved seats for fifty cents each, forming a semi-circle and enveloping about one third of the quadrangle. All around the ramparts crowded more bystanders who had paid only twenty-five cents for admission. In the center of it all, the chiefs sat around the bonfire. Some wore antlers on their heads. One sported a pair of extended heron wings. White Horse, who had been chosen to conduct the orchestra, wore two enormous horns. The flickering fires cast their black shadows against a backdrop of decaying Spanish architecture, which intensified the noir ambience of the shows.[19]

In many of their shows, the Indians offered a drama in pantomime. They divided into two acting troupes, the first consisting mostly of Cheyenne and Comanche and the second of Kiowa and Arapaho. The courtyard was their stage. After a mock battle between the warring troupes, the survivors left the field with equal dispatch, abandoning two dead warriors— one Kiowa and one Cheyenne. The Kiowa tried rising to his feet, but he fell back, writhing, to show that his leg was broken. Taking out his scalping knife, he painfully dragged himself toward the deceased enemy. Suddenly he heard a sound and relapsed into a feigned death. A company of Cheyenne entered, one of them on horseback. They approached their dead brother, dismounted, and, lifting him from the ground, laid him across the horse's back. After they departed, the Kiowa limped bravely and rapidly away. Next, a contrived war for revenge broke out between the two tribes, each of which was led by a chieftain on horseback. Little Medicine, a Cheyenne, rode up and touched an adversary with his long decorated stick, thereby counting coup on his enemy. With rich symbolism, the exhausted belligerents sat down for a council of peace. The resolution of the Indian war elicited long and continuous applause.[20]

A series of traditional dances would typically follow the applause. The dance repertoire included a Cheyenne Bird Dance, a Kiowa Horse Dance, a Kiowa Sheep Killing Dance, a Comanche Swift Dance, and a Cheyenne Rabbit Dance. Seated around the circle, the headmen led a grand vocal and instrumental band. The music consisted of a low chant accompanied by drums and tom-toms. They produced a succession of wailing calls and apparent answers, gradually swelling into a loud melody with a hypnotic rhythm. The big and burly Pile of Rocks, the general stage director, signaled for the dancers to enter. Out they came to perform their "Walk Around" for the audience. One by one, dancers bowed, swayed, and turned right and left. Their feet were always parallel with the ground, so that they came down flat-footed after shaking, leaping, and turning. Each gesture possessed meaning, representing the chasing of rabbits, the capturing of wild mustangs, the flight of birds, or the triumph of hunters. They wielded tomahawks, spears, bows, and arrows. Their buckskin was unbleached muslin while the feathers on their costumes were tails of turkeys. With an elegant and nimble gait, they reenacted the vibrant culture of the Great Plains in a mass of life, color, and sounds.[21]

During a short intermission, virtually all of the Indians prepared themselves for the grand finale—a war dance. Sometimes called the Ohomah or Grass Dance, it traditionally inspired pride in the warriors and terror in their enemies. Cheyenne and Kiowa artists at Fort Marion sketched an animated scene of bodies in motion around the courtyard. Dancers painted their faces in vivid ways with each exercising personal artistic talent. One dancer wore a massive silver cross. Another wore silver armlets like those of a bronze antique. A silver heart, from which descended two crescent shaped ornaments, nearly covered the breasts of another. Costumes were adorned with little bells and tins that jingled as they moved. Brass buttons and beads in every imaginable combination of brightness complemented the feathers and face-paint. War-bonnets—crowns of long, stiff feathers—extended in crests down the back to the feet, with each feather tipped with bits of red flannel or tiny tassels. Once the dancing concluded, White Horse turned to the multitudes to deliver a farewell speech. He offered friendly sentiments in his Kiowa tongue, but his closing words were in English: "Good night! Go'long!"[22]

Along with the carnival atmosphere of the show, Pratt encouraged the Indians to participate in competitive sports on weekends. The winners of competitions would receive three and a half dollars. Foot racing became one of the popular pastimes in the courtyard. During clear afternoons, the officer would march the prisoners down to the plaza to give an archery display. Roman Nose, one of the most athletic of the Cheyenne warriors, recalled "jolly times" shooting arrows with bows. While riding horses at full speed, they would fire arrows at a distance of 200 yards with great accuracy, perforating the small building that they used as a target. In another test of their skill, they would launch arrows by hand as javelins. Once, the champion of the competition threw his weapon 135 yards against the wind. The competitors were popular among the women of the town, and they would practice regularly with the Ladies' Archery Club.[23] Mrs. Joseph Larocque of New York visited Florida with her children and became greatly interested in obtaining archery lessons from the Indian war prisoners. She bought bows for her children and hired one of the Cheyenne to teach them how to shoot. Whatever the other benefits of competitive sports, the athletic events in St. Augustine became fine spectacles.[24]

During the winter months, the Indians helped enrich the festivals of the tourist town. While visiting the Sunshine State, vacationists could enjoy "a holiday in the old castle San Marco" far surpassing their previous experiences. A Jacksonville reporter wrote that their neighbors to the south were "alive and kicking" each weekend. Playing the Indians as "a big card" for savvy travelers, innkeepers filled their hotels with curiosity seekers. The Indians participated in several exhibitions full of pomp and circumstance, including a grand review at the Fair Grounds.[25] A full slate of activities, including an Indian yacht race on the St. Sebastian River, filled the week between Christmas and the New Year. In fact, Indians and non-Indians came together for the "Regattas." Eagle's Head, who was nearly sixty years of age, became a favorite at the yachting clubs. Described as "a noble-looking man," he possessed "a fine, grave countenance" and appeared to be "full of thought and feeling." From time to time, he visited the club rooms and participated in their sailing expeditions and yacht races. With dignified equipoise, the Cheyenne paid great attention to his status among the local aristocrats. When riding the boats, he imitated the dress popular among gentlemen of property and standing.[26]

The ladies and gentlemen of St. Augustine hosted a "Grand Gala Day" on March 18, 1876. The military outpost was closed during the day so the Indians could prepare for a big night. At 7:00 P.M. the rush to the "medicine shows" commenced. Omnibuses and carriages could not satisfy the demand. As many as two thousand people squeezed into Fort Marion at one time. The Indians appeared about half an hour later and commenced their acting, dancing, and singing, which continued until after 10:00 P.M. Amazed by the great performances, many guests remained until the last "whoop" was heard. Afterward, on the bulletin board at a club house, a statement of receipts and expenditures appeared. A balance of $233.39 was turned over to the General Management Committee for the benefit of the Indians. During one parade for local amusement, non-Indian folks decided to "go native." They dressed themselves in Indian costumes and carried a banner emblazoned with "St. Augustine Bonanza."[27]

The Indians at St. Augustine dazzled the spectators not only with their pageantry but also with their bazaars. To distinguish their booths inside and around the fortress, they decorated the premises with Indian memorabilia. Paper artifacts representing horses, braves, and buffaloes revealed "a good deal of rude artistic skill and spirit in the design and coloring." Merchandise was displayed from wall to wall, attracting the eye and opening the purses of visitors. A stand under the entrance archway welcomed newcomers and tempted them with last-minute shopping as they exited. The exiles cooperated with stereographers by posing for picture cards for sale to tourists. They also offered a vapor bath by firing stones to white heat and placing them inside a makeshift sweat lodge. One satisfied customer recalled hearing only three English words: "good," "no good," and "dollar." After greeting the strangers sauntering around the courtyard, the salesmen kept matters strictly to business.[28]

Business often turned the courtyard into a cultural meeting ground. The "Florida boys" tried to respect the local customs. When one Northern visitor tried to bargain for bows and arrows on a Sunday, he was refused. No Indians would sell to him or traffic in goods on a Sabbath, for they were careful not to dishonor "the Lord's Day." One guest of the Indians said: "They take the hand of a paleface as readily as they once went for his scalp; but there is no love in the shake, if I am any judge of character." The worst customers harangued them, particularly Buffalo Calf, who wore a large scarlet blanket over her army uniform. Indeed, a few scoundrels stood on the parapets and hurled pebbles and cement at them. Still, the Indians tolerated the annoyances and tried to make the most of their contact with the tourists. From their enterprise, they earned approximately $5,000. However, Pratt reported, they sent home only a small part of their income, most of which they spent on small purchases at the plaza. In other words, they desired to be consumers as well as producers.[29]

Because the Indians disposed of their income locally, they were important customers in the local shops. So long as they were neatly dressed, Pratt would grant them individual passes into town during business hours to make purchases as well as to make friends among the citizenry. Buffalo Meat, a Cheyenne, compiled a price list of items sold in St. Augustine. After the list circulated among his counterparts, non-Indians requested copies of the popular shopping guide as well. A merchant who sold watermelons recalled hard bargaining with the Comanche chief, Black Horse, who regularly conducted a thorough inspection of the produce and insisted upon good melons at a cheap price. Clearly, their discretionary spending gave them leverage during the off-season.[30] One wintering guest from New York described the local traffic:

The Indians are allowed to go into town. They are seen about the streets—one meets them everywhere—sometimes on their way to make a visit, sometimes returning with parcels from a shopping expedition. Not a charge can be brought against them for a misdemeanor of any kind outside or within the fort. Everywhere one meets them they are so quiet and well-behaved, so civil and dignified, that it is a pleasure to see and exchange with them a friendly greeting. In the afternoons, always busy polishing sea-beans, making bows and arrows or drawing and painting their pictures, no unpleasant word is heard from them, nothing objectionable in manners or habits seen. San Marco and the Indians supply the chief attraction for visitors, who come away gratified by the cleanliness and order prevailing within its precincts, the neatness in dress, the industry, handiwork and intelligence of the Indians, and above all the kindness and urbanity of the officer in charge.[31]

To the surprise of strangers, the Indians exercised a remarkable degree of economic autonomy.

In their spare time, the Indians peddled goods on the streets of St. Augustine without restraint. J. D. Lopez of the city council complained about their excessive trading activities, warning that it violated the interests of those who paid for licenses as merchants. The council instructed Lopez to request that Pratt require the Indians to sell their wares only within the confines of the military outpost. Otherwise, they threatened, they would pass an ordinance outlawing their vending in town. The next day, the officer investigated and found that the complaint was limited to three merchants. He reported to his commander at the post: "I am sure the grounds for it were very slight." The Indians earned less than a dollar a day in this way, and they rarely sold many items beyond the gate. Nevertheless, Pratt forbade them from selling outside of Fort Marion and further prohibited them from trading in any manner with the complainants. He even pressured the merchants, threatening to cut off Indian purchases in town and to allow the prisoners to buy their personal items elsewhere. Faced the loss of their customers, two of the complainants denied that they had ever complained to the council about the curio class.[32]

The council heard few complaints, even though some inhabitants expressed alarm about the presence of the exiles. Despite the appearance of friendly relations in public, tensions seethed beneath the surface. A handful of residents who witnessed the "medicine shows" considered them "dangerous." In private, the timid thought it "a somewhat hazardous experiment to put a band of murderers on their honor." They carped about the prisoners' appearances in "native costume— or rather its absence." During one performance, the Indians "became so excited that it was judged best to cause all the ladies to withdraw" from the premises. Without a doubt, locals fretted about "the possibilities of mutiny and general massacre." Most of all, they expressed concern about a "medicine man" conducting sun dances and "other heathenish customs." One newspaper editor, J. O. Whitney, openly fumed about the unsupervised movement of the "savages."[33]

During the spring of 1876, Pratt became suspicious about the movements of the Kiowa. Over a period of three weeks, he noticed that their eyes became "evasive" during inspections. They grew "discontented," he noted, and exhibited "restlessness" while off-duty. Meanwhile, a bottle of poison marked by a "skull and crossbones" label disappeared from the post physician's medical supplies. During a "religious ceremony" at a remote sand dune, one of the sergeants, White Horse, acted in a way that evoked particular suspicion. Whatever he suspected, Pratt continued to monitor their undercover operations. For several months, the warrior artists sketched the facilities, the island, and the countryside, possibly mapping escape routes. Pratt faced the possibility that the street vending cloaked their espionage in town. On Monday, April 3, he asked Fox to interrogate Ahkeah, or Coming to the Grove, who was ill and separated from his fellow Kiowa. That evening, the interpreter pressed the Kiowa about the disposition of his traditional leaders, particularly Lone Wolf and White Horse. Coming to the Grove broke down in tears and expressed fear of his own death. Under pressure, he divulged information about "a plot" to make their way back to their people.[34]

On condition that he receive the same punishment as his kinsmen, Coming to the Grove told Fox details of their plot. White Horse and Lone Wolf had organized them for a "breakout," though Woman's Heart and Double Vision had helped to coordinate it. The braves had expressed reluctance to join at first, but White Horse had demanded their loyalty. The Kiowa intended to act in a few days under the full moon. They had prepared bows and arrows for use in their escape attempt and were determined not to be retaken. If they failed to reach their homeland, they pledged to live in the woods or to die "at all hazards." Even though Pratt learned about the conspiracy of only the Kiowa, the Comanche may have known of their secret plan. Since their language was not well-understood by the Cheyenne and Arapaho, he presumed that the Kiowa communicated without the full knowledge of their inmates. All the Kiowa were conspirators, though, including Boy Hunting, one of Pratt's most trusted sergeants.[35]

On Tuesday, April 4, Pratt moved to foil the conspiracy. That morning, he informed Lieutenant Colonel Dent and received orders to launch a preemptive strike. A special force of one regular army sergeant and twelve seasoned bluecoats were assigned to him. Of course, he picked "large strong fellows" for the mission. At noon, they marched into Fort Marion with bayonets fixed and guns loaded. Next, Pratt invited the Cheyenne Eagle's Head and Heap of Birds to a closed conference, where they pledged to assist him "to the death." For their afternoon meal, the diners entered the mess hall without incident. Pratt, who was armed with a pistol, ordered the doors locked. He demanded information about the stolen bottle of poison, pausing to stare at White Horse and Lone Wolf. He directed a search of their quarters and their bodies. In the process, a Comanche named Wyako, or Dry Wood, threatened Fox and was taken into custody for insubordination. Standing tall with arms folded, White Horse said to the interpreter: "Tell the Captain it is all right. I understand and I want him to kill me now." Lone Wolf capitulated, too. As troops under Captain Edmund Bainbridge surrounded the fortress, twenty-four Kiowa were arrested inside. Working in the open courtyard, the post blacksmith fitted shackles and handcuffs upon them. Pratt confined the warriors separately from their chiefs, leaving Lone Wolf, White Horse, and Dry Wood to languish alone.[36]

That evening, Pratt planned what he called "a little ceremony" to abuse and humiliate the prisoners. He scheduled the post cart from St. Francis Barracks to arrive about 7:00 P.M., when its movements would escape the notice of the townspeople. At 10:00 P.M., Pratt and his associates entered Dry Wood's cell to blindfold him. Then he ordered two stalwart soldiers to take him firmly by the arms and to march the Comanche around the open courtyard, backward and forward in the moonlight, until he began to weaken. The men in blue coerced him throughout the ordeal, dragging him to his cell once he was unable to stand any longer. Lone Wolf received similar treatment and, after exhaustion, collapsed to the ground. Finally, White Horse was taken from his cell. With head erect and body firm, he marched in step despite the rough handling of his escorts. Afterward, he swaggered back to his cell on his own two feet without displaying any weakness.[37]

At Pratt's request, the post surgeon, Dr. Janeway, entered their cells to complete the ceremony. He rendered Dry Wood and Lone Wolf unconscious with a prepared solution administered with a hypodermic needle. As the doctor approached White Horse, the great warrior scrutinized the needle intently and began to speak. Pratt described the scene:

Fox interpreted: "Captain, he wants to know what you are doing to him." I said: "Tell him that I know the Indians have strong medicine and can do some wonderful things, but the white man has stronger medicine and can do more wonderful things, and I am having the doctor give him a dose of one of our strong medicines." White Horse immediately asked: "Will it make me good?" I said: "Tell him I hope so. That is the object."[38]

Without another word, White Horse fell asleep.

Once incapacitated, the three men were carried to the courtyard by four soldiers and laid side by side upon the cart. They were, to all appearances, dead, as their brethren observed Pratt's ceremony from afar under the bright moonlight. The post cart departed for the barracks, where the human cargo was unloaded for solitary confinement in the guardhouse.[39]

As the cart passed quietly through town, a group of residents became alarmed. R. A. Speissegger, a long-time inhabitant of St. Augustine, heard rumors that the prisoners had bundled and hidden arrows in their campground at Anastasia Island. Like his fellow vigilantes, he recalled charging toward the fortress prepared to "shoot to kill." However, they were interrupted by the hurried tramp of soldiers on Bay Street. He concluded that the insurrection "was a first class dud." Once he found no sign of slain guards, he went home. Another resident testified that White Horse "got a little liquor and made a big racket," although no evidence existed to substantiate such a claim. Perhaps his mistaken notion derived from his glimpse of the drugged leaders as they were rolled through town.[40]

Fort Marion closed briefly to visitors, but on Thursday, April 6, it reopened. On April 7, Pratt released fourteen of the men from custody but continued to detain ten whom he deemed security threats. He dispatched the rest to Matanzas, where they remained for two weeks. On April 30, the three "ringleaders" were returned to the casemates after reviving from slumber. Pratt impressed their accomplices with his trick of apparently resurrecting the dead. Nevertheless, they remained in irons and confined under the guard of their own people. For his role in planning the outbreak, White Horse was demoted to the rank of private.[41]

Pratt tried to keep word of the outbreak from the press, but an April 6 report in the *Florida Tri-Weekly Sun* broke the news about a "rising in St. Augustine." A party of Kiowa, "some fifteen or sixteen in number," had launched "a mutinous plot" to accomplish "serious mischief," the paper reported. Reportedly, they had planned a "general uprising and slaughter of the white inhabitants," an insurrection that was "narrowly prevented" by an armed detachment of bluecoats. Posing as guards, the "savages" would have attempted to overpower "the single soldier who remains in the Fort at night." Then they would have struck at the local populace and the sleeping soldiers stationed at the barracks. "Poisoned arrows were the weapons to be used," warned the newspaper, along with whatever "guns could be obtained." Furthermore, the Cheyenne had "plotted to murder Captain Pratt, the sergeant in the Fort, and another white man, and then escape into the city." Also, a reporter somehow determined, "a half breed" had offered to help the escapees "obtain shelter with the Seminole in the Everglades." Whatever the credibility of the coverage, the hysteria caused a number of visitors in St. Augustine to make preparations to leave the city.[42]

Indeed, townspeople experienced the hysteria for some time. As soon as one report of a prison riot made the rounds, another one came forth, then another, and so on. "The great scare about the Indians imprisoned at St. Augustine pans out rather thin," admitted the *Daily Florida Union*. The newspaper hoped "to set at rest the fabulous, vague rumors," but they continued to circulate. Apologetic about contributing to the intense fear, the *Florida Tri-Weekly Sun* offered a bit of satire to relax its readers. One storyline teased that "some disgruntled Cheyenne or Kiowa Chief must have edited the Florida press last week." The editor blamed an "inkslinger" for addled reports of sedition, positing that "Brother Lone Wolf" had been the sole culprit. With law and order restored, the Kiowa chieftain was fed for "a week on soothing syrup." Undoubtedly, the creative writers fueled the fiery situation. In fact, dispatches across the country recounted stories of a violent insurrection that had never occurred.[43]

To counter the bad news, Pratt endeavored to disseminate as much good news as possible. In his ledger dated June 1, he reported that Lone Wolf had returned to guard duty "cured of any design to escape." Next he remarked: "Discipline, general deportment and desire to learn, without fault." Likewise, he reiterated his previous statements to Lieutenant General Sheridan that "the best discipline prevails." He added: "I now think it impossible for any emergency to arise that I can not meet with my Indian Guard." Moreover, he exulted to superiors, "a majority of them" went to the barbershop to get "their hair shingled" voluntarily. "They make fine looking soldiers," he wrote. When the dramatic news of "Custer's Last Stand" at the Little Big Horn reached Florida, he reported that they "asked to be allowed to help put down the rebellious Sioux and Cheyennes." Anxious "to show their reformation and loyalty," Pratt offered to lead "a picked fifty" of them on a campaign during the summer of 1876. Lieutenant Colonel Dent declared that "they will be true as steel" and "more efficient than double the number of other Indians" used as scouts in the Northern Plains. The War Department declined the offer, even though a few locals seemed eager to see them leave St. Augustine.[44]

At 2:00 A.M. on July 15, 1876, a fire erupted at the house of M. M. Moleanor, one of the locals. The town possessed no fire department, leaving only a handful of volunteers to battle the blaze alone. It burned Moleanor's house to the ground and spread to an adjoining structure that was unoccupied and empty. About twelve feet away stood another house, to which came, "just in the nick of time," the entire company of Indian prisoners with buckets and blankets. They succeeded in extinguishing the flames before the fire spread any farther. In the process, three Indians suffered accidents, stepping upon upright nails with bare feet. They were attended by Dr. Janeway, though nothing serious stemmed from the wounds. One resident expressed his "heartfelt gratitude," because "their wonderful exertions" saved his home. Instead of disturbing the peace, the Natives had actually risked their lives to preserve it.[45]

Nonetheless, trouble continued to brew in St. Augustine. Working people around town sent a petition to Washington

asking officials to prevent the able-bodied prisoners from gaining employment off the post. They complained that the low
wages paid to gang laborers undermined their own capacities
as family breadwinners. They wanted no competition for jobs
from the Indians.[46] On August 5, 1876, Senator Charles W.
Jones of Florida introduced a resolution requesting that the
Secretary of War notify the body about the "liberty" of the
prisoners held at Fort Marion. However, Senator Roscoe Conk-
ling of New York suggested tabling the resolution, leaving it in
"innocuous desuetude" for the rest of the session. Pratt responded by increasing regulations, allowing the Indians to venture into town only to do business or to greet friends. To com-
ply, each Indian passed into town alone and without permission
to linger. A large party was permitted into town only once, and
its members were back in their quarters by 9:00 P.M. Except for
the night they fought the fire, they were not allowed to go out
after dark. In an era of "black codes" that restricted the movement of minorities in the American South, fears about the
Indians echoed provincial concerns about the mobility of any
person of color.[47]

St. Augustine benefited from the captivity of the Indians
because Americans from all over the country ventured to see
them in the ancient city. They came to the coastal paradise for
many reasons, leaving with a memorable impression of the
chiefs and the warriors in the Sunshine State. They wanted to
look upon them at the very moment that incarceration threatened to erase their "Indianness." Once the voyeurs had witnessed the charm, intelligence, and commerce on display at
the fort, though, they could associate a human face with what
they perceived to be an "Indian problem." Pratt observed that
"great publicity and favor to our red people resulted from the
three years the Indian prisoners remained in Florida." He
boasted that they created grand spectacles that "out Buffalo

Billed Mr. Cody." The Indians were playing Indians for the crowds. He mused that they "will have stories to tell when they return that will be hardly believed by the average plains white man, let alone the Indians." Perhaps the same thing could have been said of the non-Indians who saw Indians for the first time.[48]

Unfortunately, the non-Indians still saw the Indians through the inflected lens of their cultural assumptions. Their views revealed more about themselves than about the objects of their fascination. They were excited by the original inhabitants of North America, who embodied the things that the tourists craved. They patronized people perceived as wild, exotic, alluring, natural, and fantastic. With few exceptions, even the new friends of the Indians lacked the sense and the sensibilities to accept them as equals. Much like Pratt, they underestimated the capacities of groups culturally different from their own. Despite the space between them, though, the Natives and the strangers amused one another. The latter observed the improvisation and intrigue of the former, turning a brief excursion into a cross-cultural encounter. The cross-cultural encounters enriched the points of view of each party, even if they reinforced an image of the Indians that made them relics of a distant place and time. Hence, the curio class showed their gifts in St. Augustine, where they were seen as novelties in the Gilded Age.

Chapter 5
Brave Hearts
Inside the Prison School

THE WARRIOR ARTIST WOHAW SKETCHED a Plains Indian on the blank page of his drawing book. A crescent moon, a falling star, and an eclipsed sun appear at the top of the panel. On one side appears a buffalo bull, while a spotted cow poses on the other. Both beasts exhale smoke and bow toward the central figure, who embodies "Indianness." Dressed only in a red loincloth, this figure stands with one foot upon a homestead and the other beside a tipi. He hosts a council between the envoys of two different worlds and extends the gifts of a red pipe and a black pipe to his right and to his left, respectively. While bringing the bull and the cow together, he imagines their mutual coexistence. His opposing worlds neither collide nor come apart. Rather, he wisely brokers peace between them. Wohaw printed his name in upper case block letters near the center of the sketch, endorsing the "peaceable kingdom" of the medicine maker.[1]

His original Kiowa name was Guháude, or Wolf Robe, but "Wohaw" appeared among his aliases during exile. The latter term derived from "whoa-haw," that is, the sounds non-Indian teamsters yelled when admonishing their beasts of burden. The Kiowa used the colloquialism to identify the beef cattle introduced into Indian Territory by non-Indians. By 1877, the twenty-one-year-old prisoner had produced fifty-one drawings and affixed his new name to three of them. Like other Plains Indians at Fort Marion, his use of paper and books for artwork indicated an adaptation of Native hide-painting techniques. His self-titled sketch of the buffalo, the cow, and the Indian referenced a legendary tipi emblem rendered by the deceased Owl Prophet, Sky Walker. It also expressed in visual terms what Wohaw hoped to achieve through education. Indeed, the meticulously printed five-letter word hinted at his degree of literacy. To show the heart of a brave, the warrior artist counted coup with the strokes of his pencil.[2]

The warrior artists filled their ledger books while attending classes inside the old Spanish castle. Lieutenant Pratt organized classes in the chapel and the adjacent casemates close to his office on the north side of the fortress. The space evoked the aesthetics of "monkish cloisters." It contained crude wooden benches that faced the whitewashed walls, on which hung small tapestries embroidered with the Lord's Prayer and the Ten Commandments. In addition, a United States map, large spelling-cards, and a blackboard decorated the premises. Large spelling-cards decorated the classrooms.[3] To encourage the students to practice what he preached, Pratt also hosted a Bible study on Monday nights in the chapel. In day and evening classes, they gathered for prayer and sang popular hymns in the Moody and Sankey collection. The Bible represented the primary textbook for all of their lessons. Under Pratt's gaze, the students spelled out simple words in their ledgers. They sat together and recited the alphabet, vocabulary, and numerals. As they studied, Pratt watched them scribble in their books. General of the Army Sherman, who refused to detail an officer for instructional duty with Pratt, disparaged this classroom teaching as "old woman's work."[4]

No woman contributed more to the work of teaching the prisoners than Sarah A. Mather. Formerly of Hartford, Connecticut, she was a member of the first graduating class at Mount Holyoke College in Massachusetts. For more than a

decade before 1875, she had operated a young ladies' boarding
school in St. Augustine. Successful and enthusiastic, the sixty-
year-old woman earned a reputation around town as a tireless
pedagogue. One colleague described her as "a born genius for
instruction—one whose very life is in teaching." While visiting
Fort Marion, she asked Pratt for the opportunity "to educate
wild Indians." Without her, he later admitted, he would "never
have begun the work of civilizing and educating" the prisoners
of war. He considered it her labor, not his. Expressing deep
affection for "Miss Mather," the Cheyenne Bear's Heart attended her classes faithfully. He wanted to "learn good ways"
from her so that when he returned home he would "know how
to teach my friends." As the matron of the classrooms, Mather
recruited other volunteer instructors from St. Augustine.[5]

A number of these volunteers stayed in St. Augustine for
more than one season. Anna Pratt, for instance, taught alongside an assortment of "benevolent ladies." The Mother Superior at a Catholic school in town hoped to instruct any children
sent out from Indian Territory, and so she detailed a nun for
occasional service. Numerous schoolmarms applied their craft,
including Nannie Burt and Rebecca Perrit. Julia Gibbs, whose
husband had been an officer in the Confederate Army, devoted
herself to volunteering. Her sister, Laura Gibbs, who lived in
St. Augustine and Fort George Island, contributed her time
and talent as well. By early 1876, five different ladies from local
churches had arranged regular instruction for "about fifty of
the youngest men" at the fort.[6] Pratt lamented that "it would be
so much better if I could have them in a stirring New England
community," where "the best energy and intelligence of the
country" resided. Nevertheless, the cadre of volunteers touched
the heart of Boy Hunting, a Kiowa entrusted as one of Pratt's
sergeants. Despite the turnover in faculty, he was grateful for
the "kind ladies" who "helped us learn to read and write."[7]

Bishop Henry B. Whipple, a Minnesota Episcopalian wintering in Florida, joined the faculty of the "Christian school" from 1875 to 1876. Famous for his previous work among the Sioux, he taught at Fort Marion twice during weekdays. In addition to adjunct instruction, he delivered special sermons on Sundays. His primary admonition to them was "to obey," which he underscored through stories from the Bible. The pupils especially appreciated his Old Testament tale about Joseph, who had been unjustly sent into captivity. The bishop claimed that he "was never more touched than when I entered this school," where he saw the adults "sitting like docile children at the feet of women." The school showed him that "even in the most savage men there is a heart which can be reached by discipline, kindness, and Christian teaching." Thanks to the "devoted Christian women," the students behaved like an "orderly body" in the classrooms. He called the younger men "very intelligent," asserting that "they ought to be educated as teachers and craftsmen" and returned as "leaders of their people." In fact, a number of the students honored him by incorporating his animated oratory into their sketches.[8]

Amy Caruthers, a resident of Tarrytown, New York, began teaching the next winter when she and her husband, Horace, a successful physician, trekked southward. She glared at the Indian students as she entered the old Spanish castle for the first time. They were "the bronze, statue-like figures standing about, seated in the embrasures, or leaning over the parapet, the dark faces, encircled by long, straight black hair, peering down." She felt a "strange thrill" at the thought of her proximity to the "untamable and treacherous savage." Exotic sounds floated toward her from the ramparts, with Cheyenne songs coming from her right and Kiowa chants from her left. A year of schooling later, no such sounds greeted her when she arrived. Instead, fine "manly voices" sang the words to "Just as

I Am," "I Need Thee Every Hour," and "I Am Coming to the Cross." The students carried books, including hymnals and Bibles. They repeated the Lord's Prayer in concert as well as spelling and figuring out loud. She described the pupils as "eager to learn and understand," "interested," "persevering," "obedient," and "courteous." Once they completed their education, she promised them, they would return to their people "as instructors thereafter."[9]

The instructors organized four classes at Fort Marion, recruiting twelve to fifteen students for each. The students usually received their lessons five days a week, except Saturdays and Sundays. After an early morning bugle call and an assembly in the chapel, the lessons commenced in the classrooms from 10:00 A.M. to 12:00 P.M. Eventually, the schedule would expand to include seven classes and add an hour during the afternoon. The students were dismissed around 4:30 P.M. for their evening meals. Reportedly, the "docile and orderly" scholars undertook each classroom activity with great discipline.[10] At first, they depended upon an interpreter to communicate through sign language, but soon they began to write and to speak effectively on their own. A Kiowa named Koba, or Wild Horse, filled five pages of his ledger with "picture-words" illustrating each new term he learned. After months of toil, the English language became the "common tongue" for classroom discourse. Eventually, all were able to understand and to make themselves understood, although their speech remained limited. In fact, their acquisition of English as a second language rendered the interpreter's services unnecessary.[11]

The classroom pedagogy reflected the methodology of primary schools. The pupils studied in silence or responded to the call of the teacher. They practiced spelling and grammar as a group. They experienced constant drilling in phonetics. They labored to master the sounds of vowels and consonants as well as the fundamentals of spelling and reading. As a result of direct instruction, more than thirty completed the first reader in a year and a few eventually reached the third. For hand-writing, they adapted the popular "Spencerian method" and worked out of copybooks containing guidelines for heights, lengths, and slants to indicate proper lettering for reproduc-tion. They displayed a particular facility for arithmetic, and quickly mastered numeracy and figured up to one hundred. They grasped the geography of the U.S., which helped them to locate their homeland on the map. They learned "about God, about justice, and truth"—or, at least, they listened to non-Indian lectures about such concepts. They memorized pas-sages of scripture and the words to hymns, which the faculty believed touched "their hearts and minds." In ways pleasing to female pedagogues, the manly students were schooled like children inside the prison.[12]

The students were pleased with the chapel meetings, per-haps because there they could assume an active role in the proceedings. The Cheyenne Roman Nose recalled "meeting in Ft. Marion every Monday evening to pray to God to guide us in the right way." In contrast to the day-to-day study de-manded by the school teachers, the evening services featured hymn singing, group meditation, and lay preaching. The favor-ite hymns of the Indians included "Hold the Fort" and "I Am So Glad That Our Father's in Heaven," which resonated with masculine themes of vigilance and patriarchy. They repeated verses from New Testament texts, including the memorable John 3:16. On at least one occasion, they discussed the parable of "the Good Shepherd seeking the lost sheep," which they amplified by the use of sign language. Moreover, they took turns standing and testifying aloud about "the great and good spirit." Permitted to use their native tongues in prayer, they would audibly interpolate their own language with the name

"Jesus." They blessed their brethren and asked for forgiveness, petitioning a higher power to release them from their bondage. In many respects, the talks appeared syncretic with Native ceremonies around the campfires.[13]

Making Medicine, the Cheyenne first sergeant, talked about his heartfelt determination "to become a man." At the head of his class, he spoke of education as a necessary condition for the social and economic improvement of his people. He refined his nascent skills in English, although his two wives back home corresponded with him using pictographs. To address him, they used the symbol for a lodge with sticks placed horizontally at the apex, a sign denoting a medicine man's hut. Through what his mentors called "primitive correspondence," he acquired information about his family's affairs. He even learned about the first steps of his oldest child. Whenever the prisoners held councils to send "a talk" to Washington, the dog soldier's voice resonated with the warriors in captivity.[14] Making Medicine declared:

Heretofore, I have led a bad life on the plains, wandering around living in a house made of skins. I have now learned something about the Great Spirit's road and want to learn more . . . . We want Washington to give us our wives and children, our fathers and mothers and send us somewhere where we can settle down and live like white men. Washington has lots of good ground laying around loose, give us some of it and let us learn to make things grow. We want to farm the ground. We want a house and pigs and chickens and cows. We feel happy to have learned so much that we can teach our children. I speak for the young men; we want to work.[15]

Even if his homeland seemed distant, Making Medicine anticipated returning to it better prepared for leadership.

Mindful of their constraints, the braves studied the best practices of their former enemies. The Cheyenne warrior

Ouhoh, or Soaring Eagle, composed a message for inclusion in one church bulletin. Confessing that he used to "hunt, shoot, and sleep on Sundays," he said he had learned at the prison school that "God's good book has told me it was wrong." Carefully choosing his words, he wrote: "I know now to spell and read a little." Looking forward, he promised to "know more when I go home." He described a day of jubilee when "I hope to sit down and sing God's hymns, which I have been taught."[16] Likewise, the Cheyenne Roman Nose stated that it was "not bad we stayed in prison" for punishment. The school teachers, he noted, "taught them all about the good ways of the whites." They "showed us ABC," making it possible for the Indians to "understand those letters." Before exile, "we did not know how to spell anything" and relied upon pictures and signs alone. After exile, he predicted, he could "do something useful and teach the red men [to] avoid temptation."[17] Intending to use his knowledge to benefit his kinsmen, he recognized the practicality of education.

The Kiowa Tsaitkopeta, or Bear Mountain, viewed education in light of its practical benefits as well. Described by Pratt as a "tall, bright young man," the twenty-five-year-old faithfully sat in the front seat on the east side of the classroom. "I think the hardest of all languages [is] English," he later confessed. The Kiowa complained about his inability to "speak good English," fearing "that after while I cannot talk any kind of language." To practice public speaking, he led his comrades in prayer using both his native language and his second one. He expressed gratitude for the "kind ladies" who taught him English "without pay." He wished that he were "very rich and could pay them," but he added that perhaps "God will pay you all." He surmised that his life had been "pretty rough and sharp" before attending school. In the past, he had been "just like the waves of the ocean, unsteady and not sure." He de-

spised the work of "Satan," who had treated him "like an ox
with his yoke on me" and made him "a prisoner." Bear Mountain felt cheated by his tormentor, asking, "What kind of pay
did he give me?" Looking forward, he expected to earn good
wages.[18] He considered the employment prospects for an interpreter at the Kiowa agency and prepared himself to become
a voice for his people.

Eagle's Head, one of the most vocal of the Cheyenne
chiefs, declared that "our hearts are glad, our heads are bigger,
and we are all glad for what we have learned." He anticipated
that the exiles would be "bearers of all these good white man
ways to their people, who are ignorant of them." He no longer
cared that he would be "called a woman" by his chief rivals
back home. Rather, he wanted the Cheyenne at the agency to
adopt "the road of sending letters" to him. He hoped to communicate with the students at the agency school. "I want you
all to listen to this," the chieftain admonished his kinsmen in
one letter, "and the Agent to read it over very carefully to you
so you will understand it." Of course, pictography remained
common in his correspondence. From one picture letter, he
learned that Curly Head, the wife of his son, Howling Wolf,
had given birth to a child, Little Turtle. It conveyed news about
life and death, expressing a desire on the part of the writers to
speak with their absent loved ones again. Although he continued to rely upon Pratt to pen his formal statements, he
signed them with his mark. Using a blended discourse, he also
began to write his own name.[19]

Most of the prisoners seemed strongly motivated by the
desire to write their own words, and so only a few refused to
accept any schooling. Even the Cheyenne headmen attended
classes, albeit less regularly. In fact, Pratt reported, Bear Shield
was "about the last Cheyenne to fall into the traces here." The
"most serious cases" of resistance appeared among the Kiowa

and the Comanche. Some of the older men preferred to bide their time in retirement, even though many were "anxious" to compose letters.[20] The once-defiant White Horse went to school and caused only one notable classroom disruption. While trying to teach him to pronounce the word "teeth," Mather removed her complete set of false uppers and lowers to show him an object to associate with it. Horrified, the Kiowa exclaimed, "Miss Mather no good!" Pratt rushed into the classroom when he heard the commotion but was relieved to learn that the warlord merely meant that she was "defective." In fact, White Horse's talent for class clowning helped win him the affection of the faculty.[21]

The relationship between the female faculty and the so-called "blood-thirsty scalp-hunters" stirred some controversy, though. One local newspaper noted that "some of the Indians at the fort are manly and handsome" and intimated that they were "quite admired by the ladies." More alarming was the news that the women hosted "big dinners" for the students in the evenings.[22] A wag from the *New York Observer* saw "multitudes of ladies, young ones especially, while away their idle hours at the fort and throw themselves upon the red men in a way that is perhaps overdone." He worried that the "criminals" would draw the wrong lesson from such compassion and conclude that "the commission of a crime is a passport into the best society." The teachers' affection for their students insinuated "that murder entitles a man to handshakes, caresses, and compliments from fair, delicate young girls." He scrutinized the pupils carefully as they studied the alphabet "at the hands of a gray-haired lady teacher." Nevertheless, the observer also hoped that "such constant intercourse" would result in the "taming of the savage." In line with Victorian notions of domesticity, the school teachers made the classroom into a "woman's sphere."[23]

The Florida Press became concerned about the school teachers and dispatched a blue-ribbon panel of ladies and gentlemen to investigate. Auditing one class, they counted "about 15 Indians, including the two squaws and child, seated upon benches before rude school desks with books, slates, and pencils before them." The students sat in a semi-square facing the blackboard and the faculty. They appeared deeply interested in their work, to the extent that scarcely any of them glanced at the onlookers. Sitting with his family, the Comanche chief Black Horse practiced penmanship on a ledger. On the blackboard, one instructor placed simple examples of writing, spelling, and arithmetic. After hearing a battery of one-syllable words, the captive audience spelled them in unison and pronounced them correctly. For two hours, they retained their seats in deference to motherly authority. Suddenly, the sound of a small bell called them to the chapel, where Pratt received them for prayer and then dismissed them from school for the day. Closing their investigation, the blue-ribbon panel left the casemates with heartwarming praise for the prison school.[24]

Local support for the school increased over time, and Pratt reported that it was becoming increasingly popular with the prisoners as well. He declared that "rays of light are breaking in on the dark minds." During one examination, the students recited "the Lord's Prayer perfectly," he reported. A superior recitation earned one winner the prize of a Bible, although five others repeated it almost as well. The officer found them "much advanced in spelling and figures," capable of inscribing letters in a copybook "better than average children after several times effort." To reward them for their progress, he picked out five men for instruction in gardening on two acres near the post. He tried to instruct the older prisoners in carpentry, so he purchased a set of tools for them and established a carpenter's shop in one of the casemates. In addition, he promoted an "education in the wonders of the ocean." He hired a local mariner to teach a cohort to sail and to row. They captured exotic fish and sea turtles. They learned to catch sharks, which they called "water buffalo." After catching an alligator, they labeled it "a water horse." The active learning stimulated vigorous discussions among the students, including the older ones.[25]

What Pratt later termed the "outing system" increased their active learning. The officer encouraged the students to use their "off-duty" time to obtain various and sundry vocational skills. While interned, they earned money in the assorted industries around town. They became guides to visitors who wanted to go fishing, walk the beach, or venture down the bay. They toiled in saw mills, tended horses, milked cows, picked oranges, packed crates, and worked other odd jobs. One of the prisoners assisted on the locomotive between the town and the St. Johns River. They worked during the winter at the railroad station handling baggage. Others accepted seasonal construction work. They operated the block and tackle for a heavy driver, which was used to drive pipe deep underground to reach fresh water for a town well. Five prisoners were hired out to a local citizen to clear five acres of palmetto growth and prepare the soil for orange groves. They succeeded in clearing it after six hard weeks, completing their assignment despite blistered hands. Their work ethic during the "outings" impressed Pratt.[26]

To be sure, Pratt continued to examine carefully the achievements of the students. He attested to the competence of several men, including Ouksteuh, or Shave Head, Tsahdletah, or White Goose; Mohewihkio, or Buzzard; Tichkematse, or Squint Eyes; Chisiseduh, or Matches; Koweonarre, or Little Chief; and Zonekeuh, or Tooth Man. Degrees of proficiency were evident, with the younger pupils learning more easily than the older ones. Most possessed "an aptitude in learning," although he called some "very stupid." He identified "from six to ten of the best" and took steps to get them into "a good agricultural school." After a few years of schooling, he surmised, they would "make themselves useful as helpers about their agencies" in Indian Territory.[27] Able to read and to speak in English, they "would be a great civilizing element among their people." He sensed that the most talented would "take an education readily." Unwilling to ignore the potential of the rest, he suggested that about "thirty of the others can be successfully taught" at the elementary level. He never knew a "more carefully obedient and better behaved lot of men." Indeed, the school teachers schemed "to get them held longer that they might have the pleasure of seeing their efforts more fully consummated."[28]

One of the teachers' favorite students, Ahkah, was not even considered a prisoner. The ten-year-old Comanche went to class each day with her exiled family. She learned to read and write and resolved to become "a teacher to her people" someday. She began composing letters to the "Great Father" in Washington, including one to the Indian Office. It made the rounds in the Interior Department and even reached the desk of the President. She wrote:

Dear Washington:
Me love you. Me want to go home, see my little sister. Me and my people here all time three years. Me tire now. My mother's name Peonte; my father's name Black Horse, Comanche Chief; my name Ah-Kah.[29]

However, the authorities missed her point. They did not hear a plea for liberation but considered it "a great pity that Ahkah should not also be educated at some of our eastern institutions."[30]

Pratt regretted that the women and children in Indian Territory were unable "to share the progress of the men" at Fort Marion. He feared that the exiles would unlearn everything "when they go back and join their wives and families who have not advanced." By the spring of 1876, officials in Washington had renewed their internal discussions about gathering the prisoners' dependents to join them. Edward D. Townsend, the adjutant general, recommended to General John Pope, Commander of the Missouri Department, that he encourage them to relocate. By informing them about "the improving condition of their men and the kindness they would receive if they went there," he expected to change their resolution against going to Florida. On June 27, Townsend informed Pratt that, once again, they had "all declined to go." Reportedly, General of the Army Sherman refused to compel them "to go to Florida against their wishes" and closed the matter once and for all.[31] Furthermore, Pratt learned, an application for "a thorough schooling for some of the young men will not meet with favorable action." The War Department planned to return the prisoners "in a body to form the anchors for the organization and subjugation of their tribes." Despite Pratt's lobbying, the government remained ambivalent about continuing their education.[32]

Meanwhile, Pratt became preoccupied with keeping the decaying facilities intact. He found that the roof covering the barracks "leaked badly in thirty to forty places" and would require a completely new covering. In the fall of 1876, a heavy storm forced the prisoners to vacate their residence hall entirely. He worried about the deteriorating structure, fearing that its collapse would interrupt their schooling. Briefly, they returned to sleeping in the casemates. Aside from some needed masonry work, the prisoners were able to quickly repair the facilities and return to the barracks on the upper deck. They shingled the entire roof and renovated their quarters under the direction of a builder, who found them both "docile and competent." They placed large stoves in the center aisle between the bunks, providing warmth during a brisk season along the coast. After George Fox, the interpreter, left in 1877, Pratt resolved to "make better use of the Indians" to administer the place.[33]

Their physical fitness continued to concern Pratt. The post surgeon opined that "prolonged confinement" was "permanently impairing" their health. Suffering from an injury received before his imprisonment, Standing Wolf, one of the Cheyenne warriors, remained bedfast for five months from paralysis in the lower portions of his body. He died on December 5, 1876.[34] Pratt reported "the appearance of pulmonary tendencies among them," which the medical doctor attributed to the spread of tuberculosis. Spotted Elk, a Cheyenne, died on January 2, 1877, from "consumption." A number of others exhibited its symptoms and became "depressed by it." At the same time, chicken pox struck the cohort, badly scarring a few. The Arapaho White Bear suffered a particularly nagging case. Homesickness exacerbated the effects of illness, leaving the less fortunate in no condition to learn at school.[35]

Fortunately, the poor conditions moved several patrons eager to "uplift" the brave hearts. As early as the winter of 1875, Cornelius Rea Agnew, a clinical professor of eye and ear diseases at the College of Physicians and Surgeons, came to visit. Before leaving, he offered to contribute a $20 gold piece. At Pratt's suggestion, he gave the money to the volunteer teachers. During the summer of 1876, N. D. W. Miller, a New Yorker staying in Savannah, Georgia, offered to purchase school books with each student's respective name on them. He purchased a bundle and sent them to Florida along with an offering from his local Sunday school. Later, Dr. M. B. Anderson, the president of Rochester University, met Pratt in the ancient city. In one conversation, they compared the Native people to "low grade foreign emigrants." They only needed education and training to become "part of our people," or so they resolved. Lobbying for funding, Dr. Anderson sent letters of endorsement to other college presidents, to members of the U.S. House of Representatives, and to the Commissioner of Education, John Eaton.[36] A number of philanthropists promised to support Pratt's pedagogy for the oppressed.

Esther Baker Steele, the wife of Joel Dorman Steele, a prominent educator and textbook author, took an active interest in Pratt's pedagogy. She visited Fort Marion in the early months of 1877. During the mornings, she saw the classrooms "filled with earnest learners." She inquired about their families and obtained and published one of their pictographic letters in two London periodicals. She concluded that Native peoples presented as "desirable a field for missionary labor as the far-off denizens of Borrioboola-Gha." Protestant clergy, such as Presbyterian pastor J. D. Wells of Brooklyn, New York, stoked the missionary fires. After his first trip to the prison school, he returned to his congregation to spread the good news. He offered to send tracts for use in instruction, particularly one with large print titled, *The Silent Comforter*. In fact, the pastor read aloud a number of their letters during monthly council meetings.[37]

Deaconess Mary Douglas Burnham, who headed the Women's Auxiliary of the Episcopal Diocese for Central New York, became excited about the Indian students in Florida. She described them to more than 2000 members of the Auxiliary. She noted that "these were not children taken from their homes and taught and trained in Christian schools." Rather, they were "men of mature lives and experience in savage cruelty and barbarism." She praised their "habits of politeness and respect," which had surprised her. When supplied with a pencil, she reported, one had instantly replied with "Thank You." With their eyes fixed upon their books, they "light up with intelligent perceptions and are bright with frequent smiles of appreciative pleasure." She attended services in the chapel, where forty or fifty spoke with great passion. She concluded "that a large body of brave, wild, mature men can in a short period of time be taught habits of discipline and civilization, and be changed into law-abiding citizens ashamed of their uncouth and savage customs and dress." Impressed by the leading men in the classrooms, she wanted to send them to a "School for Prophets."[38]

No classroom visitor was more renowned than Harriet Beecher Stowe, the antebellum author of *Uncle Tom's Cabin*. Though originally from Connecticut, the writer resided in a cottage along the St. Johns River. She frequently accompanied Mather, her close friend, to the old Spanish castle during the winter months. After the school bell rang, she would watch "dark men in the United States uniform, neat, compact, trim, with well-brushed boots and nicely-kept clothing, and books in their hands" rush into the casemates. Sitting in a hollow square around the blackboard, they appeared "docile and eager." They read in concert and mastered perfectly the pronunciation of difficult words. They especially prided themselves in showing how plainly they could speak any "th" sound, which, Stowe noted, "embarrassed every foreigner in the English tongue." They enunciated it "with an anxious and careful precision," and successfully proceeded through reading, spelling, and vocabulary words. She called them "a strong, thoughtful, sensible race, not emotional like the negro." Whatever her prejudices, she found "not a listless face, not a wandering eye, in the whole class."[39]

Stowe also attended chapel services. After taking a seat, she would see the students produce from the breast of their coats their compact Moody and Sankey hymnbooks. They kept the tunes well, she noted, and sang several verses. A brief sermon followed, punctuated by the Cheyenne chief Eagle's Head rising and walking to the middle of the congregation. He stood before them in the "garments of civilization," wearing a long linen coat over his uniform of blue. Solemnly raising his right hand to heaven, he announced in his native tongue: "Let us pray." Immediately, the congregation knelt, bowing their heads with prostrate reverence. Even though she could not comprehend the meaning of the words, Stowe claimed to understand that "a succession of moans" conveyed "the wrongs, the cruelties, the injustice which had followed these children of the forest, driving them to wrong and cruelty in return." After giving thanks to the Great Spirit, the chief addressed her directly. "We like the white ways," he declared. "We like the dress," as he stroked his linen robe calmly. Then he drew his lecture to a close: "We would like to have farms and houses and live peaceably in the good way." As if to say amen to that, another speaker added: "The Great Spirit who sees all within us knows that we do not lie." Thus, they ended their talk at the chapel.[40]

Seduced by their talks, Stowe praised their "deep philosophy" in respect to domesticity. They longed to reunite with their families, a desire that they articulated in affectionate correspondence. In one parcel from a child, the oldest Kiowa chief, Woman's Heart, received a miniature moccasin. He tied it round his neck as a constant reminder of his beloved. Stowe celebrated their recognition that a home "is truly what every human needs to make him a good man." When she entered the "great kitchen" of the fortress, she saw Buffalo Calf, the Cheyenne "warrior woman," presiding over a Peerless cooking stove. Making a "great caldron of savory soup," she set out large dishes of boiled meat with great blocks of bread. Stowe quipped about the "pleasanter style of diet," which Buffalo Calf ostensibly preferred to "eating the hearts of enemies." At the large oven, she met the head baker, Ohettoint, a Kiowa whose name meant High Forehead but who was commonly called Charley. Stowe described the bread as "white and light and of a superior quality." Charley spoke softly: "Me make. By and by, out there, will make bread and get money."[41]

Before departing, the writer engaged in a heart-to-heart talk with the prisoners. She learned that the married men desired to return home and to have some assistance in starting "a civilized settlement." However, the unmarried men wished to further their education, which would "fit them to go back and teach their people the arts and trades of civilized life." They wanted to learn farming, blacksmithing, and other useful trades, as well as to carry on the study of language and literature. In fact, Pratt reported, "twenty-three of the most promising would elect to remain east for education, rather than go home, if such an alternative was offered." If the doors to one institution opened, then many other American Indians could "be brought up to their standard." Indeed, government assistance and private gifts would carry them "forward to a higher one."[42] To that end, Stowe concluded one of her articles:

We have tried fighting and killing the Indians, and gained little by it. We have tried feeding them as paupers in their savage state, and the result has been dishonest contractors, and invitation and provocation to war. Suppose, now, we try education; suppose we respond to the desire of these young men and give them for two or three years teaching and training in some such institution as the Amherst State Agricultural School. The government of Japan thought it worth while to send young men here to be educated—to learn our customs, manners and ideas, the government paying a commissioner to superintend and bearing their expenses. Might not the money now constantly spent on armies, forts, and frontiers be better invested in educating young men who shall return and teach their people to live like civilized beings? [43]

Echoing the sentiments of other nineteenth-century reformers, Stowe called for the national expansion of Indian education.

Stirred by Stowe's clarion call, officials in Washington began to take notice of the agile minds in the prison school. On May 8, 1877, a U.S. Inspector General, N. H. Davis, arrived at the stronghold to acquire "useful and interesting information with respect to their improvement under instruction." As he walked the courtyard with Pratt, the prisoners performed routine drills, roll calls, guard patrol, and mess detail. He found them all wearing neat uniforms and clean and bright shoes. They were "orderly and obedient in a marked degree." He scrutinized their classroom behavior, noting great progress in their studies. He vouched for their "fitness and capacity for industrious occupation and self-support," that is, if kept under "proper control." After his inspection, he reported his findings: "The success attained in the habits and knowledge of civilized life with these Indians suggests the practicability of utilizing those at our agencies in military organizations, mechanical trades, and in agriculture, and making them self-supporting." He considered their education inside the prison school highly gratifying. [44]

Meanwhile, Spencer F. Baird, a zoologist and assistant secretary at the Smithsonian Institute, visited the prison school. Accompanied by Senator George F. Edmunds of Ver-

mont, he took the prisoners on a field trip to three Indian
mounds near St. Augustine. Hoping to benefit from their tribal
knowledge, he asked them to draw the mounds and the surrounding area. In effect, the sites became outdoor classrooms.
The students excavated the site, unearthing crania, bones,
shell, pottery, ornaments, and axes. They even caught and
stuffed a sawfish sixteen feet long, which fascinated the zoologist. Baird carefully collected their findings and shipped the
artifacts in barrels to the museum in the nation's capital. The
remarkable collection appeared on display in museum cases,
but no credit was given to the Indian contributors.[45]

On May 21, 1877, Baird wrote to Pratt that "several gentlemen" in Washington were especially interested in learning
more about the Indians. He raised the possibility of sending an
expert to study the languages of the tribes. In addition, he
asked if Pratt might induce the Indians to allow plaster casts to
be taken of their faces. He added that a mask of the officer
could be made to show the mold-making process to them. He
noted: "You will not object, I suppose, to be immortalized by
being placed in a niche in the Smithsonian gallery."[46] Once
Pratt had agreed, Baird wrote to the Commissioner of Indian
Affairs. He requested permission to study the "great variety of
physiognomy among the different tribes represented" at the
prison and to examine their physical features. He believed that
a series of face casts in plaster or metal would be "an extremely
interesting contribution to Indianology." In particular, the
casts would provide molds for the faces of the mannequins
appearing in Smithsonian exhibitions.[47]

The Smithsonian hired Clark Mills, an eminent sculptor
who had crafted the statue of Andrew Jackson in Lafayette
Square outside of the White House. He took passage for St.
Augustine during the summer of 1877 and stayed for several
days. Although interested in the artistry of "life masks," Mills

appears to have been motivated in part by his passion for phrenology. This pseudo-science professed to study the relationships between character traits and skull structure. He was fascinated by the lectures of George Combe, a leading phrenology spokesman in Great Britain. To test his assumptions about racial differences, Mills made a plaster mold of each model's head. He placed an elastic cap over the hair and inserted straws in the nose. He spread over the subject a preparation of plaster, which quickly hardened. Then the mold was carefully broken and removed, to be reassembled at a later date. Finally, casts of superior finish were fashioned from the original crude ones.[48]

With Pratt's assistance, Mills experienced no difficulty in securing the cooperation of the Indians for the masking. They seemed pleased that their likenesses were destined for the city of the "Great Father at Washington, there to be preserved forever." Furthermore, Pratt intimated that there would be nothing detrimental to either soul or body in the process, subjecting himself to the masking first to reassure them. Lone Wolf, the Kiowa chief, volunteered to sit next. Mills pronounced Biter, one of the younger Kiowa, a perfect specimen of physical manhood. Enthralled with his body, he made a cast of his entire frame. The sculptor also formed a lasting impression of the Comanche Madawith, or Giving His Sister to Another Man, before he expired from "consumption" on July 21.[49]

Mills shipped to the Smithsonian eighteen packages, which contained the masks of sixty-one male Indians, one female Indian, one Indian child, and one of Pratt. He also produced about a hundred casts of fish heads and one of a nine-hundred-pound turtle. More than anything else, he seemed to fixate upon the formation of skulls and bones. As he drew closer to his subjects, he contemplated the unique structure to their crania. Upon completing his work, he wrote to Baird: "They are undoubtedly the most important collection of Indians heads in the world, and when they have become extinct, which fate is inevitable, posterity will see a fact simile [sic] of a race of men that once overrun this great country, not only their philognomes but phrenological development also." The Indian masks assumed a conspicuous place at the Smithsonian, though they were later relegated to storage.[50]

However limited their practical use, the masks thrilled their maker. "When I began taking the casts of the Indians," Mills later wrote to Baird, "I found the size of the brain fully up to the average of the white race." Seeking additional funding, he asked the Smithsonian for an opportunity to make more masks. He proposed a comparative study: "Now would it not be advisable to have a number of those civilized tribes found in the state of N.Y. taken by way of comparison to see whether a few generations of civilized life has changed their development." However, the Smithsonian expressed little interest in his phrenological curiosities. Later, Mills claimed to have discovered "that the form of the Indian head differed from the whites as much as their faces." He puzzled over "whether or not that is due to their mode of life," or "whether they are separate and distinct like the ape and horse." Whatever his previous assumptions, he asserted that "their brain power is fully equal if not superior to the whites." His "catalogue" of Indian heads, he believed, would make it possible to measure their mental capacities and determine their fitness for education. Of course, the masks revealed nothing about the inner worlds of the exiles.[51]

A far more revealing exhibition of their inner worlds was the ledger book imagery. Twenty-six of the prisoners at Fort Marion produced hundreds of illustrations. The braves tried to produce drawings that reflected the traditional function of

Plains Indian artistry. While recounting their exploits, they pictured the path to honorable manhood. They portrayed scenes of nostalgia, including camps, feasts, councils, dances, games, and ceremonies. They depicted tribal legends as well as comedic situations. They featured heroes of great wars and leaders of high esteem. More than anything else, they drew acts of gallantry. Reflecting a world beyond Indian Territory, virtually every series of sketches heralded their movement from battlefields to classrooms. With pencils, crayons, and paper, they used the two dimensional style and profile views characteristic of indigenous pictography. They incorporated blended hues and subtle shading into their extraordinary outpouring of artwork.[52] What precisely any warrior artist intended to express through his work, though, was and is a great mystery.[53]

Many warrior artists such as Wohaw excelled at the art of survival. Of course, imprisonment at Fort Marion represented a purgatory experience that placed the gifted and talented exiles in a bind. With nowhere to turn, the pupils inside the prison school stood at a crossroads. On the one hand, they confronted the threat of cultural extinction. On the other hand, they recognized opportunities to learn from others. Striking a balance, they handled the conflict artfully. They collaborated with new allies and passed their tests with brilliant colors. They wielded tools for communication that elevated them as a rising force among their people. More than passive recipients of parochial knowledge, they displayed amazing insight by imagining a world where Indians still made medicine. They found creative ways to positively channel their deepest and most profound sentiments. Their bravery transformed the casemates into classrooms and heartened almost everyone interested in their fate.

W. S. Soule, Photo.   Entered according to Act of Congress, in the year 1875, by John P. Soule, in the Office of the Librarian of Congress, at Washington.   Fort Sill, I. T.

QUIR-PAR-KO or LONE WOLFS CAMP.

KIOWA.

No. 6.

Kiowa camp in Indian Territory. Courtesy Yale Collection of Western Americana, Beinecke Rare Book and Manuscript Library.

Sketch of buffalo hunt, by Nock-ko-ist (Bear's Heart). Courtesy Yale Collection of Western Americana, Beinecke Rare Book and Manuscript Library.

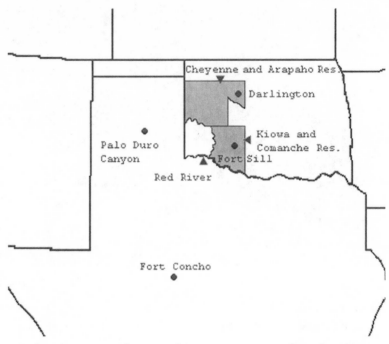

Indian Territory and surrounding area. Courtesy of Deidra Moses Lookingbill.

Richard Henry Pratt. Courtesy Yale Collection of Western Americana, Beinecke Rare Book and Manuscript Library.

Fort Marion. Courtesy Yale Collection of Western Americana, Beinecke Rare Book and Manuscript Library.

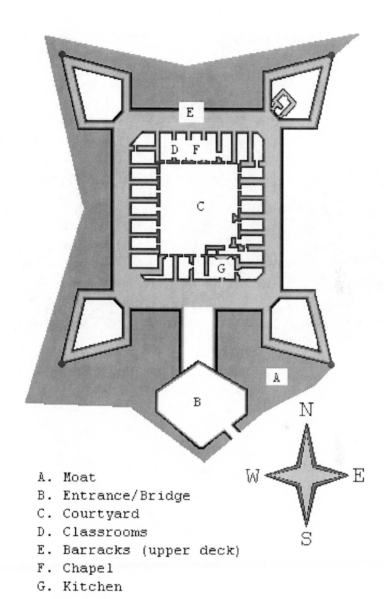

A. Moat
B. Entrance/Bridge
C. Courtyard
D. Classrooms
E. Barracks (upper deck)
F. Chapel
G. Kitchen

Diagram of Fort Marion. Courtesy of Deidra Moses Lookingbill.

Plains Indian prisoners at Fort Marion. Courtesy Yale Collection of
Western Americana, Beinecke Rare Book and Manuscript Library.

(Left to right) Pe-ah-in (Mother), Mo-chi (Buffalo Calf), Po-ka-do-ah (Black Horse), Mi-huh-heu-i-mup (Medicine Water), Minimic (Eagle's Head). Courtesy Yale Collection of Western Americana, Beinecke Rare Book and Manuscript Library.

Indian soldiers at Fort Marion. Courtesy Yale Collection of Western Americana, Beinecke Rare Book and Manuscript Library.

Prisoners making bows and arrows. Courtesy Yale Collection of
Western Americana, Beinecke Rare Book and Manuscript Library.

Sketch of photographer and visitors, by Wohaw. Courtesy Yale Collection of Western Americana, Beinecke Rare Book and Manuscript Library.

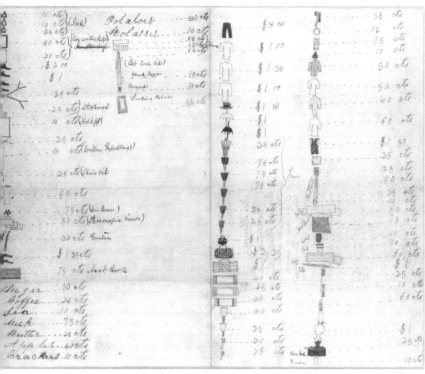

Ledger with listing of prices for local merchandise, by Buffalo Meat. Courtesy Yale Collection of Western Americana, Beinecke Rare Book and Manuscript Library.

Sketch of dance, by Etahdleuh (Boy Hunting). Courtesy Yale Collection of Western Americana, Beinecke Rare Book and Manuscript Library.

Anastasia Island, drawing by Cohoe. From *A Cheyenne Sketchbook*, by Cohoe, with commentary by E. Adamson Hoebel and Karen Daniels Petersen. Copyright 1964 by the University of Oklahoma Press, Publishing Division of the University. Courtesy University of Oklahoma Press.

Wohaw, self-portrait in pencil. Courtesy of the Missouri Historical
Society, St. Louis.

Sketch of classroom, by O-uh-oh (Soaring Eagle). Courtesy Yale Collection of Western Americana, Beinecke Rare Book and Manuscript Library.

Drawing of family of Minimic (Eagle's Head). Courtesy Yale Collection of Western Americana, Beinecke Rare Book and Manuscript Library.

Sarah Mather. Courtesy Yale Collection of Western Americana, Beinecke Rare Book and Manuscript Library.

(*Left to right*) Henry Ta-a-way-te (Telling Something), David Pendleton O-kuh-ha-tuh (Making Medicine), Paul Caryl Zotom (Biter), John Wicks O-uk-ste-uh (Shave Head). Courtesy Yale Collection of Western Americana, Beinecke Rare Book and Manuscript Library.

Chapter 6
Vision Quest
The Last Days of Exile

IN EARLY JANUARY OF 1877, THE WAR prisoners at Fort Marion gathered for an intertribal council to discuss a "change of condition." They sat around a bonfire in the open courtyard and discussed the future. As each gave "a talk," clouds of smoke billowed into the night sky. Lieutenant Pratt stared at the burning embers and listened to the exiles' request to study outside the military stronghold. "If by removal elsewhere facilities for instruction in trades and farming could be given to the retained younger ones," he recorded, then "they would cheerfully and efficiently labor to show its wisdom." They had come to terms with the lines, corners, and squares of the outpost and now desired to scout a country foreign to them. With an end to their imprisonment in sight, they pledged to continue their education at an institution of higher learning. They envisioned winning honors while studying abroad.[1]

Pratt made trips to Washington to talk to officials in the War and Interior Departments about their visions. Pratt recommended the "release of a few of the most deserving old men, and a promise of release to the others contingent on good behavior all round." Specifically, he requested clemency for at least eight prisoners able to do "the greatest good" on behalf of their people.[2] Ezra A. Hayt, the Commissioner of Indian Affairs, expressed a general interest in "education and civilization." However, he concluded "that the eventual civilization of Indians may be reached through the education of their children." In fact, he believed "that it can be brought about more speedily by that method than by any other." The students at Fort Marion learned too slowly, he surmised, although "many adult Indians can of course in the mean time be taught to raise their own subsistence from the ground, to herd cattle, or to do mechanical work." The goal of the administration was to educate "the head and heart" of an Indian child.[3] Officials undoubtedly preferred to deal with the weak, not the strong.

Officials did consider sending home Coming to the Grove, the Kiowa who had previously betrayed his kinsmen's escape attempt. He suffered from "consumption," that is, tuberculosis. Pratt feared that he "would not likely live many weeks," even though he was as "stout and promising as any when he came." The Kiowa experienced "six or seven severe hemorrhages from the lungs" and appeared to be failing rapidly. Pratt implored Lieutenant Colonel Frederick Dent, the post commander, to make "some special effort" to end his agony and predicted the prisoner's certain death "before many weeks if he remains here." On the other hand, Pratt hoped, he might recover if sent back home, and he told a friend that "we owe this effort to him." Pratt also asked that Woman's Heart accompany the ailing warrior to Indian Territory. The latter's ability to speak effectively in both Kiowa and in English, his old age, his disabled condition, and his good conduct justified an end to his exile.[4]

On April 12, 1877, E. D. Townsend, Adjutant General, announced that Coming to the Grove and Woman's Heart were to be "sent to Fort Sill in charge of a noncommissioned officer" for release. Expeditiously, the two Kiowa left on Wednesday, April 18. Under the supervision of Sergeant Dunleavy, they journeyed to Jacksonville and thence by train to Fort Sill. They arrived at the fort on April 27, when a letter to the agency announced the good news. Their supervisor reported that they had behaved "admirably on the journey, giving him no trouble whatever." Greeted by their families and friends, they were "set at liberty" immediately. A "great powwow and dance" celebrated their liberation, with "noise being kept up from dusk to dawn." Sergeant Dunleavy returned to Florida with a gift to White Horse from his wife. It was a buffalo robe, which he soon decorated with memorable scenes of hunting and fighting. One newspaper reporter wondered "whether the civilization which has come to them will have a permanent influence on their future deportment." Regardless of such doubts, the freedom of Woman's Heart and Coming to the Grove raised expectations for the return of the rest.[5]

Even in poor health, the returned Kiowa conveyed "strong talk." Agent James Haworth attended a tribal council on April 30, where he was asked to transcribe their speeches and send a message to Washington demanding the release of the prisoners in Florida. He described the council as "large and pleasant," noting that Woman's Heart spoke with eloquence. The elderly chief expressed joy at his return and promised to remember the things he had learned "over there," particularly in regard to "traveling the good road" and "making corn." Because he had "learned much about the Sabbath Day" and "about the Great Spirit and his ways," he planned to host Sunday services to lead his people "on the good way." Turning to the agent, he asked for his support to help them to "settle down in houses" and "to get the rest of the people back." As he switched from one language to another, the headman handled his words skillfully. Moved by his words, Agent Haworth requested that the Indian Office fix a time for "the immediate release of all those held as prisoners belonging to this agency." Weeks passed, however, and the distant authorities remained silent.[6]

Undaunted by the authorities, Woman's Heart continued to compose letters. On June 20, he asked Agent Haworth to

help him draft one to Pratt. "I am feeling well," he said, adding
that "I have not forgotten what you said to me before starting—
for me to keep strong heart, and not get discouraged, or tired."
The chieftain gave "his people a good talk every Sunday," re-
iterating what he had learned "on Sunday there." Woman's
Heart wanted to receive letters from "a lady," probably one of
the teachers, and he promised to write her back. However, he
wrote of tragedy as well. The length of the trip and the changes
in climate were too much for Coming to the Grove. His tuberculosis had worsened, and he died. His family cherished his
last days in Indian Territory and buried him at the agency. The
Kiowa told Pratt that "he carried your talk with him to the
grave, and I too will do the same." He closed his message,
saying: "This is all my talk now."[7]

Throughout 1877, officials in Indian Territory debated
the merits of returning the exiles to their homes. Lieutenant
Colonel John P. Hatch, commander at Fort Sill, thought that
"it would be bad policy to release any of them, if they are to be
sent here." As for the "talk" of the Indians, he said, "I attach no
value to it." No Indian intended to keep "a promise where he
thinks he can benefit himself by breaking it," he opined, adding, "Why then run again the risk of trouble by introducing an
element the elimination of which has had so good an effect?"
If the government were to free them, Hatch resolved, they
should "be put at work on a farm in New Jersey, where they can
receive the assistance of charitable people, and be held to
strict accountability for any breach of the laws." The commanding officer insisted "that none of these prisoners should
be released," preferring to keep the Indians at a distance.[8]

Agent Haworth disagreed with the post commander. "I
do not think any evil would result from the release of a part of
them now," he wrote, "and the rest after a while, say in the
Fall." Influenced by the tribal councils, he asked for the imme-

diate release of Lone Wolf, the banished Kiowa chief. He "would accomplish a great deal more by his presence than by his absence," but Haworth doubted the good conduct of the rest. "The spring of the year, when the grass is coming up and the ponies getting fat, is a restless time among wild Indians," he cautioned. Recalling the uprising of 1874, he feared that "some might feel more disposed to do wrong" once they were back on the reservation. If only "ten or twelve of the most deserving of the Kiowas" and "four or five Comanches" were returned, he would be confident of maintaining social control. Moreover, the gesture "would be an assurance to the Indians that the Government was both powerful and merciful." Rather than seek an end to their internment all at once, the agent asked for the parole of a handful into his care.[9]

The authorities at the Darlington agency outlined their plans for paroling the Cheyenne prisoners. Major J. K. Mizener, the commanding officer at Fort Reno, advised that "the release of the prisoners held in Florida should, I think be very gradual, in very small numbers, at considerable intervals." Furthermore, it should be contingent upon "good behavior on the part of the prisoners" and "faith on the part of the tribe." Otherwise, the motives "may be misjudged by the Indians," who from "their suspicious nature" would presume "that we repent having resorted to unnecessary or unjust punishment." Agent Miles recommended "that they be liberated about October 1, 1877." He preferred gradual release for a chosen few without interference from those "who may not know their real characters." He concluded: "I shall be well satisfied that the balance of the prisoners from this Agency remain where they are until the wisdom of our government may direct them otherwise." Philip McCusker, a non-Indian interpreter at the agencies, warned "be careful who you recommend for release." Although McCusker wished "to see Heap of Birds released," Pratt balked at the proposition. The latter reported to the agency that the chieftain was a "conservative force" among the Cheyenne.[10]

The Interior Department studied the plans and asked the War Department for a delay of action. The Office of Indian Affairs feared "great excitement and constant disturbance" at the agencies. While Lieutenant General Sheridan doubted that the returning Indians would cause any disturbances, he worried that "they will go back to the blanket condition." In fact, he expressed support for Harriet Beecher Stowe's suggestion that a number of them be sent to New England for further schooling. By the summer of 1877, General of the Army William T. Sherman and Secretary of War George W. McCrary were prepared to act. Reluctantly, General Sherman conceded that "there are good reasons for delay til the autumn, say October, when I recommend that the whole be transported to Fort Sill, delivered over to the Indian Agent there, and a few of the worst might be put in the guardhouse there."[11] Ignoring the risks to their health and safety, they detained the prisoners in Florida through the remainder of the year.

One Cheyenne prisoner nearly lost his vision that year. "I sometimes took the Bible and held it open before me," recalled Howling Wolf, the son of Cheyenne chief Eagle's Head. "That gave me comfort," he said, "although I could not read it." He struggled with his lessons in the prison school after he began to lose sight in his left eye. The warrior once notorious for "rambling around and raiding" sought help from the post surgeon, Dr. John Janeway, who examined the Cheyenne and certified him "competent to cure." Janeway operated using a caustic, but the patient's condition continued to degenerate. In fact, he suffered from a pterygium, a wedge-shaped fibrovascular growth that appeared on the surface tissue in the white of the eye and extended onto the cornea. His acute disorder stemmed from prolonged exposure to ultraviolet sunlight. In all likelihood, Howling Wolf had harmed himself by staring directly into the sun while seeking visions.[12]

The school teachers at the fortress undertook an extensive letter-writing campaign on behalf of Howling Wolf. They aimed to send him to an ophthalmologist for treatment. In the summer of 1877, the War Department granted permission for his transfer to New England. Alice Pendleton, the wife of an Ohio senator and a vacationer in St. Augustine, convinced authorities to ship Howling Wolf to Boston for surgery at the Massachusetts Eye and Ear Infirmary. She paid for most of his travel expenses, and other benefactors covered the medical bills. The post commander ordered Lieutenant Edmund Zalinski, who was preparing to go to Boston for his own wedding, to accompany the patient. Identified as case number 337, the Cheyenne was admitted to the Infirmary on July 20. His surgeon, Henry Lyman Shaw, found pterygia in both eyes and operated. The patient recovered in the hospital, where the "friends of the Indian" came to see him.[13]

During his convalescence, Howling Wolf was seen by philanthropists as the epitome of an Indian pupil. After his surgery, he sported a pair of blue eyeglasses and walked with "all the airs and graces of a Harvard freshman." Wherever he went, the warrior gathered intelligence about the foreign country. He recorded details of his fantastic journey with pencils and paper. He sketched steamers stopping at various ports and documented passengers changing ships. He toured the Berkshire Mountains. He surveyed the architecture and housing near Cape Cod and entered Brahman estates, including the home of historian Francis Parkman. He attended Lieutenant Zalinski's wedding ceremony and visited Back Bay and

Cambridge salons. Guided by his fellow travelers, he probably saw the galleries at the Museum of Fine Arts in Copley Square.[14]

As his vision recovered, Howling Wolf experimented with innovative techniques in his own drawings. He mailed several to his father at Fort Marion and to his wife in Indian Territory. In one remarkable pictographic letter, he rendered himself conversing with acquaintances in Massachusetts. It included a sketched map locating the highlights of his long, strange trip. The Post Office, though, inadvertently delivered it to the Cheyenne River agency in Dakota Territory, where a puzzled Lieutenant R. M. Hoyt of the Eleventh Infantry scrutinized it for clues. In an amusing example of a military intelligence failure, he detected an international plot involving the visionary Sioux war leader and holy man Sitting Bull. Incredibly, Hoyt failed to notice the printed word "Boston," which the Cheyenne had scribbled prominently on the image. The officer's alarm passed as Howling Wolf continued his reconnaissance in New England.[15]

In St. Augustine, Pratt sought to keep the prisoners occupied with various tasks. When the Presbyterian Church undertook a building project during 1877, the congregation hired them for work. Pratt, who arranged the job, commanded a crew of eighteen Indians and three non-Indians. They were hired to transfer a detached Sunday school building from its original site on South St. George to a point back of the Post Office. The building stood 48 x 28 x 22 feet in its dimensions. The prisoners made their own windlass power and rollers, obtained at low cost the necessary timbers, borrowed heavy ropes and blocks from a ported ship, and rented lifting screws from a contractor in Jacksonville. As a crew chief barked commands, they moved the structure during high tide and turned the entire frame 180 degrees. They moved it over 1100 yards, 350 of which included carrying it about four feet off the ground to keep it out of the water. Pratt mailed Agent Miles at Darlington "an Indian's picture" of the operation, calling the experience a "valuable object lesson."[16]

Meanwhile, Pratt purchased the wreck of a stranded vessel from its desperate owner. He paid only $100 for it, planning to use the Indian laborers to rescue the ship for resale. They enjoyed "fighting the waves and the great forces of the sea," he observed, but found that the wreck could not be dislodged. Thereafter, he tried to get his money back by salvaging the rigging. His wrecking crew expressed particular pleasure at "tearing to pieces this strong work of the white man." As the wreck lay in the breakers off North Beach, they could only work about two hours a day during low tide. They dropped the top mast with blocks and ropes and then cut it away. Unfortunately, it landed overboard onto a sand bar and broke in the middle. They carried away the cable chain, which was 200 yards long and weighed over 5,000 pounds. They hauled away the main anchor, which weighed 900 pounds. They appropriated over 4000 pounds of rope from the wreck, too. Finally, they reclaimed the yawls, which the exiles used to ferry around guests during the travel season at the resort community.[17]

To escape the summer doldrums, the exiles frequently boated to Anastasia Island and Matanzas Inlet. During one rendezvous, a boating party led by C. M. Bevan landed at their bivouac site. Despite the disruption to Pratt's assigned tasks, the gentlemen were greeted with "howdy" and hearty handshakes. Eagle's Head, Lone Wolf, and White Horse offered them a pipe of peace, which was about two feet long and filled with perfumed tobacco. The smokers passed the pipe and the day on the beach. As they chatted, the non-Indians asked the Indians about their jobs. The latter replied: "me fish," "me swim," "me row," "me work," and offered the motions of swimming, rowing, and other activities. To the surprise of one mariner, the Indians put on a demonstration of their nautical skills. Making Medicine piloted the boat with Eagle's Head at his side. As they sailed off the shore, the Cheyenne chief waved his hand in the air, saying: "goodbye boys."[18] Boating parties often searched for the exiles on the waters while cruising near St. Augustine.

In the late fall, a terrible outbreak of disease frightened many parties away from the St. Augustine area. A severe type of typho-malarial fever spread southward from Jacksonville, with more than forty non-Indians in the area dying from its infection. Pratt estimated that seventeen cases erupted among the Indians, referring to its spread as a "calamity."[19] On October 8, Heap of Birds died of congestion and heart disease. Also known as Many Magpies, he was the eleventh prisoner to die since leaving Indian Territory in chains. His comrades buried him the following day at the St. Francis Barracks cemetery. A eulogy in a local newspaper called him "an Indian of good ways," who was "greatly admired by those who knew him." It recalled how often he "expressed his desire to regain his family on the plains, procure a lot of ground, build him a house, and live like a white man." Eagle's Head, the last prominent Cheyenne chief still alive, made "a long talk about their past and future" after the burial of his close friend. "His heart cries out to be with his wife and children," wrote Pratt.[20] By winter, a cold snap broke the attack of the fever.

As the year 1877 closed, the wheels of bureaucracy finally began to turn. General of the Army Sherman asked Indian Commissioner Hayt to appoint "some keeper" to relieve Pratt because his "services are needed with his regiment." With the prisoners thrust into his hands, Hayt concluded on November 10 that their suffering "seems to have been of sufficient severity for all reformatory purposes." He confessed "that severe punishment may have been, and probably was, visited upon some who were innocent of deliberate crimes." He noted that "a part of them have died away from their families and friends" and that "of those remaining many are sick." He acknowledged their good behavior, though he expressed no remorse for their agony. "Believing that no possible interest will be subserved by their further imprisonment," he concluded, "I respectfully recommend that all these prisoners be returned to their tribes and released." Unfortunately, the Indian Office lacked funds for their transportation. Hayt asked the War Department "to take charge of their delivery" or to request the necessary appropriation from Congress in the next session.[21] Therefore, Hayt expected the prisoners to stay in Florida for the winter.

Howling Wolf stayed in the Boston area almost five months before arriving back at St. Augustine in December of 1877. Influenced by his experiences in New England, he saw his captivity with fresh eyes. Pratt described his return:

We saw a dapper gentleman, with hand satchel, derby hat and cane pass up the sea wall into the fort with quick step, and I went to the fort to see who it was, and found that Howling Wolf had returned unannounced, his eyes greatly benefited, and in addition, in his dress, manner, and conduct, he had imbibed a large stock of Boston qualities. In fact, I was not long in finding out that, in some respects, he had taken on altogether too much Boston for his resources and future good. He became insubordinate and insurrectionary, and I was forced to discipline him.[22]

Thanks to his corrective lenses, Howling Wolf thrived in the classroom that winter. The bespectacled brave was described as "thoroughly Bostonian," prompting a visitor to the castle to joke about hearing him reply to the stereotypical Indian greeting "How" with an affected "Nicely."[23] With his vision fully recovered, he looked forward to going home with his fellow captives.

By the beginning of 1878, rumors circulated around the ancient city concerning the possible transfer of the captives. Pratt learned that no government money was available to educate "adult prisoners," but the Indian Office offered "no objection" to an effort to solicit donations for the "younger and most promising" of his cohort. His request to give them "worn out or broken" tools—mostly shovels and axes—was denied, and so he sold them at an auction, where the whole lot fetched only forty cents.[24] Alice Pendleton, who had previously underwritten Howling Wolf's trip to Boston, promised to sponsor a student. Pratt proudly observed that "Mr. Making Medicine" mailed her a letter of "thank you" and courted the favor of the senator's wife. One after another, visitors began offering money for scholarships to aid others. Walking on the sea-wall one day, Pratt met a gentleman from Illinois who asked: "How much does it take to send one to school?" The officer gave him an estimate, prompting the fellow to pledge to send a check for one year's expense.[25]

Amy Caruthers, who returned to teach her class, pledged to sponsor two students. Exhibiting great enterprise, she raised money from philanthropists in the North and wrote to Commissioner Hayt to obtain his approval. As a result of her vigorous effort, she collected about $500. Furthermore, she and several ladies in town hosted a "Mother Goose" pageant for the fundraising campaign. About twenty-five boys and girls less than eight-years-old volunteered to help. The town buzzed with excitement as people rallied to see the pageantry. The first show was held on March 4, 1878, at the Magnolia Hotel. Because of the great turnout, two performances were held before audiences numbering over 700 people. An encore followed the next evening. The hosts had hoped to raise $180, but they took in $220. They donated the extra money to the "Indian fund" for the education of additional students.[26]

The audiences rushed to the shows because Pratt had permitted the Indians to perform with local children. Even though the officer had forbidden any more "Indian dances," the ladies of the town had convinced him to lift his ban for this powwow. In addition to the children's nursery rhymes, the program consisted of a traditional recital by four of the best dancers, a war whoop by White Horse, a love song by Boy Hunting, and a public talk in sign language by Bear Mountain. Before his grand entrance, Boy Hunting donned his native garb. He had preserved the braids of his once-long hair, which had been cut at the beginning of his training. In a packed hall, he stood in full regalia with moccasins, buckskin leggings, beaded coat, war paint, eagle feather, and tethered braids. He joined with Biter, Bear Mountain, and Roman Nose in a quartet, harmonizing an American-style ballad written by one of the teachers.[27] Perhaps with tongue in cheek, the ensemble sang:

> *Lo we Red Men to your home,*
> *Came in silent sadness.*
> *From the far-off Plains where roam*
> *All our tribes in gladness.*
> *In this genial happy land*
> *Chiefs of many a nation,*
> *We find the welcome friendly hand,*
> *We find the true salvation.*
> *Here we've learned a nobler life,*
> *To do unto each other,*
> *The good we can,*
> *To conquer strife,*
> *And call the white man brother.*[28]

This song represented their last great performance in St. Augustine.

The next day, Pratt wrote to Commissioner Hayt about Boy Hunting, requesting that the Kiowa be placed under the officer's guardianship for two years. His protégé looked forward to completing a formal education and wanted to become a teacher. Pratt contacted friends in Massachusetts about aiding him, stating: "I want him to see and learn the very best side of civilization." As Boy Hunting's people had been "consigned to agriculture for a living," Pratt tried to send him to a state agricultural college. In fact, he offered to pay for the Kiowa's tuition and expenses in advance. However, he found that institutions of higher learning were reluctant to take "the bad Indians." Lacking the vision of Pratt, Commissioner Hayt and the "friends of the Indians" preferred to educate children, not men.[29]

Major General Winfield S. Hancock, who commanded the Division of the Atlantic, expressed interest in the "young men who wanted to go to school." He came to St. Augustine on March 15, entering the castle unannounced during drill hour. As he watched the marching troops in the courtyard, he observed the "laudable precision" of the uniformed Indians. Carefully eyeing the rank and file, General Hancock asked: "How many wish to remain and be educated?" Most of those who stepped forward were bachelors, sacrificing their immediate return in order to join the vanguard of education. Nineteen declared: "We want to go to school and learn books and learn to till the ground." Later, three more volunteered to make their total number twenty-two. "There is no question about their earnestness in the matter," Pratt told Hancock. The latter, though, emphasized the youth of the vanguard in his report to General of the Army Sherman. Hancock concluded that their schooling was "worthy of consideration," pledging his support for "their wishes in this respect" after leaving Fort Marion. He noted that five had been promised funding by private parties, but that the other seventeen needed help to continue their education. In fact, the division commander talked with each individually about their aspirations.[30]

Sarah Mather, the matron of the prison school, talked with General Samuel C. Armstrong, the superintendent of Hampton Normal and Industrial Institute in Virginia, about admitting the students. The American Missionary Association (AMA) had opened Hampton for former slaves in 1868, and in 1877 it had enrolled an Indian pupil, a Ute sent by a scholarship donor. Responding to Mather in early 1878, General Armstrong agreed to accept one Indian from Fort Marion, and after hearing from Pratt directly, he offered "to take all he could get." Because "army officers are gentlemen of character, force, of experience with the red man," Armstrong wrote, they were "better fitted than any others to settle the Indian question." With the destructive work of warfare accomplished, their military experience "fitted them for the constructive work to be done." Education, he later reasoned, was "indirectly doing more than any two regiments for the pacification of the Indian—the army's special business." That spring, the American Missionary Association agreed to fund at least thirteen of the Native students for enrollment at the historically black institution.[31]

Pratt arranged for a three-year course of study for twenty-two students at various locations. Hampton prepared to admit Boy Hunting as well as High Forehead, Bear's Heart, Big Nose, Wild Horse, Hail Stone, Limpy, White Goose, Buzzard, and Squint Eyes. Good Talk, White Bear, Matches, Little Chief, and Soaring Eagle also planned to stay at Hampton until September before going on to the school of Bishop Henry Whipple at Faribault, Minnesota. Because the Bishop later asked General Armstrong to retain his students under Hampton's tutelage, the total number of Indians studying there reached fifteen. At Tarrytown, New York, Amy and Horace Caruthers hosted and home-schooled Bear Mountain, Roman Nose, and Tooth Man. Making Medicine, Biter, Telling Something, and Shave Head were accepted by an Episcopalian school operated by John B. Wicks, rector at St. Paul's Church in Paris Hill, New York. Pratt offered all the students the chance to change their minds and return home with the other prisoners upon release, but they all declined.[32]

Pratt exchanged a series of telegraphs with his superiors about arranging transportation for the prisoners. On March 25, the Interior Department announced its approval of "the proposition of the General of the Army in relation to return of the prisoners to Fort Sill and the reimbursement of the expenses under future legislation." A few days later, the War Department authorized Pratt "to take such measures as may be necessary to accomplish the object in view." On April 5, Adjutant General Townsend directed Pratt to release only the men "whose education is provided for under sanction of the Indian department." The War Department refused to transport the rest to Fort Sill due to the cost, while the Indian Office expressed reluctance to assume the expense. Commissioner Hayt offered to receive the lot at Norfolk, Virginia, if they could be sent without cost to his office. Pratt immediately prepared the sixty-two Indians in his charge for departure, fearing that officials would change their mind.[33]

Pratt found an excursion steamer that plied the St. Johns River during winters and the Chesapeake Bay during summers. The pilot, Captain Starke, operated the ship christened the *Hampton* and offered to carry the prisoners at no charge. On Monday, April 8, Pratt received permission from his superiors to take them as far as Norfolk, with the government reluctantly agreeing to pay for their food. The next day, "practically all St. Augustine" gathered on the waterfront to see them depart. With tears in their eyes, the ladies of the town said farewell to their band of brothers. As they embarked, the Indians began to sing the hymn, "In the Sweet By and By." Pratt and his family climbed aboard with them. At once, the steamer rolled into the harbor and steered toward the ocean. The exiles would spend their last days together cruising the Atlantic seaboard.[34]

As the exiles passed through the Chesapeake Bay, a correspondent for the *New York Times* breezily issued a dispatch. He confused them with members of "Big Red Foot's gang of outlawed Indians." Their headman, the correspondent wrote, had led a run-away band of "Nauvoos" and, with "scalps dangling from his belt," had died ten days after capture. Adding insult to injury, the reporter claimed that the "savages" had refused "to eat or to touch a white man's hand." They had originally been banished to "the Dry Tortugas," where forty-eight had died in the hands of their captors. Though released from captivity, the reporter considered them a menace to society. His story contained inaccurate information about the steamer's passengers, and no editor at the newspaper bothered to check the facts.[35]

The steamer ported at Old Point in Virginia on Saturday evening, April 13, and the Hampton faculty and students gave the Indians a warm reception. The *Southern Workman*, the campus newspaper, featured a story about the "midnight raid of red men." The next morning, the newcomers wandered the grounds, lounged under trees, and enjoyed the Sunday. In their uniforms, they appeared before a capacity crowd at the chapel of Virginia Hall, where they performed several songs—including a "shrill and startling" Kiowa war song—for the nervous audience. The Hampton choir then sang a number of hymns, accentuating the sounds of racial harmony. Afterward,

Pratt delivered an address. "Is there going to be a war of races here?" he bluntly asked. No, he answered, because the Indians "had come to work." As testimony, the officer invited them to speak at the platform. Matches, a twenty-two year-old Cheyenne brave, announced: "I like here all these girls—good girls!" The gallant words of the freshman brought down the house with laughter.[36]

To conduct the "home-goers" back to Indian Territory, the Indian Office sent General James H. O'Bierne, a Washington correspondent of the *New York Herald*. O'Bierne reached Fortress Monroe on April 14 and proceeded to relieve Pratt from duty. Pratt sent his own family to New York, and prepared to accompany the returning exiles as far as Indianapolis. He extended his best wishes to those who were to remain at Hampton, and they, in turn, put their arms around the officer's neck and wept. Pratt then boarded a steamer with O'Bierne, and the party launched from Old Point. They cruised through Washington to Baltimore, where they transferred to a railroad car for their final passage westward. Pratt parted company with the group in Indiana, and the remaining passengers rode the "Iron Horse" to Wichita, Kansas, where they arrived at 1:00 A.M. on April 18. O'Bierne turned them over to Agent Miles, who receipted him for forty Indians.[37]

Three Indians arrived in Tarrytown for schooling under the watchful eye of Amy Caruthers. She wrote to a colleague in Florida on June 20, informing her about the "effect the change from the old San Marcos life is having upon them." Every morning and afternoon, she would conduct classes in her sitting room, just "as we did at the Fort." She considered Roman Nose "the brightest of the three," calling him "very ambitious and persevering." Tooth Man seemed "a dear good, bright boy, always pleasant and improving every day." Bear Mountain appeared "much more cheerful" but complained often about the

"pain in one lung that used to trouble him when at the Fort."
By January 24, 1879, though, he had recovered sufficiently to
travel to New York and to deliver a speech at a Young Men's
Christian Association meeting. Meanwhile, Roman Nose and
Tooth Man left to enter school at Hampton with their fifteen
counterparts.[38]

Four other Indians made "steady progress" at the Episcopalian "School for the Prophets" in Paris Hill, New York.
Deaconess Mary Douglas Burnham collaborated with Bishop
Frederick Huntington and Reverend John Wicks to deliver a
three-year course of study that prepared them to return to the
agencies as missionaries. She anticipated that their efforts
would contribute to "the conversion and assimilation of the
Plains Indians within a generation." Biter testified about his
desire "to be pure in heart" and to become a "holy man." He
chose a new name, "Paul Caryl." At the same time, Making
Medicine chose "David Pendleton," Shave Head chose "John
Wicks," and Telling Something chose "Henry Pratt." On October 6, 1878, the Bishop baptized them at Grace Church in
Syracuse, and they were confirmed at St. Paul's Church two
weeks later. After a careful and satisfactory examination by two
clergy on June 7, 1881, Making Medicine and Biter were
admitted to the Deaconate, the first order of Episcopalian
ministry.[39]

During their three years at Hampton, seventeen of the
"St. Augustines" were admitted to "the Indian program." The
War Department detailed Captain Henry Romeyn of the Fifth
Infantry for duty as "Instructor in Tactics." Reverend J. J.
Gravatt, the rector of St. John's Church, mentored them.
Booker T. Washington, a graduate of Hampton and famous
black educator, noted their progress: "Praised be all that band
of prisoners, for the transformation begun in your Florida
prison has roused the nation to think that it is its duty to edu-

cate all your brethren." Typically, they remained segregated from blacks in the classrooms, dormitories, and chapel. Each week, they received "book instruction" for four days and labor lessons for two days. Teachers found them earnest, quick, and diligent. They wrote and understood English quite well, but they spoke it with difficulty. They passed examinations in spelling, reading, writing, and geography. They used "the hoe and the spade energetically" and evinced mechanical ingenuity. Bear's Heart became the Indian sergeant, seemingly as careful "as any West-Pointer" to maintain the honor of his stripes. To the satisfaction of General Armstrong, they were baptized and confirmed. They agreed to stop smoking "the Indian weed," that is, tobacco. Most, though not all, adopted Anglicized names.[40]

Each year at Hampton, the Indians participated in the great fanfare of anniversary exercises. In May of 1878, Pratt, President Rutherford B. Hayes, Mrs. Hayes, and several members of his cabinet came down from Washington to attend. Under the direction of General Armstrong, the dignitaries toured the campus and perused the students' projects. President Hayes singled out several of the "big warriors" for praise, while Pratt observed that they "acquitted themselves with great credit." They stood before the dignitaries proudly wearing the school gray uniform. Boy Hunting, who had assumed the alias "Edwin," delivered a captivating speech at commencement. "When the educated young brave returns to his tribe," declared one reporter, "he will, no doubt, be regarded somewhat as a medicine man and will be a person of influence among his people." After finishing school at Hampton, the students intended to bring honor to their brethren back home.[41]

During their first summer at Hampton, Pratt urged the General to place the pupils with "good families to work." Alexander Hyde of Lee, Massachusetts, one of Hampton's trustees, sought homes for "the Florida squad" in Berkshire County. Pratt traveled with Boy Hunting to meet farmers from the locale at a Congregational church. After talking with the Kiowa personally, a number of farmers agreed to board them. Soon, the young men from the Great Plains found themselves in an unfamiliar landscape of rugged mountains and lush woodlands. Wild Horse, who declined to use a non-Indian name, worked as a farmhand in Stockbridge, Massachusetts. He confessed that he feared the townspeople, who appeared to be even more afraid of him. To fraternize with the locals, the Indians met at church on Sundays and shared lunch. They also participated in "the Lee Farmers Club" and attended community picnics, including one in which "William" Limpy won first prize of two dollars as the best runner. Sadly, White Goose died from tuberculosis on October 6, 1879, and was buried at the Hyde family plot. In fact, the colder climate caused several to fall ill in New England.[42]

Although he suffered from bouts of illness, "James" Bear's Heart survived his New England "outings." Assigned to a farmer, he cut corn stalks, dug potatoes, picked apples, and learned to work with a mowing machine. Once, the Cheyenne wrote to a former teacher in Florida: "As I am out of seabeans now and can't get any, I wish you would send me five and tell me how much they cost, and I will send you the money for them." Bear's Heart wanted to collect curios during his stay in Massachusetts, venturing on a "vacation" to Boston. "I saw the governor in the state and went in a house and saw some old flags and some of the books in the State House," he wrote. From the top of the cupola of the State House, he gazed upon the metropolis. He "saw a great many beautiful things," concluding that "Boston is a good city." He met "a great many white people and shook hands with them and spoke with them." He rode "in horse cars" to Norwich, Connecticut, where he sang hymns at a meeting of the American Missionary Association. Next, he went to New York City to a meeting of Episcopal ministers. After singing for them, he checked in to a hotel for the evening. He then returned to Hampton to prepare for his journey home, packing a trunk full of assorted gifts and a chest of carpenter tools for the road ahead.[43]

Meanwhile, Pratt was deployed to aid General Armstrong with the Indians at Hampton for one year. During his tenure, he escorted them on fundraising expeditions to New England and took five students to Washington to meet President Hayes. In the fall of 1878, he successfully recruited forty-nine youths, chiefly Sioux, from the upper Missouri River agencies. "William" Little Chief welcomed the freshmen to school: "Look at me; I will give you the road." Big Nose, who received the name "Nick Pratt," died at school on May 31, 1879, from congestion of the lungs and was interred at the Hampton cemetery. In June, Commissioner Hayt dispatched Pratt to Florida in order to establish relations with the Seminole. Accompanied by "John" Squint Eyes, they held councils with village chieftains. After he returned, General Armstrong took Pratt over to Back Bay and showed him a large farm. He envisioned schooling "up to 250 to 300 young Indians," and asked Pratt to develop "a branch of Hampton Institute." Pratt declined the General's offer, however, and insisted upon returning to his regiment.[44]

Pratt knew that the Commissioner of Education, John Eaton, desired to establish an institution solely for Indians. Secretary of War McCrary, Secretary of Interior Carl Schurz, and Indian Commissioner Hayt decided to submit a proposal to Congress. Senator George H. Pendleton, whose wife had helped save Howling Wolf's vision, introduced a bill to turn the abandoned Carlisle army barracks in Pennsylvania into a campus for Native people. With congressional approval, Gen-

eral of the Army Sherman and Major General Hancock authorized the transfer of the facilities to the new boarding school.
Pratt, assigned to "Indian educational duty," was appointed its
head. The officer, who was visiting Washington at the time,
called the occasion "one of the most eventful days of my life."[45]

On September 8, 1879, Pratt contacted Mather in St.
Augustine about his vision for Carlisle. She agreed to travel
with him to the Dakota Territory "to bring in children" and "to
look after the girls." He dispatched Boy Hunting to the Kiowa
and Comanche agency and Making Medicine to the Cheyenne
and Arapaho agency on recruiting missions. On October 17,
they joined Pratt and Mather at Wichita, Kansas, with twenty-
nine Cheyenne and Arapaho and sixteen Kiowa children for
the boarding school. Afterward, Making Medicine returned to
New York with his wife and child. With a different objective in
mind, Boy Hunting endeavored "to bring back a sweetheart" to
Pennsylvania for courting. Among the rank and file, Pratt was
pleased to find "a number of the children of my Florida prisoners, which proved their confidence in their former jailor."
Although the officer took credit for the recruiting drive, the
support of the former prisoners from Fort Marion helped him
to realize his vision.[46]

Pratt was further gratified when eleven of the former
prisoners came to assist him at Carlisle Barracks. They built a
picket fence seven feet high around the twenty-seven acre
campus to "keep the Indians in and the whites out." They
repaired and remodeled the facilities in time to receive the
first class of pupils. "Walter" Matches and "Charley" High
Forehead provided orientation, translation, and direction for
the new arrivals. The Carlisle Indian School opened on November 1, 1879, and soon would enroll 158 students from
twelve different tribes. Even though Pratt considered Hampton a "stepping stone for Carlisle," he borrowed his "practical

ideas in regard to industrial training" directly from his "experiences in Florida." His boarding school offered an elementary education with vocational courses in agriculture, mechanics, and nursing. Once the school became fully operational, the officer began returning the last of the former prisoners to their reservations. Passing through Carlisle on his way home, Tooth Man died of tuberculosis on April 27, 1880. He was buried at the military cemetery, where numerous children struck by infectious diseases at Carlisle later rested.[47]

Roman Nose, who took the baptized name "Henry Caruthers," studied briefly at Hampton and Carlisle and traveled widely on the East Coast. Wherever he traveled, he spoke fondly of his "old home in Indian Territory." On one visit to New York, he became seasick from a boat ride on the Atlantic Ocean. The Cheyenne preferred hiking the trails of the Hudson Valley. Helen Ludlow, one of his former teachers at Hampton, looked for him at his hotel but found that he had left the building. According to the clerk, Roman Nose had inquired about the "way to New York" and headed to the ferry at Hoboken to reach the city. He toured Jersey City and Brooklyn before reaching Manhattan. While sightseeing with a fellow traveler, he explored the aquarium and the zoo. He rode an elevator to the top of the Equitable Life Insurance Building on Broadway and looked around the "very handsome" city from the skyscraper. Laughing about his restlessness, Ludlow mused that Roman Nose proved "the noble red man can be made a Yankee."[48]

Bear Mountain adopted the baptized name "Paul Caruthers" while residing in New York for three years. On December 5, 1881, he visited St. Augustine to look upon the old Spanish castle once again. After locating Mather, they undertook "a delightful ride all over the town" in her carriage. They enjoyed the afternoon sunshine and the oceanside view as they reminisced about his years of exile. The Kiowa also saw a "good many old friends, and they seemed glad to see me."[49] They passed through the town plaza and arrived at the military stronghold, which Bear Mountain vividly described:

It seemed very strange to see the old Fort! Our house where we slept is gone. No one is there! It is only inhabited by rats, bats and owls, and they have piled up the cannon balls in the square inside. I felt as if I was born in that place. I felt something like Rip Van Winkle, as if I just wake up after a long time, and found things different some ways, but the same in others.[50]

Bear Mountain completed his quest, which had taken him to Fort Marion and back again.

The vision quest constituted an essential rite of passage among Plains Indians, including the war prisoners at Fort Marion. Young warriors would customarily seek guidance from spiritual forces, but they would also search for power with respect to tradition. It traditionally involved isolation, fasting, and dreaming during times of trouble. It would not produce changes in character. Rather, it would summon forth capabilities already present within an individual. It would bring healing, discovery, and growth and reveal how one fits into a grander scheme to life.[51] Many of the exiles, though certainly not all, obtained a new vision in this way. Outside circles known to their ancestors, they added another dimension to their identities by acquiring Anglicized names. Their great adventure took them to unexpected places, where they blazed a trail for others to follow. Indeed, their study abroad allowed them to infiltrate a foreign country and to gather intelligence during their last days of exile. Beyond the facade of the military outpost, they saw an America big enough to accommodate the people of the buffalo-hunting nations.

Chapter 7
Homeward Bound
The Exiles Return

ON APRIL 18, 1878, A PARTY OF FORTY Plains Indians arrived
in Wichita, Kansas. Under an open sky, they basked in the
warm sunshine and felt a familiar wind brush against their
cheeks. Tears of jubilation poured from their eyes. Attired in
U.S. Army uniforms and conversant in English, the former
prisoners of war were welcomed by Agent John Miles from
Darlington and by Wichita's mayor. A crowd gathered for a
reception to celebrate what Miles described as their "thorough reformation" at Fort Marion. Another reunion occurred
four days later at the territorial boundary, where family and
friends greeted the caravan on an overland trail. Between 200
and 300 Cheyenne and Arapaho escorted them into Darlington. They disembarked from the wagons and paraded at the
head of a joyous procession. Meanwhile, the Kiowa and the
Comanche proceeded to Fort Sill for their homecoming day
on April 25. "Our people were all glad to see us," the Kiowa
Wise wrote to Boy Hunting, "and when we told them you were
going to school to learn more, they were glad again."[1]

The chiefs and the warriors were prepared for their repatriation. They had acquired a mastery of English during
their captivity, removing their dependence upon non-Indian
interpreters. They also understood the native tongues of the
Cheyenne, Arapaho, Comanche, and Kiowa. Likewise, they
felt empowered by their new knowledge of economics, geography, arithmetic, science, and religion.[2] However, the reser-

vations provided limited opportunities for employment, no matter what their skills or their determination. Faced with widespread corruption and chronic neglect, the freed men became increasingly ambivalent about the broken promises of government officials. They achieved a great deal with their education, but they succeeded in terms that non-Indians often failed to recognize. They were determined to do much more than simply march upon the "white man's road."

The homecoming proved very difficult for a number of the elders. The Kiowa chief Lone Wolf conferred succession of his title upon his adopted son Mamadayte and gave him the name Lone Wolf the Younger. A few months later, the elder died and was buried at Mount Scott. Reports from the Kiowa and Comanche agency called his death in 1879 "a great blessing." Government agents had discerned "a slight spirit of restlessness and opposition" before Lone Wolf died and had worried that his presence might bring "trouble in the spring." In fact, Woman's Heart did call upon his kinsmen to participate in Native ceremonies and raiding parties.[3] The sun dance of 1879 was labeled on the Kiowa calendar as the "horse-eating dance." No major migration of bison passed through their homeland that year, which forced the Kiowa to sacrifice their ponies to save themselves from starvation. The changes in the land threatened to destroy their traditional way of life.[4]

So long as the Kiowa and Comanche abandoned their traditional ways, the agency at Anadarko offered them support. The younger men, in particular, were praised for dedication to their "Augustine teachings." Agent P. B. Hunt appreciated Toosape, or Bull With Holes in His Ears, calling him "industrious and perfectly reliable." He noted the cooperation of Onkoeht among the Kiowa and Pile of Rocks among the Comanche. However, a quarrel with their boss erupted when the cohort complained that "the pay was too small" for police work. The agent promised Wise the captaincy if he served, but he reneged and awarded it to another man. Nevertheless, most of the returnees eventually signed on for duty. Lieutenant Colonel John W. Davidson at Fort Sill observed that the "St. Augustine Indians can write a few words, sing a hymn or two, but are wanting in a knowledge of the industrial pursuits of life." Since the agency offered them little more than rations, he expected them to "lapse into their former savage ways of life." Despite their detractors, they maintained a strong sense of duty while serving on the Indian police force.[5]

In addition to policing the reservation, the former exiles worked to develop the local economy. The Comanche chief Black Horse, for instance, plowed a field and fenced it. Though he was eager to build a house, the materials failed to arrive. He split several hundred rails, but he could not convey them from the woods before prairie fires destroyed them. Unable to acquire horses, mules, and wagons, he borrowed them from the army at Fort Sill. Even though he refused to allow her to attend Hampton or Carlisle, he sent his daughter, Ahkah, to the agency school in Anadarko.[6] Pile of Rocks, who was forty-eight-years-old, tried to use what he had learned at Fort Marion. However, he confessed: "I am again a Comanche." Living "very poor and disconsolate," he hired himself out to area farmers and chopped wood. He toiled to little avail, stating that "this is a poor country and a bad ground." Briefly, he received a position with the agency police but not adequate pay. Although he tried to follow the instructions of the agent, he soon felt "compelled to go back to the old road."[7] Black Horse and his fellow Comanche found few opportunities to make a decent living.

The Kiowa warrior Wohaw returned to the reservation to find that his wife had passed away during his banishment. He married the widow of the prisoner Wolf Stomach, who had died at Fort Marion. Later, Wohaw took a Mexican captive as an additional wife. He served on the agency police force, earning about five dollars per month in pay. One agency report noted that he "held up quite a long while, and even went to school with the children here, but he could not hold out; he got into a scrape which rather disgraces him; he left school, and now wanders around almost worthless; he wears his uniform, but also a blanket and al-string." Although the reasons for his "disgrace" were undocumented, the agency terminated his service.[8]

The record of the returning Kiowa at the agency was mixed. Good Talk adapted the name "Paul" and arrived at Anadarko on March 2, 1880, after attending Hampton and Carlisle. Despite his schooling, the agent complained, he was "a perfect failure." He remained "unable to forego the cherished allurements of indolent camp life" or to resist "sensuality." He refused to wear pants or a coat, preferring instead to wrap himself in a "sheet much soiled." The agent expressed doubt about their educational achievements and believed that they needed "a paternal, watchful, and sustaining hand" to urge them forward. A different opinion was rendered by "Charley" High Forehead, who returned to the reservation on June 29, 1880, after a year at Carlisle. He joined the agency police force and wrote optimistic letters to his peers at the boarding schools. He reported that his people were "advancing towards civilization rapidly" and "going to meetings every Sunday."[9] Indeed, they appeared predisposed to embrace any movement that might help them to survive the nightmare of the disappearing bison.

The released Cheyenne and Arapaho fared little better. Chief Killer, a Cheyenne, wrote to Lieutenant Pratt in 1879: "We all still love you and your family and have not forgotten you." As soon as the spring generated warmer weather, he wrote, he planned "to make a corn field and raise corn in

earnest" in cooperation with his brethren. He also planned to
send his six children to the agency school at Darlington. "I
have nothing, no horses and no money," he confessed, "but I
am going to work to get some." Adhering to Cheyenne custom,
he measured wealth in terms of horses. He invited Pratt to visit
him, promising "by that time I want to have four horses, and
show you how I can make corn." With the buffalo gone, his
hunger intensified. Because of the dishonesty and fraud surrounding the issuance of agency rations, the Cheyenne who
looked to the government often received adulterated beef[10]

Buffalo Meat, a Cheyenne who eventually would become
a head chief and a deacon in the Baptist church, also corresponded with Pratt.[11] In one letter, he praised the bygone days
at Fort Marion:

*Dear Friend: A long time ago you were my father. You were very
good to me. Since I have been here I have never written to you. Now I
want to send you a letter. I want to tell you that the white man's road
which a long time ago you gave to me, I have not thrown away, but
am still holding to it. The paper you gave me with the verses from the
Bible, I have not lost, nor what the Bible says in those verses. I know
they are good talks. I have tried to give that road to all the Cheyennes. Have worked hard to get them to take hold of it. Have taught it
to my child, and all the English I know I have talked to my son, and
he now understands most of it and will follow it . . . . If you could get
me a suit of white man's clothes, I would like to have them. I have my
soldier's uniform yet, but it is worn badly, and the clothes the agent
gives me do not wear long, and I can get no more till next winter.
When we were in Florida with you, we were not hungry or poor; the
white women and all white people were our friends; but here we are
often hungry and always poor.[12]*

Thus, the Cheyenne struggled to find employment, to raise
crops, and to get ahead.

After leaving Fort Marion, Howling Wolf returned to his wife and his four-year-old child. He declared himself "a great man" and acted arrogantly at the agency. "I threw away my old road and took the road of the Bible," he insisted, "which I believe to be God's road." With relentless fervor, he urged the Cheyenne and the Arapaho to accept "the good Bible road," which he foresaw would bring them happiness and prosperity.[13] Writing to one of the school teachers at Fort Marion, he promised "that I have been trying and am now trying to lead the good life I found away East." He added that "the good road I learned there I have traveled myself and have done my best since I came here to induce all the Cheyennes to take hold of and love." He claimed to have convinced "a large number of young men to go to work in earnest and also to throw away the old way of dressing and put on the white man's clothes." Philanthropists sent non-Indian clothes to his wife, who donned them at her husband's insistence. He placed his daughter in the agency school, because "I want her to know all about books when she grows up." The freed man pledged his service to the agency, working as a teacher, policeman, butcher, farmer, and freighter.[14]

After initially embracing the agency, though, Howling Wolf began to express concerns about the injustices he observed. In 1879, he complained to Pratt: "I am on the white man's road but have got the Cheyenne on my back and am getting behind." He compared the quality of life in Indian Territory with what he saw elsewhere and found it wanting. He grumbled: "We don't get as much for five cents as I did in the states." Even though he had "abandoned the blanket," he longed to follow the herds of buffalo. "I would like to go out on the planes [sic] again," he declared, "where I could rome [sic] at will and not come back again." He presumed that wild horses grazed in Mexico and said that "if I should go there I

could capture a herd and bring them back here, then I would
not be poor." He promised "to not harm any man" on such a
raid but would remain "friendly" to the non-Indians. In addition to the lack of horses, wagons, clothing, shelter, and food,
he complained about the cheating traders at Darlington. With
provisions running low, he slaughtered his last beef cow. Suspicious of the non-Indians at the agency, he called the chiefs to
his lodge to "have a talk and make a road."[15]

No chief expressed greater support for the agency than
Eagle's Head, Howling Wolf's father. Once reunited with his
wives, he lobbied his kin to cut their hair, to adapt new clothes,
to seek work, and to attend school. Despite the lobbying, he
wrote to Pratt, "a great many of my friends and relatives were
still 'Indians.'" In one letter, he confessed: "I often find that
the Cheyennes do not do as they ought to, and I get discouraged." As a personal reminder of the lessons of Fort Marion,
the chief carried a photo of Pratt with him. He applauded the
off-reservation education at Hampton and Carlisle and read
aloud the letters sent to him by the students. He praised "my
old friends at St. Augustine" and desired to "visit them at their
houses." He told his poor neighbors of the abundance beyond
Indian Territory, although he observed that no Indians he
knew lived in such comfort.[16]

Trying to make a living in Indian Territory, Eagle's Head
organized a company of tribesmen. They camped in the woods
and cut down trees, which were chopped or sawed into cord
wood lengths, then split, corded up for measurement, and
finally hauled to delivery points. During his first year at home,
they undertook and filled contracts for the cutting and delivery
of 1,500 cords of wood to Fort Reno and to the agency at Darlington. The next year, his company cut, sawed, split, stacked,
and hauled 2,400 cords of wood at $1.25 for each.[17] Proud of
his accomplishments, Eagle's Head wrote to Pratt in 1880:

"The good road you gave me I have not thrown away." He added that he wore "white man's clothes," which were "getting old and ragged" after all of his laboring. "I pray all the day and I work," which became his mantra. He regularly attended Sunday church services and led the meditations of the congregation. Struck by a grave illness and bedridden for days, he slept with the "Jesus Book" given to him in Florida over his forehead. He died in the spring of 1881.[18]

The last of the Cheyenne exiles came home with little more than the clothes on their backs. "Walter" Matches left Carlisle in September of 1880 to marry Emma, a young scholar at the agency school. The teachers at Darlington, where the wedding took place, prepared an event to which "all the Florida boys were invited." Not all were able to attend: Wild Horse, a Kiowa who returned with the Cheyenne, and "John Wicks" Shave Head, his Cheyenne counterpart, had in the meantime both died of tuberculosis.[19] One of their fellows, "James" Bear's Heart, left Hampton the next spring and obtained work at the agency, mastering carpentry and driving wagons to and from the train station. Exhausted and afflicted by tuberculosis, he succumbed to "consumption" on January 25, 1882. At his funeral, a government agent called him "a good man" with an excellent reputation. Whatever the educational advantages of the former Hampton and Carlisle students, few were able to escape the misfortunes of reservation life.[20]

Little Chief, a Cheyenne who assumed the proper name "William," worked at the reservation as an interpreter and general assistant. The son of the headman Little Chief and nephew of the deceased Heap of Birds, he also served as an army scout and agency policeman. His wife, Standing Twenty, died in 1880, but he married Anna Gentle Horse the next year. Reportedly, he lived "like a white man, dresses like one and in all ways shows he holds fast to what he has learned and is still learning, for he keeps up his studies and correspondence." In 1883, he was selected as an apprentice for an agency physician. The physician promised to help him to advance his studies in medicine. Little Chief learned to keep the dispensatory in good order, producing pills and deciphering remedies such as quinine, castor oil, and cough syrup. In fact, the agent predicted that he would eventually be called "Dr." Little Chief. An honored man among his people, the medicine maker remained close to his companions from Fort Marion.[21]

Another honored Cheyenne was "Henry" Roman Nose, who arrived home on March 15, 1881. "I will teach the Indians what I have learned at school," he once declared. While working at the agency, he met and married a woman named Red Paint. Agent John Miles offered to purchase tools for Roman Nose to practice the tinsmith trade, believing that his success would be more than commensurate with the outlay. Unfortunately, the tinsmith found that his knowledge of the trade was insufficient to warrant his operation of an agency shop. By the fall, he approached the agent about returning to Carlisle to finish his training. Miles convinced a reluctant Pratt to take him back as an apprentice, pointing out that "it is my judgment that such a course would pay big in the end." The next year, Roman Nose finished another term at Carlisle and returned to the agency again on September 18, 1883. He set up a mill room and acquired tools—albeit an incomplete set—for his trade.[22]

Three of the most dedicated "Florida boys" returned to Indian Territory on June 7, 1881. Deacons "David Pendleton" Making Medicine and "Paul Caryl" Biter were joined by "Henry Pratt" Telling Something. They traveled by rail for three days to Caldwell, Kansas, where they were met by Bear's Heart shortly before he died. Accompanied by their friend and teacher, Reverend John B. Wicks, they sought to establish Episcopalian missions. They had returned upon the eve of an annual sun dance, which was marked by hysteria about the messages of a buffalo prophet. Patepte, a son of Woman's Heart, had promised that he would "make medicine" to resurrect the buffalo in 1881, but his ceremonies were opposed by the "younger men among the returned prisoners from the east." Exhibiting diplomatic skill as well as leadership ambition, they addressed their people at the tribal councils in many tongues.[23]

The missionaries spoke earnestly about their plans to lead their people out of bondage, impressing the non-Indians running the agencies. Although they roomed at the agency school house, they fraternized with their brethren in the camps. They conducted Sunday church services, instructed children, read scripture to elders, and visited the sick in their lodges. Although Agent P. B. Hunt called Biter "the brightest of the lot," he complained that he seemed too sympathetic to "the savage superstitions of his people." He claimed that Biter "retrograded perceptibly," but the Kiowa deacon saw things differently. In fact, he wrote to Deaconess Mary Burnham that he endeavored to pray and to preach using "the new medicine." Remaining aloof of the agency, he drew a $150 stipend annually from the Episcopal Church. Telling Something, the missionary to the Comanche, chose a different path. Although he showed "much courage and strength at first," he exhibited "a falling off from the standard," the agent observed. Telling Something left the mission and started a small farm.[24] Even for the dedicated missionaries, the contradictions of reservation life were difficult to resolve.

Making Medicine lived an exemplary life with his special blend of Christian dogma and Cheyenne tradition. His first wife, Nomee, died in 1880, and he married Nahepo, or Susie Anna Bent, in 1882. He began offering Sunday School services

to his people. After receiving a barrel of clothing from Episcopalians in the East, he distributed the gifts among the women
attending services. Among those in regular attendance was his
aged mother, one of his first converts. She regularly walked
three miles each way to attend the crowded services of her son.
At the close of one service in the schoolhouse, the elderly
woman went to Reverend Wicks and said: "When my son
gone, my heart cry; I not sleep; I walk about; I think very hard
all the time. Now he come and my heart sings; I sleep good; I
do not think at all." Like his counterpart, Biter, Making Medicine received a stipend from the church to perpetuate the
missionary work.[25]

Of course, Making Medicine's employment with the mission reduced his dependence on the agency ration system. Un-
tethered from both the agency and the traditional chiefs, the
former dog soldier was free to become a new kind of holy man.
Though once a great artist, he abandoned the pictographic
work entirely in pursuit of converts. In one dramatic event, the
Cheyenne addressed more than fifty men and a host of women
and children at a sun dance.[26] He spoke with great passion:

*You remember when I led you out to war, I always went first and
what I told you was true. Now I have been away to the east and I have
learned about another captain, the Lord Jesus Christ, and he is my
leader. He goes first and all he tells me is true. I come back to my
people to tell them about him, and I want you to go with me now in
this new road, a war that makes all for peace and where we never
have only victory.*[27]

Girding his loins for spiritual combat, Making Medicine summoned the Cheyenne to his side.

After 1884, the Cheyenne deacon's challenges increased.
That year, Reverend Wicks left the reservation to resume his

duties at Paris Hill, New York, leaving "the finest man" he ever knew to continue missionary work on his own. While losing seven of his own children over the years, Making Medicine persevered and kept his faith. He continued to represent the mission by christening babies and conducting funerals in both English and Cheyenne. For instance, in 1889 he preached at the funeral of Robert Bent. Standing at the open grave, he recited John 14:1–3, which promised the survivors that their "Father's house" contained many mansions for the dead. One non-Indian informant at the service praised his timely message, calling him "faithful and competent." Driven by his convictions, the deacon continued to walk "the better way" among his people.[28]

While still at Carlisle in the summer of 1882, "Edwin" Boy Hunting received a letter from the Kiowa, Comanche, and Wichita agency. The letter called him home to assist at the agency school. The Kiowa accepted the call, motivated by "a strong purpose to do some good for my people." On August 7, 1882, he arrived at Anadarko with his wife, Laura, whom he had married at Carlisle in an elaborate ceremony. While assisting the superintendent of the school, he also began farming. He ventured into the camps and attended tribal councils, talking "to greater numbers and relating to them the old, old story of Jesus and his love, and they always listened very attentively." However, he became a target of "witchcraft" after the elders warned him to cease his exhortations.[29] To the Carlisle students he wrote:

I have heard many times that the Indians make fun of those who have been at school in east and returned home. I think the reason the Indians make fun of those returned is because some of them do not try to exercise their influence and the experience they had East at school, or set their example of living right and doing right. I thought the Indians had a great respect toward me, while I was at home. They would come to me to hear the ways of civilization, religion and salvation, and they said that they were wrong to live in such low estate. A great number of Indians are doing excellently in farm pursuits, and are gaining much cattle. The cattle business is increasing very rapidly and the Indians are taking a great interest in that course. A great many Indians are employed to assist the cattle men to herd and earn a large amount of money in cattle and some of them have large herds of cattle . . . . I am glad to say that some of the old Florida prisoners are doing remarkably well, they have built small log-cabins on their farms, and they raise cattle, horses, pigs, chickens, and attend to their own business.[30]

With the former prisoners working at the agency, Boy Hunting expected the Carlisle graduates to prosper in Indian Territory.

In 1882, Pratt sent his seventeen-year-old son to visit the former prisoners living in Indian Territory. From July 8 to July 12, Mason Pratt toured the agencies at Darlington and Anadarko. After a ride across the prairies, he was met by "Howard" Buzzard's parents and "Paul" Bear Mountain's mother. He encountered several "Florida boys," including many who were "dressed in full Indian rig" and residing in "the medicine camp about 5 miles from the agency." At a school house, he met Woman's Heart, whom he could not distinguish from "a regular Indian." The chief, who had turned against the agency, passed away later that year. While traveling along a river, he encountered Pile of Rocks, the Comanche who had conducted grand shows in St. Augustine. "He is as large as ever," noted the younger Pratt, adding that he "would wear white man's clothes if he had them." White Horse, the once-formidable Kiowa sergeant at Fort Marion, "weighs 350 if not more." Onkoeht "dresses like an Indian," he observed, but the Kiowa farmer was "raising corn."[31]

Among the Cheyenne and Arapaho, Mason found many signs of "camp life." He observed that many of the "Florida boys" resided in tents and lamented that "nearly all stay together in a small village of their own." They continued to practice their traditional customs, including communal living and seasonal migration. At the Cheyenne agency, he found Chief Killer, who had obtained work as a butcher for twenty dollars a month. The Cheyenne said that "he was anxious to come to Carlisle now, that he would do anything Papa would give him." The young Pratt also encountered a disorderly Howling Wolf, who appeared to have "forgotten all his English" and "does nothing." On the other hand, he found Matches and his family in good shape. Accompanied by Whit, Agent Miles's son, he watched the beef issuance early one morning. In contrast to the spectacles in St. Augustine, the mock "buffalo hunt" performed at the agency seemed rather unexciting to the youth.[32]

In fact, the agencies offered the Indians little more than a precarious existence. Buffalo Calf, a Cheyenne "warrior woman" to the last, passed away in 1882. Her husband, Medicine Water, joined Antelope, Left Hand, and Rising Bull on the police force and in the freighting business. Little Medicine was elected to the position of police captain and emerged as an active voice in the community. Agent Miles lamented that Soaring Eagle and White Bear, though, "lost ground, and they more from lack of opportunity than perhaps from lack of spirit." Meanwhile, Buffalo Meat, Bear Killer, Chief Killer, Hail Stone, and Star toiled at various jobs. They teamed, herded, carpentered, dug wells, manufactured brick, cut wood, and cultivated corn. By the end of 1883, however, the agency at Darlington had discharged all of them for lack of funds. Left with the sense that "the government has gone back on us," they brooded over what they considered a grave betrayal. Laura

Gibbs, one of the faculty at Fort Marion, ceased to receive letters from them and feared that they had returned to "camp life."[33]

Pratt was disappointed by the negative reports he received from the agencies. He seemed to empathize with the suffering of the Indians, positing that they had received few chances to earn a living on the reservations. On one occasion, he encouraged readers of the *Southern Workman* to send clothing to them. He admitted that "a few have gone back to the blanket condition," but he maintained that "there is abundant testimony" in the reports that "they continue to form a useful and leading industrious element among their people." Nevertheless, he became increasingly critical of the Bureau of Indian Affairs and its policies. He believed that agency schools lacked the capacity to enforce the systematic regimentation of body and mind. In contrast, the Carlisle Indian School represented a "civilization mill." He told one confidante that "to get the best results in our educational work among Indian children, as many as possible should be removed from reservation and tribal influences and placed in an atmosphere of civilized life."[34] He refused to believe that his experiment with adults at Fort Marion had failed, but he increasingly advocated off-reservation education for all Indian children.

While Pratt decried the reservation system, he remained confidant in his most steadfast pupil, Boy Hunting. However, fate was unkind to the Kiowa known as "Edwin." After losing a newborn child, he contracted chills and fever. Fearing for his life in his homeland, he and his wife returned to Carlisle on December 15, 1884, to recover. He at once began to improve and worked with the students and remained a visible figure on the campus. After the birth of another child named Richard Henry in 1886, he returned to Indian Territory in time to plant spring crops on his farm near the agency. As the buffalo prophets in 1887 renewed their ceremonies to resurrect the bison herds, he lamented "that some have been attending the superstitious rites." He watched as those expecting the miraculous return of the buffalo were disappointed, although variations of the "Ghost Dancing" movement continued to resonate among traditionalists. Desiring to build a house and till the soil, the Kiowa prophesied to his tribesmen that he would be the "happiest man in the world" by the next harvest. Joined by his family at his homestead on January 3, 1888, he renewed his teaching at the agency school.[35]

In the spring of 1888, though, Pratt received a devastating letter about his protégé from Reverend J. J. Methvin, a Methodist minister at Anadarko. The Reverend wrote: "Etahdleuh Doanmoe, a former pupil of yours, died at his home here of congestion of bowels." His death occurred suddenly, taking everyone by surprise, though he himself seemed to have expected it. Mysteriously sensing the end of his days, he had given direction as to his burial and for the estate of his family. During the previous afternoon, the Kiowa had appeared at a church meeting where he exhorted the congregation. In his final words, he said: "Lord if it is thy will, I would remain here and continue work among my people, but if it is thy will to take me I am ready to go and I can say thy will be done." A large concourse of both Indians and non-Indians attended his funeral and followed his casket to a high hill across the river from his homestead for burial. "I feel his loss myself beyond measure," lamented the minister, adding that "there is nobody to take his place." The evening after the burial, "the superstitious Indians" destroyed his property by burning everything the deceased had owned. The agent threatened to make the Indians pay for the family's losses but to little avail. His wife and child were left with virtually nothing.[36]

Meanwhile, the Kiowa warlord White Horse became

known as the "very worst character" around the agency. Legendary for his military prowess, he remained unrepentant about the bloody, daring deeds of his past. Bitterly, Pratt himself decided in later years that the educational experiment in Florida would have been strengthened if White Horse and his ilk had "met a fate more in keeping with their crimes." Reservation life left him "the same big lazy Indian that he was in Augustine," according to one observer. After many years of repose at his lodge, he added several layers of fat to his waistline. Suffering from "some old war injury" in his abdomen, he summoned the Kiowa healer Taybodal, who performed emergency surgery. Plunging a sharp, narrow-pointed knife into a bundle of swelling flesh, the healer made an incision. He squeezed the afflicted area, which caused pus to drain through his fingers. Then he dressed the wound that had caused White Horse great pain. The patient eventually died of a stomach ailment in 1892, leaving as his only heirs the family of an adopted Navajo son.[37]

The death of Eagle's Head seemingly triggered his son's turn against the Cheyenne and Arapaho agency, which posted Howling Wolf as a frequent malefactor. Agent Miles, who retired from agency service in 1884, complained that he appeared "as uncivilized, but not as hostile, as he ever was." The Cheyenne married and divorced several times, seemingly exhibiting restlessness about domestic life. He became a leader of the dog soldiers and a participant in traditional military societies. His eyesight continued to decline, though, and he was eventually deemed "one-eyed." In 1893, he was arrested and indicted for an assault on a fourteen-year-old "white girl" near Watonga in Indian Territory. While in jail, the Cheyenne confessed his crime but stated defiantly: "The white men did that way with the squaws." Narrowly escaping a lynching party while awaiting trial, he broke free from jail. A sheriff pursued him to an Indian camp until a band of 200 warriors rebuffed the posse. The lawmen, loathe to provoke more spirited resistance, dropped the matter. Howling Wolf remained a fugitive for another seven years until the charges were finally dismissed.[38]

Although Pratt expressed great disappointment with the Cheyenne fugitive, the superintendent of Carlisle defended his austere institution in Pennsylvania. For almost a quarter century, Pratt and his cadre of teachers tried to spread "civilization" by boarding Native students off the reservations. An exuberant graduate even hailed him as "one of the greatest medicine men living." Federal appropriations for boarding schools soared to millions of dollars, though legislators complained about squandering money on Indians who "returned to the blanket." While day schools and parochial schools in Indian Territory multiplied, institutions patterned after Carlisle proliferated as well. By 1903, the enrollment at Carlisle reached more than 1,200. During Pratt's twenty-four-year tenure, it educated 4,903 Indian boys and girls from seventy-seven tribes. However, Pratt openly rebuked the authority of the Commissioner of Indian Affairs and called for the "complete destruction of the Bureau." He decried the "scant and lax methods of progress the Indian system provides." Pratt, though appointed Brigadier General on January 24, 1903, was retired from active service by President Theodore Roosevelt the following year.[39]

Even in retirement, though, the champion of boarding schools refused to fade away. Pratt addressed numerous audiences about his odyssey since he first led the Plains Indians to imprisonment. Whenever he spoke or wrote about off-reservation education, the officer often began with a word about the war prisoners. They were among the thousands of educated Indians employed in schools and agencies—or so he said. They stood among the heads of boarding schools, assistant superintendents, teachers, disciplinarians, farm and mechanical instructors, clerks, and translators. "No influence contributed as much to the inception and accomplishment of these results as the Indian prisoners," he declared. Their ranks grew "to an army of thousands of young Indians, hurrying on to good American citizenship ability under the practical training of the qualified schools and their experiences among citizens." Francis Leupp, Commissioner of Indian Affairs, alleged that "little can be done to change the Indian who has already passed middle life," but Pratt dismissed his statement as "twaddle." He argued that even mature thinkers could be "completely changed in their habits of thought and action" by discipline and punishment. Unlike most of his contemporaries, Pratt insisted that Indian education "civilized" the young as well as the old.[40]

Pratt clung to the notion that Plains Indians would complete their journey to full equality with the abolition of tribal governments and the allotment of reservation lands the Plains Indians. In 1907, he planned a trip to see "my old Florida boys" and retired government agent John Miles, who had by then relocated to Kingfisher, Oklahoma. With the entry of the new state into the union that year, Pratt considered moving there "with a view of trying to get into Congress, where I could have possibly done some effective work for our old charges." However, he decided to continue his crusade against the mismanagement of Indian affairs in Washington. Privately, he even contemplated an appointment to the Bureau. In 1910, he still pointed to his record of success with "the hardened old Indian prisoners," saying that "three years can be made to settle our Indian problem."[41]

Among the former prisoners of war, Pratt admired the constancy shown by Bear Mountain. Following his homecoming on July 31, 1882, the Kiowa labored for decades as a school employee, wood cutter, army scout, and dirt farmer. He married and divorced several times, fathering three children who survived and fourteen who did not. He became a missionary assistant for Reverend Methvin and an informant for anthropologist James Mooney. Like many of his kinsmen, he belonged to the peyote cult. He became a skillful orator, evincing a sense of sarcasm and irony even in his English rhetoric. Once, the Kiowa observed that "the people all over this country choose one man for President." He asked: "Why can't he do what he knows is good and right, if he is the greatest man in our country?" Promising to make "this fighting stop," he eschewed violence and advocated a pan-Indian form of pacifism. On April 7, 1910, he passed away at the age of fifty-eight and was buried in a cemetery south of Anadarko.[42]

Biter, the once-promising Episcopal deacon, abandoned his mission to the Kiowa when Reverend Wicks departed. In 1894, he formally put into writing his renunciation of the ministry. Two years later, he was baptized again and assisted with the founding of a Baptist mission. He married multiple wives and raised a son. For most of his remaining years, he was considered a "medicine man" and openly practiced the peyote cult. As an officer in the Kiowa Gourd Clan, he blew a bugle—a talent he had acquired at Fort Marion—for tribal ceremonies. At the request of the Smithsonian, he fashioned and painted model tipis for the Omaha Exposition of 1898. He subsequently suffered a decline in health, which was probably exacerbated by lapses into alcoholism. He died in Caddo County, Oklahoma, on April 27, 1913.[43]

Over time, Roman Nose lost interest in his tinsmith trade. After his first wife died, he married again in 1887 and fathered two children. He became an army scout, a policeman, and a delegate to Washington, D.C. In 1890, he began wearing a

"Messiah hat" of gray felt to identify with the pan-Indian Ghost Dance religion, which had spread among the Cheyenne and Arapaho. One government agent referred to him as a "non-progressive" Indian. In 1897, a Cheyenne graduate of Carlisle told Pratt that Roman Nose was emerging as one of the voices critical of federal government policies. In 1899, he officially became chief of the Southern Cheyenne and kept the title for almost two decades. A savvy businessman, he helped to organize the Roman Nose Gypsum Company in 1903. On June 13, 1917, he died during a peyote meeting on the allot-ment of "William" Cohoe, who had been called "Limpy" at Fort Marion. Roman Nose was interred at Baptist Indian Mis-sion near Watonga, Oklahoma, where a state park was later established in his honor.[44]

One by one, other "Florida boys" also passed away. Buf-falo Meat, who had briefly served as head chief of the Southern Cheyenne, died of tuberculosis on October 2, 1917 and was buried at the Indian mission in Kingfisher, Oklahoma. Chief Killer, who had sat for a romantic oil-on-canvas portrait by artist Elbridge Ayer Burbank, passed away on July 24, 1922. He was interred in the cemetery at Concho, Oklahoma. Little Chief joined the traditionalist War Dancers society, a frater-nity that evolved from the performances that had amazed the tourists at St. Augustine, while Cohoe became headman of the War Dancers society and a prominent peyotist. Little Chief perished on December 24, 1923, at Clinton, Oklahoma, and Cohoe followed on March 18, 1924, at his allotment near Bick-ford, Oklahoma. The leader of the Bowstring society, Medi-cine Water, died the same year. According to his associates, the scars caused by the chains that had been placed around his ankles by Pratt never disappeared.[45]

As the years passed, Pratt lost track of the Indians once held at Fort Marion. After 1909, he began to sort through his collected photographs, scrapbooks, and stereocards from St. Augustine to prepare an account of his life. He asked for assistance from a Bureau employee at Darlington in identifying their names, confessing that his failing memory left him uncertain of what had become of them. He watched as the Bureau closed Carlisle in 1918 and as Hampton abandoned its Indian program by 1923. He dictated the last chapters of his memoirs as he struggled with fifty years of disparate notes and fading recollections. On April 24, 1924, he gave his last breath at an army hospital in San Francisco, California. He was buried in Arlington National Cemetery, where a granite monument marks his gravesite with the words: "Erected in Loving Memory by his Students and Other Indians." His biographer dubbed him "the Red Man's Moses," who had delivered Native people out of captivity.[46]

One of those Natives led into captivity, Wohaw, subsequently lived a long and fascinating life. He joined the Ohomah society, a Kiowa dancing organization that performed a routine popularized at Fort Marion. Known for a unique repertoire incorporating a captured army saber, Wohaw espoused the Ghost Dance religion even after it faded in popularity. When Troop L of the Seventh U.S. Cavalry was organized, he enlisted and served from 1891 to 1895. Obtaining an allotment of land under the Jerome Agreement in 1900, he leased his 160 acres to local farmers. With a steady income stream in retirement, he built a two-room house. After receiving an injury in a mock Indian battle conducted at Fort Sill in 1917, he again proclaimed, "I'm a warrior!" A member of the Native American Church in Oklahoma, the ailing Kiowa died on October 29, 1924.[47]

Blind in his left eye, the Cheyenne Howling Wolf lived for many years in exile among the Kiowa in Oklahoma. After the turn of the century, he reappeared at his allotment near Kingfisher. He attended a Baptist camp meeting in 1911 and talked of his weariness with what he called the "crooked road." After his last wife died, he lived at Cantonment, known as a stronghold of the traditionalists among the Southern Cheyenne. Late in his life, he traveled great distances to dance for a small salary. He made a long trip to a "wild west show" in the municipal park of Houston, Texas. On the return trip, his automobile was struck by an unknown vehicle about seventeen miles from Waurika, Oklahoma. As a result of the hit-and-run accident, Howling Wolf expired in a hospital on July 5, 1927.[48]

Making Medicine, who preferred to go by the name David Pendleton, continued to serve as a deacon for the Episcopal Church. The Cheyenne proselytized for thirty-eight years despite a lack of support from his distant church officials. His wife, Susie Bent, passed away in 1890 and his older brother, Little Medicine, renounced the "progressives" before his sudden death in 1893 during a measles epidemic. Among the seven new converts made by the deacon in 1894 stood White Buffalo Woman, also known as Minnie, whom he married the next year. Their son, Frank Pendleton, was born in 1905. Beginning in 1904, he worked at an Episcopal day school at Fay. In 1917, the church abandoned its ministry to the Southern Cheyenne altogether and formally retired his services. He moved to Watonga, Oklahoma, where he continued to preach in his home and at other locations until his death on August 31, 1931. Years later, Episcopalians officially declared the Cheyenne deacon a "saint" and dedicated a memorial window to him at Grace Church in Syracuse, New York.[49]

Squint Eyes, who became better known as John Tichkematse, saw more of the country than any other ex-prisoner. After attending Hampton and traveling with Pratt to meet the Seminole, he worked for the Smithsonian Institution as a taxidermist. In that capacity, he journeyed with anthropologist

Frank Hamilton Cushing to study the Native people of New Mexico and Arizona. On the trip, he danced with the Navajo and clashed with the Apache. Despite his frequent travels, he served in cavalry and police forces. After resettling in Montana, he acquired a ranch and became a successful cattleman. He married a woman named Nellie in 1891 and, after her death in 1924, married Josie Whistling Elk in 1929 and adopted a child, Besie Americanhorse. He also accepted baptism by a Mennonite congregation. He died on November 7, 1932, at Lame Deer, Montana.[50]

The first student to enroll at Carlisle, High Forehead, lived longer than any other Fort Marion inmate. Often conflated in official records with his twin brother, White Buffalo, the Kiowa was commonly recognized by the name "Charley Buffalo." For many years, he resided in a room at the agency school, recruited children for the classes, and became a fine teacher. The agent reported that he possessed "a well-balanced mind" and praised his good character. An officer for the Indian police, he found that the position earned him the respect of non-Indians as well as his kinsmen. The position afforded him high status, signified by the uniform, the weapons, and the horses. He acquired a plurality of wives, which unfortunately resulted in his discharge from the police force. At his four-room home west of Anadarko, he designed tipi coverings and models for public exhibition. He remained a warrior artist on the vanguard of creative expression, whether donning buckskin and headdress or uniform and cap. His life ended on May 13, 1934, and his body rested at Red Stone Baptist Cemetery. He was the last of the prisoners of war to die.[51]

Even if a number of the former prisoners vanished into obscurity, the repatriated exiles honored their friends and families with their lives. They joined police forces, formed scout companies, organized ceremonial dances, founded Christian missions, created local businesses, taught at agency schools, planted rows of corn, raised herds of livestock, headed tribal councils, preserved traditional societies, and promoted Indian fellowship. More than anything else, they attempted to find an alternative to cultural extinction. Prior to their banishment, none had ventured outside their homelands or had associated with their enemies. Afterward, they moved courageously along their own distinct yet parallel paths toward self-determination. They opened a road for others to follow by reaching across the lines of division to mediate with non-Indians. They turned to one another for strength. They remained linked by bonds that crossed the boundaries of tribal and religious differences. Their descendants in later years continued their long walk, never forgetting the prisoners of war who came home from Fort Marion.

Epilogue

THE CHIEFS AND WARRIORS OF THE buffalo-hunting nations survived many dark days. The resistance leaders suffered great losses in the Buffalo War but lived to fight their battles on a shore far away. Once incarcerated at Fort Marion, the prisoners of war rose to the challenge of their exile. Their meeting ground off the reservation facilitated a spirit of collaboration. Their flexible responses to a coercive regime demonstrated the strengths and the capabilities of Plains Indians. They met and exceeded the rigorous standards of the military authorities. They forged cultural bridges and crossed great divides. They emerged from the old Spanish castle prepared to guide and to serve their people. As they looked to the horizon, they envisioned a way out of captivity. However, they returned to the reservations with little or no assistance from officials in Washington. Federal Indian policy never embraced the power of adult learning, concentrating instead upon erecting institutions to board their children. At the dawn of America's Gilded Age, policymakers missed an opportunity to build something creative rather than destructive.

During the late nineteenth century, policymakers built powerful institutions to fulfill their "final promise" to assimilate Native people. Of course, their assumptions resonated with widespread prejudice toward the offspring of immigrants, blacks, Hispanics, and other minorities. They often described non-English speakers as barbaric, ignorant, and backward.

The "Great Father" in Washington propagated the ideology of "manifest destiny" and inspired the national expansion of the boarding school system. The children of "primitive" cultures were selected for immersion in "Anglo Saxon civilization," a kind of baptism into the mainstream of an industrial society. The "lower sort" required cultural uplift through elementary education. The classroom instruction elevated the hearts and the minds of the most unfortunate ones, or so the Bureau of Indian Affairs presumed. Nevertheless, confining children to institutions was a tragic solution to the "Indian problem."[1]

The confinement of another group of American Indians turned Fort Marion into a monument of tragedy. Between 1886 to 1887, over five hundred Apache were imprisoned there. Although the legendary warrior Geronimo was not among them, one of his wives and more than four hundred women and children suffered inside the stronghold. At least twenty-four Apache died and were buried in the sands of North Beach. Sarah A. Mather, who had taught the adults from the Great Plains at the same location, provided instruction to the Apache children. In fact, the Sisters of St. Joseph established a primary school for them. After thirteen months in captivity, most left Fort Marion on a train bound for other military outposts. Their offspring headed to Carlisle Indian School, making their stay in St. Augustine a sorrowful point of departure.[2]

After being turned over to the National Parks Service in 1933, the Castillo de San Marcos became a historic landmark. While stationed in St. Augustine during World War II, James Auchiah, a Kiowa Apache who served in the U.S. Coast Guard, attempted to recover "a lot of unwritten history" for the park museum. He studied the unusual markings on the coquina walls and sought clues about the war prisoners who had once lived inside the fortress. He found a black-and-white photograph featuring the Kiowa, Comanche, Cheyenne, and Arapaho and requested information about their identities from tribal elders. In 1943, Auchiah contacted John P. Aunko, a Kiowa residing in Saddle Mountain, Oklahoma. In his return correspondence, Aunko noted that "they were all men of sciences." He listed them as farmers, ranchers, ministers, interpreters, and policemen. He opined that they "learned many good things" during their years away from the reservation. The prison school at old Fort Marion had given them an opportunity—albeit a limited one—to learn.[3]

Meanwhile, Mason D. Pratt began to assemble materials for a book about his deceased father, the prison school's supervisor. In the process, he contacted the Missouri Historical Society in search of newspaper articles about the transportation of the Plains Indians to Florida. The librarian replied that she had found no information about them in the local media. She questioned his recollection of their overland journey, although she confessed that "it might be more reliable" than the sources she had consulted. Pratt wrote to Julien Yonge, the editor of the *Florida Historical Quarterly*, concerning the prisoners' experiences in captivity during the 1870s. "I do not recall any Indian prisoners in St. Augustine at that time," the editor responded, "but of course there may have been some." Eventually, Richard Henry Pratt's memoirs were published by Yale University Press under the title of *Battlefield and Classroom* in 1964. Thanks to the editorial work of Robert M. Utley, the incarceration of the war prisoners became a familiar subject to historians of Native America.[4]

In 1984, Kiowa leaders commissioned a mural project commemorating the artistic tradition "reborn" during their incarceration. Comprising ten six-by-eight canvasses, the colorful murals distinguished the Kiowa Tribal Museum and Complex at Carnegie, Oklahoma. Sherman Chaddlesone, a Kiowa artist who participated in the project, reproduced a drawing by the war prisoner Wohaw. He called the particular acrylic rendering "Transition," in which light tones of gray accentuated the ambivalence of conquest. Along with the traditional dances, peyote ceremonies, and Native American churches, Wohaw's self-portrait captured "what it was, and is, to be Kiowa." In a sense, his art illustrated the emergence of a people and a nation. It reminded each generation about the Kiowa saying: "Behold, I stand in good relation to all things."[5]

About a dozen descendants of the war prisoners stood inside the Castillo de San Marcos for a ceremony in 1993. K. D. Edwards, dressed in the full regalia of his Comanche forefathers, gazed at the exhibited photographs of the warriors and the chiefs. Accompanied by a small crowd, he walked the park grounds and offered a few words about the place. "Coming here is like a Jewish person going to Treblinka or Auschwitz," he mused with deep emotion. As he led them from casemate to casemate, he wielded a ceremonial feather to cast smoke from a burning pot. It was a symbolic act of purification for the facility. They dispatched the Indian dead into another world. Those who could still hear the voices of their ancestors made medicine, promising to never forget their story.[6]

Even if the coquina walls of the fortress remain silent, the Plains Indians who once dwelled there can be understood. In the shadows of the facade, the prisoners of war enhanced their powers in ways they found enriching and meaningful. Their exile enlarged a sense of "Indianness" among the rank and file at the same time the institution confined their bodies. Indeed, their cultural ideals became transcendent to a great extent. Provisioned with uniforms, books, and pencils, they made history at Fort Marion. Drawing upon a collaborative spirit, they grasped a bigger picture than the narrow one painted for them by military authorities. They listened and learned, marched and danced, and adapted and overcame. The bold and clever fighters emerged from incarceration prepared to count coups once again. They defied the odds against them and lived honorably in America's Gilded Age. Their destiny was not to stop the Indian war that never ends but to survive it.

List of Indian Prisoners

Cheyenne (33)

1. Heap of Birds: Mo-e-yau-hay-ist. Also known as Many Magpies.
2. Bear Shield: Nock-o-yo-uh.
3. Eagle's Head: Minimic.
4. Medicine Water: Mi-huh-heu-i-mup.
5. Long Back: Cha-se-yun-nuh.
6. Hail Stone: Ow-us-sait, or Ah-sit. Also known as White Man and Hail.
7. Rising Bull: O-to-as-tuh-hos.
8. Limpy: Co-hoe, or Mo-he. Also known as Broken Leg, Moose, Elk, Nohnicas, and William.
9. Bear's Heart: Nock-ko-ist. Also known as James.
10. Star: Ho-i-toich.
11. Howling Wolf: Ho-na-nist-to.
12. Making Medicine: O-kuh-ha-tuh, Oakahaton, or Oakerhater. Also known as Sun Dancer, Bear Going Straight, Noksowist, and David Pendleton.
13. Antelope: Wuh-ah.
14. Wolf's Marrow: Come-uh-see-vah.
15. Little Medicine: Ma-ha-ih-ha-chit.
16. Shave Head: O-uk-ste-uh. Also known as John Wicks.
17. Roman Nose: Wo-uh-hun-nih. Also known as Henry Caruthers.
18. Big Nose: Pa-e-yis. Also known as Nick Pratt.

19. Squint Eyes: Ouch-ke-i-mus, or Tichkematse. Also known as John.

20. Little Chief: Ko-we-o-narre. Also known as William.

21. Matches: Chis-i-se-duh, or Wan-hi-yurs. Also known as Walter.

22. Buffalo Meat: O-e-wo-toh.

23. Buzzard: Mo-he-wih-kio. Also known as Black Lodge, Moqtaruhiyumeni, and Howard Charlton.

24. Soaring Eagle: O-uh-oh.

25. Bear Killer: No-co-mis-ta.

26. Left Hand: No-mohst, or Newat.

27. Chief Killer: Noh-hu-nah-wih.

28. Buffalo Calf: Mo-chi. Also known as Warrior Woman. The wife of Medicine Water.

29. Gray Beard.

30. Big Moccasin.

31. Lean Bear: Ouachita.

32. Standing Wolf. Also known as Starving Wolf and Shaving Wolf.

33. Spotted Elk.

Arapaho (2)

34. Packer: Nun-ne-ti-yuh. Also known as Backer and Backei.

35. White Bear: Huh-noh-uh-co-aj. Also known as Albino Bear.

Caddo (1)

36. Hu-wah-nee.

Kiowa (27)

37. Woman's Heart: Mányi-ten.

38. White Horse: Tsa-tah, Isa-tah, or Tsen-t-ainte.

39. Wohaw: Wo-ha-te. Also known as Beef, Pah-a-ko-eh, Gu-háu-de, and Wolf Robe.

40. Bad Eye: Ta-na-ti, or The-ne-tai-de. Also known as Eagle Chief, Bird Chief, Bird Medicine, or Bad Eye.

41. Double Vision: Yi-saum, So-gau-se, or To-zance.

42. Bear in the Clouds: Saet-mi, or Sa-a-mi-a-da.

43. Lone Wolf: Cui-fa-gaui, Gui-pah-ko, or E-si-sim-ers.

44. Biter: Zo-tom. Also known as Podal-adalte, Snake Head, and Paul Caryl.

45. Ankle: Un-koi-a-dee, On-ko-eht, or Aun-caui-de. Also known as Aun-kawy-day and Aun-cauit.

46. High Forehead: Ohet-toint, or Aut-thaui. Also known as Bare Head, Twin, and Charley Buffalo.

47. Boy Hunting: E-tah-dle-uh, Et-ta-lyi-don-maui, or Atala. Also known as Edwin Dunmoe.

48. Toothless: Zo-pe-he, or Zo-pa-he.

49. White Goose: Tsah-dle-tah, or Chal-thai. Also known as Swan.

50. Tooth Man: Zone-ke-uh, or Zo-qi. Also known as Ki-sau-he, Zokia, Kinasahekia, and the Green Shield Man.

51. Old Man: Beah-ko, Be-ah-ko, or Bi-ko. Also known as Red Thunder.

52. Good Talk: Taung-ke-i-hi, To-un-ke-uh, To-keah-hi, To-un-keah, or To-keah. Also known as Waterman and Paul Tounkeuh.

53. Wild Horse: Ko-ba, Gobe, or Coby.

54. Flat Nose: Mau-ko-pedal.

55. Wise: Au-lih.

56. Kicking: Ko-ho, or Goho. Also known as Club Foot.

57. Bull with Holes in his Ears: To-o-sape. Also known as Pau-tau-sape and Paddy.

58. Bear Mountain: Tsait-kope-ta, Set-k'opte, or Sait-kopeta. Also known as Paul Caruthers.

59. Pedro: Palo.

60. Straightening an Arrow: Ih-pa-yah, or E-pea.

61. Wolf Stomach: Co-a-bote-ta, or Cuibotje. Also known as Pi-a-ti-ty and Sun Chief.

62. Coming to the Grove: Ah-ke-ah, or Pah-oh-ka.

63. Sky Walker: Ma-mante. Also known as Do-hat-ti, Owl Prophet, and Swan.

Comanche (9)

64. Buck: Eck-e-nah-ats, or Ek-a-wah-ats. Also known as Red Antelope.

65. Dry Wood: Wy-a-ko.

66. Black Horse: Po-ka-do-ah.

67. Giving His Sister to Another Man: Mad-a-with-t, or Nad-a-with-t.

68. Telling Something: Ta-a-way-te. Also known as Buffalo Scout and Henry Pratt.

69. Tail Feathers: Pe-eh-chip. Also known as Little Feather.

70. Always Sitting Down in a Bad Place: Tis-cha-kah-da.

71. Pile of Rocks: Quoi-yo-uh.

72. Little Prairie Hill: Pa-voor-ite, or Looking Glass.

Nonprisoners (3)

73. Pe-ah-in. A wife of Black Horse and mother of Ahkah.

74. Ahkah. A female child of Black Horse and Pe-ah-in.

75. Dick. A black captive of Lone Wolf.

Notes

Prologue

1. Benjamin Kracht, "Kiowa Religion in Historical Perspective," *American Indian Quarterly* 21 (Winter 1997): 15–34; Maurice Boyd, ed., *Kiowa Voices*, Volume 2 (Fort Worth: Texas Christian University Press, 1981), 14–21, 47–59; Wilbur S. Nye, ed., *Bad Medicine and Good: Tales of the Kiowas* (Norman: University of Oklahoma Press, 1962); see also Mildred Mayhall, *The Kiowas* (Norman: University of Oklahoma Press, 1962).

2. Clyde Ellis, "We Don't Want Your Rations, We Want this Dance: The Changing Use of Song and Dance on the Southern Plains," *Western Historical Quarterly* 30 (Summer 1999): 133–154; Henrietta Mann, *Cheyenne-Arapaho Education, 1871–1982* (Boulder: University Press of Colorado, 1997), 1–17; John Moore, *The Cheyenne Nation: A Social and Demographic History* (Lincoln: University of Nebraska Press, 1987); see also Clyde Ellis, *A Dancing People: Powwow Culture on the Southern Plains* (Lawrence: University Press of Kansas, 2003).

3. Gerald McMaster and Clifford E. Trafzer, eds., *Native Universe: Voices of Indian America* (Washington, D.C.: National Museum of the American Indian, 2004), 24–28; see also Joel W. Martin, *The Land Looks After Us: A History of Native American Religion* (New York: Oxford University Press, 1999).

4. Richard Drinnon, *Facing West: The Metaphysics of Indian Hating and Empire Building* (Minneapolis: University of Minnesota Press, 1980); Clifford Trafzer, *As Long as the Grass Shall Grow and Rivers Flow: A History of Native Americans* (New York: Harcourt, 2000); Philip J. Deloria and Neal Salisbury, eds., *A Companion to American Indian History* (Malden, Mass.: Blackwell, 2002); R. David Edmunds, "Native Americans, New Voices: American Indian History, 1895–1995,"

American Historical Review 100 (June 1995): 717–740; Frederick E. Hoxie, "Thinking Like an Indian: Exploring American Indian Views of American History," *Reviews in American History* 29 (March 2001): 1–14.

5. D'Arcy McNickle, *They Came Here First: The Epic of the American Indian* (New York: Harper & Row, 1949; reprint, New York: Octagon Books, 1975).

6. Evelyn C. Adams, *American Indian Education* (New York: King's Crown Press, 1946), 34–37; see also Francis Paul Prucha, *The Great Father: The United States Government and the American Indians*, 2 vols. (Lincoln: University of Nebraska Press, 1984).

7. James L. Haley, *The Buffalo War: The History of the Red River Uprising of 1874* (Garden City, N.Y.: Doubleday, 1976; reprint, Austin: State House Press, 1998); Karen Daniels Petersen, *Plains Indian Art from Fort Marion* (Norman: University of Oklahoma Press, 1971); David Wallace Adams, *Education for Extinction: American Indians and the Boarding School Experience, 1875–1928* (Lawrence: University Press of Kansas, 1995); see also Arrell Morgan Gibson, "St. Augustine Prisoners," *Red River Valley Historical Review* 3 (1978): 259–270; Pam Oestricher, "On the White Man's Road? Acculturation and the Fort Marion Southern Plains Prisoners" (Ph.D. dissertation, Michigan State University, 1981).

8. Richard Henry Pratt, "To the Friends of Indian Education," *Eadle Keatah Toh* 1 (June 1881): 2; Richard H. Pratt, *Battlefield and Classroom: Four Decades with the American Indian, 1867–1904*, edited by Robert Utley (New Haven, Conn.: Yale University Press, 1964); see also Frederick J. Stefon, "Richard Henry Pratt and His Indians," *Journal of Ethnic Studies* 15 (Summer 1987): 86–112.

9. Richard Pratt to Rutherford B. Hayes, 9 March 1880, Box 10, Folder 341, Richard Henry Pratt Papers, Beinecke Library; For the typical attitudes of military officers toward Indians in the trans-Mississippi West, see Sherry Smith, *The View from Officers' Row: Army Perceptions of Western Indians* (Tucson: University of Arizona Press, 1990).

10. Richard Henry Pratt, "Address by Captain Pratt before the National Convention of Charities and Correction," (Denver, Colo., 28 June 1892).

11. Robert F. Berkhofer, *The White Man's Indian: Images of the*

American Indian from Columbus to the Present (New York: Alfred A. Knopf, 1978).

12. Michel Foucault, *Discipline and Punish: The Birth of the Prison*, trans. Alan Sheridan. (New York: Vintage, 1979).

Chapter 1

1. My account of the military campaign from 1874 to 1875 derives primarily from James Haley, *The Buffalo War: The History of the Red River Uprising of 1874* (Garden City, N.Y.: Doubleday, 1976; reprint, Austin: State House Press, 1998).

2. N. Scott Momaday, *Way to Rainy Mountain* (Albuquerque: University of New Mexico Press, 1969), 10. For a fine study of indigenous strategies for survival, see Gregory Evans Dowd, *A Spirited Resistance: The North American Indian Struggle for Unity, 1745–1815* (Baltimore: Johns Hopkins University Press, 1993).

3. Paul H. Carlson, *The Plains Indians* (College Station: Texas A&M University Press, 1998), 1–66; Henrietta Mann, *Cheyenne-Arapaho Education, 1871–1982* (Boulder: University Press of Colorado, 1997), 1–17; Donald Berthrong, *The Southern Cheyennes* (Norman: University of Oklahoma Press, 1963); John Moore, *The Cheyenne Nation: A Social and Demographic History* (Lincoln: University of Nebraska Press, 1987).

4. Bear's Heart, "Indian Talk," *Southern Workman* 9 (July 1880): 77; see also Burton Supree, ed., *Bear's Heart: Scenes from the Life of a Cheyenne Artist of One Hundred Years Ago with Pictures by Himself* (Philadelphia: J. B. Lippincott, 1977).

5. Roman Nose, "An Indian Boy's Camp Life," *School News* 1 (June 1880): 1; Karen Daniels Petersen, "The Writings of Henry Roman Nose," *Chronicles of Oklahoma* 42 (Winter 1964–65): 458–478; Ellsworth Collings, "Roman Nose: Chief of the Southern Cheyenne," *Chronicles of Oklahoma* 42 (Winter 1964–65): 429–457.

6. Carlson, *The Plains Indians*, 135–162; Duane Gage, "Black Kettle: A Noble Savage?" *Chronicles of Oklahoma* 45 (1967): 244–251; see also Elliott West, *The Contested Plains: Indians, Goldseekers, and the Rush to Colorado* (Lawrence: University Press of Kansas, 1998).

7. Dee Brown, *Bury My Heart at Wounded Knee* (New York:

Holt, Rinehart and Winston, 1970), 10, 67–99, 144–169; Karen Daniels Petersen, "Cheyenne Soldier Societies," *Plains Anthropologist* 9 (August 1964): 146–172; see also Jean Afton, et. al. eds., *Cheyenne Dog Soldiers: A Ledgerbook History of Coups and Combats* (Boulder: University Press of Colorado, 1997).

    8. Alvin O. Turner, "Journey to Sainthood: David Pendleton Oakerhater's Better Way," *Chronicles of Oklahoma* 70 (Summer 1992): 116–143; Karen Daniels Petersen, ed., *Plains Indian Art from Fort Marion* (Norman: University of Oklahoma Press, 1971), 225–226; Herman Viola, ed., *Warrior Artists: Historic Cheyenne and Kiowa Ledger Art Drawn by Making Medicine and Zotom* (Washington, D.C.: National Geographic Society, 1998), 18–51; see also Richard Aquila, "Plains Indian War Medicine," *Journal of the West* 13 (April 1974): 19–43.

    9. Brown, *Bury My Heart*, 67–99, 144–169; Stan Hoig, *The Sand Creek Massacre* (Norman: University of Oklahoma Press, 1977); Jerome A. Greene, *Washita: The U.S. Army and the Southern Cheyenne, 1867–1869* (Norman: University of Oklahoma Press, 2004); see also William Leckie, *Military Conquest of the Southern Plains* (Norman: University of Oklahoma Press, 1963).

    10. Wilbur S. Nye, ed., *Bad Medicine and Good: Tales of the Kiowas* (Norman: University of Oklahoma Press, 1962), vii–xxii; Maurice Boyd, ed., *Kiowa Voices*, Volume 2 (Fort Worth: Texas Christian University Press, 1981), 14–21, 47–59; Nye, *Bad Medicine and Good*, 49–76; Carlson, *The Plains Indians*, 30–31, 133; Mildred Mayhall, *The Kiowas* (Norman: University of Oklahoma Press, 1962), 1–145; Alice Marriott, *Kiowa Years: A Study in Culture Impact* (New York: MacMillan, 1968); see also James F. Brooks, *Captives and Cousins: Slavery, Kinship, and Community in the Southwest Borderlands* (Chapel Hill: University of North Carolina Press, 2002).

    11. Etahdleuh, quoted in "Anniversary Exercises at Hampton Institute," *Southern Workman* 8 (June 1879): 71–72; Petersen, *Plains Indian Art from Fort Marion*, 135–159; Kiowa POW File, Parker MacKenzie Collection, Oklahoma Historical Society, Oklahoma City, Okla.; see also William C. Meadows, *Kiowa, Comanche, and Apache Military Societies: Enduring Veterans, 1800 to the Present* (Austin: University of Texas Press, 1999).

    12. Lone Wolf, "I Am the Man That Makes It Rain," quoted in

Indian Oratory, ed. W. C. Vanderwerth (Norman: University of Oklahoma Press, 1971), 147–148; Hugh Corwin, ed., *The Kiowa Indians: Their History and Life Stories* (Lawton, Okla.: privately published, 1958), 163–180; Haley, *Buffalo War*, 16–18, 50–51.

13. Nye, *Bad Medicine and Good*, 46–48, 123–126, 151–154, 190, 222–226; Boyd, *Kiowa Voices*, 95–106, 249–253; Haley, *Buffalo War*, 18–19, 80–81; Brown, *Bury My Heart*, 243–244.

14. Nye, *Bad Medicine and Good*, 151–154, 222–226; Boyd, *Kiowa Voices*, 252–253; Haley, *Buffalo War*, 154–214, 220; John Ewers, ed., *Murals in the Round: Painted Tipis of the Kiowa and Kiowa Apache Indians* (Washington, D.C.: Smithsonian Institution Press, 1978), 6–12, 33–34, 50–53; see also Lee Irwin, *The Dream Seekers: Native American Visionary Traditions of the Great Plains* (Norman: University of Oklahoma Press, 1994).

15. Mamanti, quoted in Nye, *Bad Medicine and Good*, 224–225.

16. Haley, *Buffalo War*, 14–16, 52–55; William T. Hagan, *Quanah Parker, Comanche Chief* (Norman: University of Oklahoma Press, 1993), 3–15; Ernest Wallace and E. Adamson Hoebel, *The Comanches: The Lords of the South Plains* (Norman: University of Oklahoma Press, 1952); Thomas W. Kavanagh, *Comanche Political History: An Ethnohistorical Approach, 1706–1875* (Lincoln: University of Nebraska Press, 1996); see also "List of Indians" in Richard H. Pratt, *Battlefield and Classroom: Four Decades with the American Indian, 1867–1904*, edited by Robert Utley (New Haven, Conn.: Yale University Press, 1964), 138–144.

17. Don Rickey, *Forty Miles a Day on Beans and Hay: The Enlisted Soldier Fighting the Indian Wars* (Norman: University of Oklahoma Press, 1963), 280–285; Robert Wooster, *The Military and United States Indian Policy, 1865–1903* (New Haven, Conn.: Yale University Press, 1988), 13–72, 11–143; Sherry Smith, *The View From Officers' Row: Army Perceptions of Western Indians* (Tucson: University of Arizona Press, 1990), 1–89; see also Paul Andrew Hutton, *Phil Sheridan and His Army* (Lincoln: University of Nebraska Press, 1985).

18. Arrell Morgan Gibson, "St. Augustine Prisoners," *Red River Valley Historical Review* 3 (1978): 259–270; Haley, *Buffalo War*, 37–50, 186; Wilbur S. Nye, *Carbine and Lance: The Story of Old Fort Sill* (Norman: University of Oklahoma Press, 1937), 1–186; see also Rob-

ert M. Utley, *Frontier Regulars: The United States Army and the Indian, 1866–1891* (New York: Macmillan, 1973).

19. Gibson, "St. Augustine Prisoners," 259–270; T. Ashley Zwink, "On the White Man's Road: Lawrie Tatum and the Formative Years of the Kiowa Agency, 1869–1873," *Chronicles of Oklahoma* 56 (Winter 1978–79): 431–441; William D. Pennington, "Government Policy and Indian Farming on the Cheyenne and Arapaho Reservation: 1869–1880," *Chronicles of Oklahoma* 57 (Summer 1979): 171–189; Robert H. Keller, *American Protestantism and United States Indian Policy, 1869–1882* (Lincoln: University of Nebraska Press, 1983), 47–128; see also Francis Paul Prucha, *The Great Father: The United States Government and the American Indians*, 2 volumes (Lincoln: University of Nebraska Press, 1984).

20. Gibson, "St. Augustine Prisoners," 259–270; Haley, *Buffalo War*, 17, 83; Wooster, *The Military and United States Indian Policy*, 151–152; see also Charles M. Robinson, *The Indian Trial: The Complete Story of the Warren Train Massacre and the Fall of the Kiowa Nation* (Spokane, Wash.: Arthur H. Clark, 1997).

21. Gibson, "St. Augustine Prisoners," 259–270; Haley, *Buffalo War*, 170; Ernest Wallace, *Ranald S. MacKenzie on the Texas Frontier* (College Station: Texas A&M University Press, 1993), 1–127.

22. The communications between officials is located in the dated microfilm rolls for Letters Received by the Office of the Adjutant General, M666, Record Group 94, National Archives and Records Administration. It was compiled by Joe Taylor in a series of published articles; see Joe F. Taylor, "The Indian Campaign on the Staked Plains, 1874–1875: Military Correspondence from the War Department, Adjutant General's Office, File 2815–1874," *Panhandle-Plains Historical Review* 34 (1961): 1–216.

23. Gibson, "St. Augustine Prisoners," 259–270; Haley, *Buffalo War*, 95–106; Wooster, *The Military and United States Indian Policy*, 152–159.

24. Haley, *Buffalo War*, 79–93, 107–123, 139–143; Carlson, *The Plains Indians*, 159–160; Robert Wooster, *Nelson A. Miles and the Twilight of the Frontier Army* (Lincoln: University of Nebraska Press, 1996), 61–75.

25. Arlene Feldmann Jauken, *The Moccasin Speaks: Living as*

Captive of the Dog Soldier Warriors (Lincoln: Dageforde Publishing, 1998), 39–69, 104; Haley, *Buffalo War*, 139–146.

26. Jauken, *The Moccasin Speaks*, 39–109; Haley, *Buffalo War*, 139–146; "Additional Indian News," *Leavenworth Daily Commercial*, 5 May 1875.

27. Haley, *Buffalo War*, 147–167, 185–188; Nye, *Bad Medicine and Good*, 184–207; Boyd, *Kiowa Voices*, 247–248; see also Chris Newton, "Archaeologists Provide New Indian War Views," *Bryan-College Station Eagle*, 10 October 1999, A9, A14.

28. Haley, *Buffalo War*, 169–183; Nye, *Bad Medicine and Good*, 184–221; Nye, *Carbine and Lance*, 187–239; Wallace, *Ranald S. MacKenzie on the Texas Frontier*, 128–149; Taylor, "The Indian Campaign on the Staked Plains," 77–78.

29. Jauken, *The Moccasin Speaks*, 110–119; Haley, *Buffalo War*, 188–196; Wooster, *Nelson A. Miles and the Twilight of the Frontier Army*, 61–75; Taylor, "The Indian Campaign," 83–86.

30. Taylor, "The Indian Campaign," 91, 102, 130–131.

31. Taylor, "The Indian Campaign," 131–133.

32. Taylor, "The Indian Campaign," 131–133.

33. Taylor, "The Indian Campaign," 133, 151–152, 180–182; see also "Surrendered Savages," *Leavenworth Daily Commercial*, 9 March 1875.

34. "The Indian Problem-A Change," *Leavenworth Daily Commercial*, 4 March 1875; "The Indian Problem," *Leavenworth Daily Commercial*, 9 March 1875; "Surrendered Savages," *Leavenworth Daily Commercial*, 9 March 1875.

35. Taylor, "The Indian Campaign," 92, 171–173; *Report of the Commissioner of Indian Affairs for 1875* (Washington, D.C.: U.S. Government Printing Office, 1875), 12, 49–50, 263–264, 267–268; see also *Wichita Eagle*, 6 May 1875.

36. Taylor, "The Indian Campaign," 179, 183–184, 186.

37. Jauken, *The Moccasin Speaks*, 120–170; Haley, *Buffalo War*, 197–209.

38. Jauken, *The Moccasin Speaks*, 171–214; Wooster, *Nelson A. Miles*, 61–75; Nelson A. Miles, *Personal Recollections and Observations* (Chicago: Werner Co., 1896), 179–181; *Kansas City Times*, 9 April 1875; Taylor, "The Indian Campaign," 158–159.

39. *Report of the Commissioner for 1875*, 59, 65, 264–265, 271–275; Haley, *Buffalo War*, 204–221; Gibson, "St. Augustine Prisoners," 259–270; Pratt, *Battlefield and Classroom*, 92.

40. G. Butler, "A Day Among the Kiowas and Comanches," *Catholic World* 23 (September 1876): 837–848; Haley, *Buffalo War*, 204–221.

41. *Report of the Commissioner for 1875*, 49–50, 268–271; Haley, *Buffalo War*, 204–221; Jauken, *The Moccasin Speaks*, 171–214; Mann, *Cheyenne-Arapaho Education*, 64.

42. *Report of the Commissioner for 1875*, 49–50, 268–271; Haley, *Buffalo War*, 215–220; Jauken, *The Moccasin Speaks*, 171–214; *Leavenworth Daily Commercial*, 11 April 1875; *Wichita Eagle*, 15 April 1875.

43. Haley, *Buffalo War*, 215–220; Jauken, *The Moccasin Speaks*, 177–181; John H. Monnett, *Massacre at Cheyenne Hole: Lieutenant Austin Henely and the Sappa Creek Controversy* (Boulder: University Press of Colorado, 1999); William Y. Chalfant, *Cheyennes at Dark Water Creek: The Last Fight of the Red River War* (Norman: University of Oklahoma Press, 1997).

44. James Mooney, *Calendar History of the Kiowa Indians, Seventeenth Annual Report of the Bureau of American Ethnology, 1895–1896*, Part 1 (Washington, D.C.: U.S. Government Printing Office, 1898; reprint, Washington, D.C.: Smithsonian Institution Press, 1979), 181–213, 327–346; Haley, *Buffalo War*, 124–196; Dan Flores, "Bison Ecology and Bison Diplomacy: The Southern Plains from 1800 to 1850," *Journal of American History* 78 (September 1991): 465–485.

45. Old Lady Horse, "The Last Buffalo Herd," quoted in Colin Calloway, ed., *Our Hearts Fell to the Ground: Plains Indian Views of How the West Was Lost* (New York: St. Martin's Press, 1996), 129–130.

Chapter 2

1. Richard Henry Pratt, "An Indian Dance," Box 19, Folder 677, Richard Henry Pratt Papers, Beinecke Library.

2. Pratt, "An Indian Dance"; see also Kiowa POW File, Parker MacKenzie Collection, Oklahoma Historical Society.

3. Richard H. Pratt, *Battlefield and Classroom: Four Decades with the American Indian, 1867–1904*, edited by Robert Utley (New Haven, Conn.: Yale University Press, 1964), 3–8, 97; see also Everett A. Gilcreast, "Richard Henry Pratt and American Indian Policy, 1877–

1906: A Study of the Assimilation Movement" (Ph.D. dissertation, Yale University, 1967); Elaine G. Eastman, *Pratt: The Red Man's Moses* (Norman: University of Oklahoma Press, 1935).

4. A brevet signified an honorary rank awarded for distinguished service, but it presents a source of confusion for scholars writing about Pratt. Although the honorary rank seldom reflected the actual authority and status of an officer, servicemen often used it in conversations and in records. In this study, I refer to Pratt according to his official rank on duty.

5. Pratt, *Battlefield and Classroom*, 1–103; see also Thomas Dunlay, *Wolves for the Blue Soldiers: Indian Scouts and Auxiliaries with the United States Army, 1860–1890* (Lincoln: University of Nebraska Press, 1982).

6. Pratt, *Battlefield and Classroom*, 91–93, 104–106; Arrell Gibson, "St. Augustine Prisoners," *Red River Valley Historical Review* 3 (1978): 259–270; Joe F. Taylor, "The Indian Campaign on the Staked Plains, 1874–1875: Military Correspondence from the War Department, Adjutant General's Office, File 2815–1874," *Panhandle-Plains Historical Review* 34 (1961): 134–135; see also Notebook, List of Indian Prisoners, 1874, Box 22, Folder 713, Richard Henry Pratt Papers, Beinecke Library; Notebook, List of Indian Prisoners, 1874, Box 22, Folder 714, Richard Henry Pratt Papers, Beinecke Library.

7. C. D. Emory to R. Mackenzie, 30 March 1875, Box 14, Folder 489, Richard Henry Pratt Papers, Beinecke Library; Pratt, *Battlefield and Classroom*, 104–106; Gibson, "St. Augustine Prisoners," 259–270.

8. Memorandum on Sending Indian Prisoners to Fort Marion, Roll 45, M565, Letters Sent by the Office of the Adjutant General, Main Series, 1800–1890, Volume 58, Record Group 94, National Archives and Records Administration; Richard Henry Pratt, "American Indians, Chained and Unchained, Address before the Pennsylvania Commandery of the Military Order of the Loyal Legion at the Union League," (Philadelphia, Pa., 23 October 1912), passim; Pratt, *Battlefield and Classroom*, 104–106; Gibson, "St. Augustine Prisoners," 259–270; Joe F. Taylor, "The Indian Campaign on the Staked Plains, 1874–1875: Military Correspondence from the War Department, Adjutant General's Office, File 2815–1874, Conclusion," *Panhandle-Plains Historical Review* 35 (1962): 272–274.

9. *Report of the Commissioner of Indian Affairs for 1875* (Wash-

ington, D.C.: U.S. Government Printing Office, 1875), 49–50, 268–271; James Haley, *The Buffalo War: The History of the Red River Uprising of 1874* (Garden City, N.Y.: Doubleday, 1976; reprint, Austin: State House Press, 1998), 204–221; Arlene Feldmann Jauken, *The Moccasin Speaks: Living as Captive of the Dog Soldier Warriors* (Lincoln: Dageforde Publishing, 1998), 171–214; Henrietta Mann, *Cheyenne-Arapaho Education, 1871–1982* (Boulder: University Press of Colorado, 1997), 64; *Wichita Eagle*, 6 May 1875.

10. "Anniversary Exercises at Hampton Institute," *Southern Workman* 8 (June 1879): 71–72; Gibson, "St. Augustine Prisoners," 259–270; Haley, *The Buffalo War*, 212–214; see also Stan Hoig, *The Kiowas and the Legend of Kicking Bird* (Boulder: University Press of Colorado, 2000).

11. Gibson, "St. Augustine Prisoners," 259–270; Taylor, "The Indian Campaign, Conclusion," 279–280; The wording of the original letter is slightly recast in Pratt, *Battlefield and Classroom*, 106–107.

12. Gibson, "St. Augustine Prisoners," 259–270; Pratt, *Battlefield and Classroom*, 91–92, 105–106, 138–144; Wilbur S. Nye, *Carbine and Lance: The Story of Old Fort Sill* (Norman: University of Oklahoma Press, 1937), 231–233.

13. List of Indian Prisoners, 19 May 1875, Roll 162, M666, Letters Received by the Office of the Adjutant General, Record Group 94, National Archives and Records Administration; List of Indian Prisoners, 19 May 1875, Box 14, Folder 490, Richard Henry Pratt Pratt Papers, Beinecke Library; Maurice Boyd, ed., *Kiowa Voices*, Volume 2 (Fort Worth: Texas Christian University Press, 1981), 250–253; see also "List of Indians" in Pratt, *Battlefield and Classroom*, 138–144; Kiowa POW File, Parker MacKenzie Collection, Oklahoma Historical Society.

14. Richard Henry Pratt, "The Florida Indian Prisoners of 1875 to 1878," Box 19, Folder 676, Richard Henry Pratt Papers, Beinecke Library; Pratt, "American Indians, Chained and Unchained"; Gibson, "St. Augustine Prisoners," 259–270.

15. Nye, *Carbine and Lance*, 233.

16. Nye, *Carbine and Lance*, 233.

17. Pratt, "The Florida Indian Prisoners of 1875 to 1878"; Pratt, "American Indians, Chained and Unchained"; Pratt, *Battlefield and Classroom*, 108–109.

18. "The Nation's Wards," *Kansas City Times*, 11 May 1875; Boyd, *Kiowa Voices*, 250–253; Nye, *Carbine and Lance*, 233–234; Hoig, *The Kiowas and the Legend of Kicking Bird*, 239–248.

19. Pratt, *Battlefield and Classroom*, 108–109; "The Nation's Wards," *Kansas City Times*, 11 May 1875; Bear's Heart, "Indian Talk," *Southern Workman* 9 (July 1880): 77; see also Brent Ashabranner, *A Strange and Distant Shore: Indians of the Great Plains in Exile* (New York: Cobblehill Books, 1996).

20. "The Nation's Wards," *Kansas City Times*, 11 May 1875.

21. *Leavenworth Daily Commercial*, 5 May 1875.

22. *St. Louis Daily Globe*, 11 May 1875; "The Cheyenne Murderers," *Leavenworth Daily Commercial*, 14 May 1875; see also J. Patrick Hughes, *Fort Leavenworth: Gateway to the West* (Topeka: Kansas State Historical Society, 2000).

23. *St. Louis Republican*, 5 May 1875.

24. Richard Henry Pratt to John Miles, May 9, 1875, Cheyenne-Arapaho Indian Prisoners Vertical File, Section X, Oklahoma Historical Society.

25. Pratt, *Battlefield and Classroom*, 109.

26. Nelson A. Miles, *Personal Recollections and Observations* (Chicago: Werner Co., 1896), 179–181; see also Nelson A. Miles, "The Indian Problem," *North American Review* 128 (March 1879): 304–314.

27. Richard H. Pratt to Assistant Adjutant General, 10 May 1875, Box 14, Folder 490, Richard Henry Pratt Papers, Beinecke Library; Richard H. Pratt to William Stickney, 9 February 1880, Box 10, Folder 341, Richard Henry Pratt Papers, Beinecke Library.

28. Orders, Box 14, Folder 499, Richard Henry Pratt Papers, Beinecke Library; Taylor, "The Indian Campaign, Conclusion," 281–283; Pratt, *Battlefield and Classroom*, 109–111.

29. Pratt, *Battlefield and Classroom*, 111; Richard H. Pratt to Secretary of Interior, Receipts, 25 September 1875, Roll 66, M234, Letters Received by the Office of Indian Affairs, Central Superintendency, Record Group 75, National Archives and Records Administration.

30. "Poor Lo," *Leavenworth Daily Commercial*, 18 May 1875.

31. Herman Viola, ed., *Warrior Artists: Historic Cheyenne and Kiowa Ledger Art Drawn by Making Medicine and Zotom* (Washington,

D.C.: National Geographic Society, 1998), 78–79; Gibson, "St. Augustine Prisoners," 259–270.

32. "Bad Indians," *Indianapolis Sentinel*, 19 May 1875; "Redskins," *Indianapolis Journal*, 19 May 1875; Pratt, *Battlefield and Classroom*, 111.

33. "Bad Indians," *Indianapolis Sentinel*, 19 May 1875; *The Evening News*, 19 May 1875; Pratt, *Battlefield and Classroom*, 111.

34. "Lo, The Poor Indian," *The Daily Louisville Commercial*, 19 May 1875.

35. "Rascally Red Men," *Louisville Courier-Journal*, 20 May 1875.

36. *The Daily Louisville Commercial*, 26 May 1875.

37. Pratt, "The Florida Indian Prisoners of 1875 to 1878"; "The Last Sensation!! The Captive Indians," *The Florida Press*, 29 May 1875.

38. Pratt, "The Florida Indian Prisoners of 1875 to 1878"; "Crime," *St. Louis Daily Times*, 20 May 1875; "Lo, The Poor Indian!" *Leavenworth Daily Commercial*, 21 May 1875; "The Last Sensation!! The Captive Indians," *The Florida Press*, 29 May 1875.

39. Pratt, *Battlefield and Classroom*, 113–115; Viola, *Warrior Artists*, 86–87; Gibson, "St. Augustine Prisoners," 259–270.

40. Pratt, "The Florida Indian Prisoners of 1875 to 1878."

41. Pratt, "The Florida Indian Prisoners of 1875 to 1878"; Viola, *Warrior Artists*, 86–87; *The Daily Louisville Commercial*, 22 May 1875; "The Last Sensation!! The Captive Indians," *The Florida Press*, 29 May 1875.

42. "The Indians," *Tri-Weekly Florida Union*, 25 May 1875; "The Last Sensation!! The Captive Indians," *The Florida Press*, 29 May 1875.

43. National Parks Service, *Castillo de San Marcos: A Guide to Castillo de San Marcos National Monument Florida*, Handbook 149, U.S. Department of the Interior (Washington, D.C.: U.S. Government Printing Office, n.d.).

44. Taylor, "The Indian Campaign, Conclusion," 274–279.

45. "The Last Sensation!! The Captive Indians," *The Florida Press*, 29 May 1875; Viola, *Warrior Artists*, 92–93.

Chapter 3

1. List of Indian Prisoners, 19 May 1875, Roll 162, M666, Letters Received by the Office of the Adjutant General, Record Group 94, Na-

tional Archives and Records Administration; List of Indian Prisoners, 19 May 1875, Box 14, Folder 490, Richard Henry Pratt Pratt Papers, Beinecke Library; "List of Indians" in Richard H. Pratt, *Battlefield and Classroom: Four Decades with the American Indian, 1867–1904*, edited by Robert Utley (New Haven, Conn.: Yale University Press, 1964), 138–144; Herman Viola, ed., *Warrior Artists: Historic Cheyenne and Kiowa Ledger Art Drawn by Making Medicine and Zotom* (Washington, D.C.: National Geographic Society, 1998), 6–7; Much of the data on the prisoner's bodies was recorded on July 9, 1877.

2. Arrell Gibson, "St. Augustine Prisoners," *Red River Valley Historical Review* 3 (1978): 259–270; "A Glimpse at the Indians," *Florida Press*, 3 July 1875.

3. "A Glimpse at the Indians," *Florida Press*, 3 July 1875; Abstract of Provisions, October 1876, Letters Received by the Office of Indian Affairs, Central Superintendency, Record Group 75, M234, Roll 68, National Archives and Records Administration; Richard Pratt to General Stark, 18 May 1876, Box 14, Folder 493a, Richard Henry Pratt Papers, Beinecke Library; Pratt, *Battlefield and Classroom*, 124–126; Wilbur S. Nye, *Carbine and Lance: The Story of Old Fort Sill* (Norman: University of Oklahoma Press, 1937), 251.

4. "The Last Sensation," *Florida Press*, 29 May 1875; "A Glimpse at the Indians," *Florida Press*, 3 July 1875.

5. Richard Pratt to House of Representatives, 14 June 1880, Box 10, Folder 341, Richard Henry Pratt Papers, Beinecke Library; Richard Henry Pratt, "An Indian Dance," Box 19, Folder 677, Richard Henry Pratt Papers, Beinecke Library; see also Pratt, *Battlefield and Classroom*, 97–98.

6. Pratt, "An Indian Dance"; see also Pratt, *Battlefield and Classroom*, 97–98.

7. David Wallace Adams, *Education for Extinction: American Indians and the Boarding School Experience, 1875–1928* (Lawrence: University Press of Kansas, 1995), 51–55; Joel Pfister, *Individuality Incorporated: Indians and the Multicultural Modern* (Durham, N.C.: Duke University Press, 2004), 31–132; see also Frederick J. Stefon, "Richard Henry Pratt and His Indians," *Journal of Ethnic Studies* 15 (Summer 1987): 86–112.

8. Esther Baker Steele, "The Indian Prisoners at Fort Marion,"

National Teachers Monthly 3 (August 1877): 290; Richard Pratt to R. C. Drum, 25 July 1875, Box 14, Folder 493a, Richard Henry Pratt Papers, Beinecke Library; Chauncey McKeever to Commanding Officer, 24 May 1875, Box 14, Folder 490, Richard Henry Pratt Papers, Beinecke Library; Joe F. Taylor, "The Indian Campaign on the Staked Plains, 1874–1875: Military Correspondence from the War Department, Adjutant General's Office, File 2815–1874, Conclusion," *Panhandle-Plains Historical Review* 35 (1962): 281–289, 342.

9. Chauncey McKeever to Post Commander, 21 July 1875, Box 14, Folder 491, Richard Henry Pratt Papers, Beinecke Library; Richard Pratt to Post Adjutant, 26 October 1875, Box 14, Folder 493a, Richard Henry Pratt Papers, Beinecke Library; Pratt, *Battlefield and Classroom*, 111, 119; Taylor, "The Indian Campaign," 289–296.

10. Alphonso Taft to Secretary of the Interior, 30 March 1876, Letters Received by the Office of Indian Affairs, Central Superintendency, Record Group 75, M234, Roll 68, National Archives and Records Administration; R. MacFeely to the Secretary of War, 17 May 1876, 18 July 1876, Letters Received by the Office of Indian Affairs, Central Superintendency, Record Group 75, M234, Roll 68, National Archives and Records Administration; Forwarded Endorsements from Post Surgeon, 14 December 1875, Letters Received by the Office of Indian Affairs, Central Superintendency, Record Group 75, M234, Roll 67, National Archives and Records Administration; Taylor, "The Indian Campaign," 276–279.

11. "The Last Sensation," *Florida Press*, 29 May 1875.

12. Taylor, "The Indian Campaign," 296–300; Gibson, "St. Augustine Prisoners," 259–270; "Scenes from the Sun-Lands," *Frank Leslie's Illustrated Newspaper*, 11 May 1878.

13. Richard Henry Pratt, "The Florida Indian Prisoners of 1875 to 1878," Box 19, Folder 676, Richard Henry Pratt Papers, Beinecke Library; Richard Pratt to Post Adjutant, 30 June 1875, Letters Received by the Office of Indian Affairs, Cheyenne and Arapaho Agency, Record Group 75, M234, Roll 120, National Archives and Records Administration; John Janeway to Post Adjutant, 1 July 1875, Letters Received by the Office of Indian Affairs, Cheyenne and Arapaho Agency, Record Group 75, M234, Roll 120, National Archives and Records Administration; J. A. Covington to Richard Pratt, 4 September 1875, Box 2, Folder 63, Rich-

ard Henry Pratt Papers, Beinecke Library; Richard Pratt to John Miles, 25 June 1875, Cheyenne-Arapaho Indian Prisoners Vertical File, Section X, Oklahoma Historical Society; Taylor, "The Indian Campaign," 303–304.

14. Richard Pratt to Adjutant General, 11 June 1875, Box 14, Folder 490, Richard Henry Pratt Papers, Beinecke Library; Taylor, "The Indian Campaign," 305–308; Pratt, *Battlefield and Classroom*, 122–123.

15. Richard Pratt to Adjutant General, 11 June 1875, Box 14, Folder 490, Richard Henry Pratt Papers, Beinecke Library; Taylor, "The Indian Campaign," 305–308; Pratt, *Battlefield and Classroom*, 122–123.

16. Wilbur S. Nye, ed., *Bad Medicine and Good: Tales of the Kiowas* (Norman: University of Oklahoma Press, 1962), 223–226; Richard Pratt to R. C. Drum, 31 July 1875, Box 14, Folder 491, Richard Henry Pratt Papers, Beinecke Library; J. M. Haworth to Richard Pratt, 30 August 1875, Box 4, Folder 126, Richard Henry Pratt Papers, Beinecke Library; Taylor, "The Indian Campaign," 317.

17. Memorandum on Sending Indian Prisoners to Fort Marion, Roll 45, M565, Letters Sent by the Office of the Adjutant General, Main Series, 1800–1890, Volume 58, Record Group 94, National Archives and Records Administration; James Haworth to E. P. Smith, 6 August 1875, Roll 380, Letters Received by the Office of Indian Affairs, Kiowa Agency, M234, Record Group 75, National Archives and Records Administration; J. A. Covington to E. P. Smith, 20 August 1875, Roll 120, Letters Received by the Office of Indian Affairs, Cheyenne and Arapaho Agency, M234, Record Group 75, National Archives and Records Administration; Taylor, "The Indian Campaign," 314–323; Gibson, "St. Augustine Prisoners," 259–270.

18. Memorandum on Sending Indian Prisoners to Fort Marion, Roll 45, M565, Letters Sent by the Office of the Adjutant General, Main Series, 1800–1890, Volume 58, Record Group 94, National Archives and Records Administration; Richard Pratt to R. C. Drum, 31 July 1875, Box 14, Folder 491, Richard Henry Pratt Papers, Beinecke Library; E. D. Townsend to Phil Sheridan, 13 August 1875, Letters Sent by the Office of the Adjutant General, Main Series, 1800–1890, Vol. 58, Roll 45, Record Group 94, National Archives and Records Administration; Taylor, "The Indian Campaign," 314–323.

19. Richard Pratt to J. A. Covington, 14 August 1875, Cheyenne-

Arapaho Indian Prisoners Vertical File, Section X, Oklahoma Historical Society; J. M. Haworth to Richard Pratt, 30 August 1875, Box 4, Folder 126, Richard Henry Pratt Papers, Beinecke Library; Richard Pratt to Adjutant General, 6 September 1875, Box 14, Folder 493a, Richard Henry Pratt Papers, Beinecke Library; Pratt, *Battlefield and Classroom*, 124.

20. Richard Pratt to E. Townsend, 29 June 1875, Box 14, Folder 493a, Richard Henry Pratt Papers, Beinecke Library; Richard Pratt to Adjutant General, 17 July 1875, Box 14, Folder 490, Richard Henry Pratt Papers, Beinecke Library; Taylor, "The Indian Campaign," 309–314; see also Michel Foucault, *Discipline and Punish: The Birth of the Prison*, Translated by Alan Sheridan (New York: Vintage, 1979).

21. Pratt, *Battlefield and Classroom*, 117–119, 125; Richard Pratt to Commissioner, 20 October 20, 1876, Letters Received by the Office of Indian Affairs, Central Superintendency, Record Group 75, M234, Roll 67, National Archives and Records Administration; Taylor, "The Indian Campaign," 296–302; Gibson, "St. Augustine Prisoners," 259–270; Brent Ashabranner, *A Strange and Distant Shore: Indians of the Great Plains in Exile* (New York: Cobblehill Books, 1996), 22–23.

22. "A Glimpse at the Indians," *Florida Press*, 3 July 1875; Richard Henry Pratt, "The Florida Indian Prisoners of 1875 to 1878," Box 19, Folder 676, Richard Henry Pratt Papers, Beinecke Library; Gibson, "St. Augustine Prisoners," 259–270; Richard Henry Pratt, "American Indians, Chained and Unchained, Address before the Pennsylvania Commandery of the Military Order of the Loyal Legion at the Union League," (Philadelphia, Pa., 23 October 1912); Pratt, *Battlefield and Classroom*, 118–120, 132.

23. Alphonso Taft to the Secretary of the Interior, 30 March 1876, Letters Received by the Office of Indian Affairs, Central Superintendency, Record Group 75, M234, Roll 68, National Archives and Records Administration; Receipts, Quartermaster General to Secretary of War, 24 February 1877, Letters Received by the Office of Indian Affairs, Central Superintendency, Record Group 75, M234, Roll 69, National Archives and Records Administration.

24. Pratt, "The Florida Indian Prisoners of 1875 to 1878"; "The Indians," *The Florida Press*, 19 August 1876; Richard Pratt to Adjutant General, 17 July 1875, Box 14, Folder 490, Richard Henry Pratt Papers,

Beinecke Library; see also Thomas Dunlay, *Wolves for the Blue Soldiers: Indian Scouts and Auxiliaries with the United States Army, 1860–1890* (Lincoln: University of Nebraska Press, 1982).

25. "Echoes from St. Augustine," *Daily Florida Union*, 17 March 1877; Amy Caruthers, "The Indian Prisoners at St. Augustine," *The Christian at Work* 11 (23 August 1877): 678–679; Pratt, *Battlefield and Classroom*, 118–120.

26. Pratt, *Battlefield and Classroom*, 119–120, 185–187; Pratt, "The Florida Indian Prisoners of 1875 to 1878"; Alvin O. Turner, "Journey to Sainthood: David Pendleton Oakerhater's Better Way," *Chronicles of Oklahoma* 70 (Summer 1992): 116–143; Karen Daniels Petersen, ed., *Plains Indian Art from Fort Marion* (Norman: University of Oklahoma Press, 1971), 135–159, 225–226; Viola, *Warrior Artists*, 106, 109, 117, 119; see also Janet Catherine Berlo, ed., *Plains Indian Drawings, 1865–1935: Pages from a Visual History* (New York: Harry B. Abrams, 1996).

27. Pratt, *Battlefield and Classroom*, 147, 187; Dunlay, *Wolves for the Blue Soldiers*, 190–191.

28. Pratt, *Battlefield and Classroom*, 185–186; Viola, *Warrior Artists*, 15.

29. "Echoes from St. Augustine," *Daily Florida Union*, 17 March 1877; Richard Pratt to General Stark, 18 May 1876, Box 14, Folder 493a, Richard Henry Pratt Papers, Beinecke Library; Richard Pratt Interview by *New York Sun* reporter, 7 October 1896, Box 19, Folder 679, Richard Henry Pratt Papers, Beinecke Library.

30. James Haworth to Enoch Hoag, 30 September 1875, Roll 380, Letters Received by the Office of Indian Affairs, Kiowa Agency, M234, Record Group 75, National Archives and Records Administration; Taylor, "The Indian Campaign," 323–328; Gibson, "St. Augustine Prisoners," 259–270.

31. Richard Pratt to J. A. Covington, 14 August 1875, Cheyenne-Arapaho Indian Prisoners Vertical File, Section X, Oklahoma Historical Society; J. A. Covington to Richard Pratt, 4 September 1875, Box 2, Folder 63, Richard Henry Pratt Papers, Beinecke Library.

32. Richard Pratt to J. A. Covington, 14 August 1875, Cheyenne-Arapaho Indian Prisoners Vertical File, Section X, Oklahoma Historical Society; Richard Pratt to J. A. Covington, 17 September 1875,

Cheyenne-Arapaho Indian Prisoners Vertical File, Section X, Oklahoma Historical Society.

33. Richard Pratt to Post Adjutant, 23 October 1875, Box 14, Folder 493, Richard Henry Pratt Papers, Beinecke Library; Report, 4 November 1875, Letters Received by the Office of Indian Affairs, Central Superintendency, Record Group 75, M234, Roll 66, National Archives and Records Administration; C. M. Bevan to Editor, 27 August 1877, Box 25, Folder 789, Richard Henry Pratt Papers, Beinecke Library; Pratt, *Battlefield and Classroom*, 124–127.

34. Richard Pratt to Post Adjutant, 23 October 1875, Box 14, Folder 493, Richard Henry Pratt Papers, Beinecke Library; Report, 4 November 1875, Letters Received by the Office of Indian Affairs, Central Superintendency, Record Group 75, M234, Roll 66, National Archives and Records Administration; Pratt, *Battlefield and Classroom*, 124–127.

35. E. Adamson Hoebel and Karen Daniels Petersen, eds., *A Cheyenne Sketchbook by Cohoe* (Norman: University of Oklahoma Press, 1964), 73–75.

36. Report, 1 December 1875, Letters Received by the Office of Indian Affairs, Central Superintendency, Record Group 75, M234, Roll 66, National Archives and Records Administration; Report, 1 September 1876, Letters Received by the Office of Indian Affairs, Central Superintendency, Record Group 75, M234, Roll 68, National Archives and Records Administration; Taylor, "The Indian Campaign," 333–336.

37. Richard Pratt to Adjutant General, 5 November 1875, Letters Received by the Office of Indian Affairs, Cheyenne and Arapaho Agency, Group 75, M234, Roll 120, National Archives and Records Administration; Richard Pratt to J. D. Miles, 3 January 1876, Cheyenne-Arapaho Indian Prisoners Vertical File, Section X, Oklahoma Historical Society; Taylor, "The Indian Campaign," 334–335.

38. Richard Pratt to J. D. Miles, 3 January 1876, Cheyenne-Arapaho Indian Prisoners Vertical File, Section X, Oklahoma Historical Society.

39. Richard Pratt to J. D. Miles, 3 January 1876, Cheyenne-Arapaho Indian Prisoners Vertical File, Section X, Oklahoma Historical Society.

40. Richard Pratt to Frederick Dent, 6 January 1876, Box 14,

Folder 493, Richard Henry Pratt Papers, Beinecke Library; Richard Pratt to J. D. Miles, 3 January 1876, Cheyenne-Arapaho Indian Prisoners Vertical File, Section X, Oklahoma Historical Society; Taylor, "The Indian Campaign," 336.

41. Richard Pratt to Phil Sheridan, 17 January 1876, Box 14, Folder 493, Richard Henry Pratt Papers, Beinecke Library; Report, 1 February 1876, Letters Received by the Office of Indian Affairs, Central Superintendency, Record Group 75, M234, Roll 68, National Archives and Records Administration; Richard Pratt to Phil Sheridan, 17 March 1876, Letters Received by the Office of Indian Affairs, Central Superintendency, Record Group 75, M234, Roll 68, National Archives and Records Administration; Taylor, "The Indian Campaign," 336–342.

42. Richard Pratt to Commissioner, 21 March 1876, Letters Received by the Office of Indian Affairs, Central Superintendency, Record Group 75, M234, Roll 69, National Archives and Records Administration; Richard Pratt to Frederick Dent, 6 January 1876, Box 14, Folder 493, Richard Henry Pratt Papers, Beinecke Library; Richard Pratt to Phil Sheridan, 1 May 1876, Box 14, Folder 493a, Richard Henry Pratt Papers, Beinecke Library; Richard Pratt to William Sherman, 31 October 1876, Box 14, Folder 493a, Richard Henry Pratt Papers, Beinecke Library; Taylor, "The Indian Campaign," 340–342, 348–351.

Chapter 4

1. Richard H. Pratt, *Battlefield and Classroom: Four Decades with the American Indian, 1867–1904*, edited by Robert Utley (New Haven, Conn.: Yale University Press, 1964), 118; see also Maggi Hall and the St. Augustine Historical Society, *Images of America: St. Augustine* (Charleston, S.C.: Arcadia, 2002).

2. The literature on American Indians and the exchange economy of the Great Plains is extensive. For an introduction to the subject, see Paul H. Carlson, *The Plains Indians* (College Station: Texas A&M University Press, 1998), 51–66, 124–141; Colin Calloway, "The Intertribal Balance of Powers on the Great Plains," *Journal of American Studies* 16 (April 1982): 25–47.

3. Roman Nose, "Experiences of H.C. Roman Nose," *School News* 1 (December 1880): 1.

4. William W. Dewhurst, *The History of Saint Augustine, Florida*

(New York: G. P. Putnam's Sons, 1885), 143–182. For a history of modern tourism, see Marguerite Shaffer, *See America First: Tourism and National Identity, 1880–1940* (Washington, D.C.: Smithsonian Institution Press, 2001).

5. "Excursion to St. Augustine," *Daily Florida Union*, 10 March 1876; "An Indian Raid on Hampton Institute," *Southern Workman* 7 (May 1878): 36; Richard Pratt to A. Richardson, 15 June 1875, Box 14, Folder 493a, Richard Henry Pratt Papers, Beinecke Library; Richard Pratt to Adjutant General, 17 July 1875, Box 14, Folder 490, Richard Henry Pratt Papers, Beinecke Library; William T. Sherman to Richard Pratt, 5 January 1877, Box 8, Folder 281, Richard Henry Pratt Papers, Beinecke Library; Richard Pratt to Jo Chapple, 11 February 1908, Box 10, Folder 352, Richard Henry Pratt Papers, Beinecke Library; General Order 51, 16 August 1875, Box 14, Folder 497, Richard Henry Pratt Papers, Beinecke Library; Joe F. Taylor, "The Indian Campaign on the Staked Plains, 1874–1875: Military Correspondence from the War Department, Adjutant General's Office, File 2815-1874, Conclusion," *Panhandle-Plains Historical Review* 35 (1962): 305; see also Frank L. Kalesnik, "Caged Tigers: Native American Prisoners in Florida, 1875–1888," *Journal of America's Military Past* 28 (Spring/Summer 2001): 60–76.

6. Sidney Lanier, *Florida: Its Scenery, Climate, and History*, a facsimile of the 1875 edition with introduction and index by Jerrell H. Shofner (Gainesville: University of Florida Press, 1973), 50–54; Sydney Lanier to Mary Day Lanier, 22 May 1875, in Charles Anderson, ed., *The Centennial Edition of the Works of Sidney Lanier* (Baltimore: Johns Hopkins University Press, 1945), 198.

7. Lanier, *Florida*, 52.

8. E. R. Townsend, "Aboriginal Junketing," *Daily Graphic* 10 (6 January 1876): 519; E. R. Townsend, "A City of the South," *Daily Graphic* 10 (30 March 1876): 239; Amy Caruthers, "The Indian Prisoners at St. Augustine," *The Christian at Work* 11 (23 August 1877): 678–679; Frank H. Taylor, "Indian Chiefs as Prisoners," *Daily Graphic* 16 (26 April 1878): 396; Karen Daniels Petersen, ed., *Plains Indian Art from Fort Marion* (Norman: University of Oklahoma Press, 1971), 40–41, 66–67, 75–76.

9. William T. Sherman to Richard Pratt, 10 January 1876, Box 8,

Folder 281, Richard Henry Pratt Papers, Beinecke Library; William E. Doyle to Richard Pratt, 27 March 1877, Box 2, Folder 67, Richard Henry Pratt Papers, Beinecke Library; Dorothy Dunn, ed., *1877: Plains Indian Sketch Books of Zo-tom and Howling Wolf* (Flagstaff, Ariz.: Northland Press, 1969), 10–11.

10. Richard H. Pratt, "The Florida Indian Prisoners of 1875 to 1878," Box 19, Folder 676, Richard Henry Pratt Papers, Beinecke Library; Richard H. Pratt, "American Indians, Chained and Unchained, Address before the Pennsylvania Commandery of the Military Order of the Loyal Legion at the Union League," (Philadelphia, Pa., 23 October 1912); Pratt, *Battlefield and Classroom*, 119–128.

11. Bear's Heart, "Indian Talk," *Southern Workman* 9 (July 1880): 77; *Florida Weekly Press*, 4 March 1876.

12. Pratt, *Battlefield and Classroom*, 119–128; Richard H. Pratt to Adjutant General, 17 July 1875, Box 14, Folder 490, Richard Henry Pratt Papers, Beinecke Library; Peterson, *Plains Indian Art from Fort Marion*, 40–41, 66–67; Roman Nose, "Experiences of H. C. Roman Nose," 1; see also Karen Daniels Petersen, "The Writings of Henry Roman Nose," *Chronicles of Oklahoma* 42 (Winter 1964–65): 458–478.

13. Richard Pratt to J. A. Covington, 15 August 1875, Cheyenne-Arapaho Indian Prisoners Vertical File, Section X, Oklahoma Historical Society; John Miles to Richard Pratt, 23 August 1876, Box 6, Folder 198, Richard Henry Pratt Papers, Beinecke Library.

14. Richard Pratt to John Miles, 24 July 1875, Cheyenne-Arapaho Indian Prisoners Vertical File, Section X, Oklahoma Historical Society; Richard Pratt to J. A. Covington, August 15, 1875, Cheyenne-Arapaho Indian Prisoners Vertical File, Section X, Oklahoma Historical Society; John Miles to Richard Pratt, August 23, 1876, Box 6, Folder 198, Richard Henry Pratt Papers, Beinecke Library; James Haworth to Richard Pratt, 20 June 1877, Box 8, Folder 331, Richard Henry Pratt Papers, Beinecke Library; George Fox to Henry Field, 15 January 1877, Box 14, 493a, Richard Henry Pratt Papers, Beinecke Library.

15. Pratt, *Battlefield and Classroom*, 120–121; Richard Pratt to Cornelius Agnew, 23 February 1876, in "Two Letters From Captain Pratt," *El Escribano* 10 (April 1973): 29–49; James W. Champney, "Home Correspondence," *Weekly Transcript*, 2 April 1878; see also

Clyde Ellis, *A Dancing People: Powwow Culture on the Southern Plains* (Lawrence: University Press of Kansas, 2003).

16. "Fourth of July Celebration in St. Augustine," *The Florida Press*, 10 July 1875; anonymous, "Petals Plucked from Sunny Climes," n.d., Box 17, Folder 577, Richard Henry Pratt Papers, Beinecke Library.

17. Wilbur S. Nye, *Carbine and Lance: The Story of Old Fort Sill* (Norman: University of Oklahoma Press, 1937), 250–253.

18. Nye, *Carbine and Lance*, 250–253. Mason Pratt, Richard Henry Pratt's son, called Nye's account a "cock and bull story"; see Mason Pratt to Wilbur S. Nye, 20 August 1943, Box 17, Folder 577, Richard Henry Pratt Papers, Beinecke Library.

19. Townsend, "Aboriginal Junketing," 519; anonymous, "The Regatta," n.d., Box 25, Folder 789, Richard Henry Pratt Papers, Beinecke Library; E. Adamson Hoebel and Karen Daniels Petersen, *A Cheyenne Sketchbook by Cohoe* (Norman: University of Oklahoma Press, 1964), 85–90.

20. Lizzie W. Champney, "The Indians at San Marco," *Independent* 30 (13 June 1878): 27–28; anonymous, "The Regatta," n.d., Box 25, Folder 789, Richard Henry Pratt Papers, Beinecke Library.

21. Champney, "The Indians at San Marco," 27–28; anonymous, "The Regatta," n.d., Box 25, Folder 789, Richard Henry Pratt Papers, Beinecke Library; "Fourth of July Celebration in St. Augustine," *The Florida Press*, 10 July 1875.

22. Champney, "The Indians at San Marco," 27–28; anonymous, "The Regatta," Box 25, Folder 789, Richard Henry Pratt Papers, Beinecke Library; "Fourth of July Celebration in St. Augustine," *The Florida Press*, 10 July 1875; Hoebel and Petersen, *A Cheyenne Sketchbook by Cohoe*, 67–69, 85–90; Indian Drawings, Box 23, Folder 735, Richard Henry Pratt Papers, Beinecke Library.

23. Roman Nose, "Experiences of H. C. Roman Nose," 1; J. Wells Champney, "Indian School at Fort Marion," *Harpers Weekly* 22 (11 May 1878): 373, 375; "Home Correspondence"; *Daily Florida Union*, 22 January 1876.

24. Richard H. Pratt, *The Indian Industrial School: Its Origin, Purposes, Progress and the Difficulties Surmounted* (Carlisle, Pa.: Hamilton County Library Association, 1908), 31–32; Pratt, *Battlefield and Classroom*, 184–185.

25. "About St. Augustine, Mostly," *Daily Florida Union*, 15 March 1877; Townsend, "Aboriginal Junketing," 519; *Florida Tri-Weekly Sun*, 24 February 1876; Richard Pratt to J. D. Miles, 3 January 1876, Cheyenne-Arapaho Indian Prisoners Vertical File, Section X, Oklahoma Historical Society.

26. "Excitement in St. Augustine," *The Florida Press*, 1 January 1876; Richard Pratt, "Address by Captain Pratt before the National Convention of Charities and Correction," (Denver Colo., 28 June 1892).

27. "Excursion to St. Augustine," *Daily Florida Union*, 11 March 1876; "The Grand Gala Day," *The Florida Press*, 18 March 1876; "The Comic Parade," *Daily Florida Union*, 6 July 1876; Caruthers, "The Indian Prisoners at St. Augustine," 678–679.

28. Harriet Beecher Stowe, "The Indians at St. Augustine," *Christian Union* 15 (18 April 1877): 345; *Christian Union* 15 (25 April 1877): 372–373; "State News," *The Weekly Floridian*, 22 May 1877; "About St. Augustine, Mostly," *Daily Florida Union*, 15 March 1877; W. H. Cushing stereogram, Box 23a, Folder 746, Richard Henry Pratt Papers, Beinecke Library; Richard Pratt to John Miles, 25 June 1875, Cheyenne-Arapaho Indian Prisoners Vertical File, Section X, Oklahoma Historical Society.

29. Mary D. Burnham, "A Story from Fort San Marco," *The Gospel Messenger and Church Journal*, April 1878, 221–223; "About St. Augustine, Mostly," *Daily Florida Union*, 15 March 1877; "Visitors to the Fort," *The Florida Press*, 5 June 1875; M. E. Winslow, "Taming the Savage," *New York Observer* 54 (9 March 1876): 77; Champney, "The Indians at San Marco," 27–28; Richard Pratt to Harriet Beecher Stowe, 30 April 1877, Box 10, Folder 341, Richard Henry Pratt Papers, Beinecke Library.

30. Pratt, "American Indians, Chained and Unchained"; Buffalo Meat Price List, Box 33, Folder 834, Richard Henry Pratt Papers, Beinecke Library; R. F. Sabate, Transcript, Josephine Burgess Jacobs, "Indian Prisoners at Fort Marion from 1875–1878," St. Augustine, 8 March 1949, in Indian Prisoner Files, St. Augustine Historical Society; Peterson, *Plains Indian Art from Fort Marion*, 65, 228–229.

31. Caruthers, "The Indian Prisoners at St. Augustine," 678–679.

32. J. D. Lopez to Richard Pratt, 23 January 1877, Box 14, Folder 493a, Richard Henry Pratt Papers, Beinecke Library; Richard Pratt to

F. T. Dent, 24 January 1877, Box 14, Folder 493a, Richard Henry Pratt Papers, Beinecke Library.

33. Winslow, "Taming the Savage," 77.

34. "About the Indians," *Florida Press*, 8 April 1876; Richard Pratt to John Miles, 27 March 1876, Cheyenne-Arapaho Indian Prisoners Vertical File, Section X, Oklahoma Historical Society; Report and Enclosures, 7 April 1876, Letters Received by the Office of Indian Affairs, Central Superintendency, Record Group 75, M234, Roll 68, National Archives and Records Administration; Alphonso Taft to the Secretary of Interior, 17 April 1876, Letters Received by the Office of Indian Affairs, Central Superintendency, Record Group 75, M234, Roll 68, National Archives and Records Administration; Pratt, *Battlefield and Classroom*, 147–153.

35. "About the Indians," *Florida Press*, 8 April 1876; Report, 1 May 1876, Letters Received by the Office of Indian Affairs, Central Superintendency, Record Group 75, M234, Roll 68, National Archives and Records Administration; Report and Enclosures, 7 April 1876, Letters Received by the Office of Indian Affairs, Central Superintendency, Record Group 75, M234, Roll 68, National Archives and Records Administration; Alphonso Taft to the Secretary of Interior, 17 April 1876, Letters Received by the Office of Indian Affairs, Central Superintendency, Record Group 75, M234, Roll 68, National Archives and Records Administration.

36. Pratt, *Battlefield and Classroom*, 147–153.

37. Pratt, *Battlefield and Classroom*, 147–153.

38. Pratt, *Battlefield and Classroom*, 150–151.

39. Pratt, *Battlefield and Classroom*, 151.

40. R. A. Speissegger, "The Last Indian Dance," Transcription, 1934, Western Indian Prisoners at Fort Marion, Miscellaneous File, St. Augustine Historical Society; Sabate, Transcript, in Indian Prisoner Files, St. Augustine Historical Society.

41. Report, 1 May 1876, Letters Received by the Office of Indian Affairs, Central Superintendency, Record Group 75, M234, Roll 68, National Archives and Records Administration; Richard Pratt to General Stark, 18 May 1876, Box 14, Folder 493a, Richard Henry Pratt Papers, Beinecke Library; *Daily Florida Union*, 24 April 1876.

42. "Indians Rising in St. Augustine," *Florida Tri-Weekly Sun*,

6 April 1876; see also "About the Indians," *The Florida Press*, 8 April 1876; "Rebellious Redskins," *St. Louis Republican* 17 April 1876.

43. "The St. Augustine Indians," *Daily Florida Union*, 11 April 1876; *Florida Tri-Weekly Sun*, 13 April 1876; Pratt, *Battlefield and Classroom*, 153.

44. Richard Pratt to General Stark, 18 May 1876, Box 14, Folder 493a, Richard Henry Pratt Papers, Beinecke Library; Richard Pratt to General Sheridan, 26 May 1876, Box 14, Folder 493a, Richard Henry Pratt Papers, Beinecke Library; Richard Pratt to General Sheridan, 31 July 1876, Box 14, Folder 493a, Richard Henry Pratt Papers, Beinecke Library; Report, 1 June 1876, Letters Received by the Office of Indian Affairs, Central Superintendency, Record Group 75, M234, Roll 68, National Archives and Records Administration.

45. "Fire at St. Augustine," *Daily Florida Union*, 18 July 1876; *Daily Florida Union*, 26 July 1876; Pratt, *Battlefield and Classroom*, 133–135.

46. Pratt, "American Indians, Chained and Unchained"; Richard Pratt to John Eaton, 23 January 1883, Box 10, Folder 342, Richard Henry Pratt Papers, Beinecke Library.

47. Pratt, *Battlefield and Classroom*, 134–135; *The Morning News*, 5 August 1876. For an introduction to black codes, see William Cohen, *At Freedom's Edge: Black Mobility and the Southern White Quest for Racial Control, 1861–1915* (Baton Rouge: Louisiana State University Press, 1991).

48. Pratt, "American Indians, Chained and Unchained"; Richard Pratt to Mary Pratt, 15 December 1877, Box 10, Folder 341, Richard Henry Pratt Papers, Beinecke Library; Pratt, *Battlefield and Classroom*, 121; see also Philip Deloria, *Playing Indian* (New Haven, Conn.: Yale University Press, 1999); L. G. Moses, *Wild West Shows and the Images of American Indians, 1883–1933* (Albuquerque: University of New Mexico Press, 1999); Joy S. Kasson, *Buffalo Bill's Wild West: Celebrity, Memory, and Popular History* (New York: Hill and Wang, 2000).

Chapter 5

1. Moira Harris, ed., *Between Two Cultures: Kiowa Art from Fort Marion* (Minneapolis: Pogo Press, 1989), 128–129; Janet Catherine Berlo, "Wo-Haw's Notebooks: Nineteenth Century Kiowa Indian Draw-

ings in the Collections of the Missouri Historical Society," *Gateway Heritage* 3 (February 1982): 3–13; Dana O. Jensen, "Wo-Haw: Kiowa Warrior," *Missouri Historical Society Bulletin* 7 (October 1950): 76–88.

2. Harris, ed., *Between Two Cultures: Kiowa Art from Fort Marion*, 9–25, 128; Karen Daniels Petersen, ed., *Plains Indian Art from Fort Marion* (Norman: University of Oklahoma Press, 1971), 90–91, 207–214; John Ewers, ed., *Murals in the Round: Painted Tipis of the Kiowa and Kiowa Apache Indians* (Washington, D.C.: Smithsonian Institution Press, 1978), 6–12, 33–34, 50–53; Kiowa POW File, Parker MacKenzie Collection, Oklahoma Historical Society; see also Hertha Dawn Wong, *Sending My Heart Back Across the Years: Tradition and Innovation in Native American Autobiography* (Norman: University of Oklahoma Press, 1989).

3. Richard H. Pratt, *Battlefield and Classroom: Four Decades with the American Indian, 1867–1904*, edited by Robert Utley (New Haven, Conn.: Yale University Press, 1964), 154–155; "The Indians," *The Florida Press*, 19 August 1876; Frank H. Taylor, "Indian Chiefs as Prisoners," *Daily Graphic* 16 (26 April 1878): 396; Mary D. Burnham, "A Story from Fort San Marco," *The Gospel Messenger and Church Journal*, April 1878, 221–223; Harriet Beecher Stowe, "The Indians at St. Augustine," *Christian Union* 15 (18 April 1877): 345.

4. Richard Henry Pratt, "The Florida Indian Prisoners of 1875 to 1878," Box 19, Folder 676, Richard Henry Pratt Papers, Beinecke Library; Richard Pratt to Adjutant General, 6 September 1875, Box 14, Folder 493a, Richard Henry Pratt Papers, Beinecke Library; J. Wells Champney, "Home Correspondence," *Weekly Transcript*, 2 April 1878; J. Wells Champney, "Indian School at Fort Marion," *Harper's Weekly* 22 (11 May 1878): 373, 375; Richard Henry Pratt, *The Indian Industrial School: Its Origin, Purposes, Progress and the Difficulties Surmounted* (Carlisle: Hamilton County Library Association, 1908), 8; Samuel C. Armstrong, *The Indian Question* (Hampton, Va.: Hampton Normal School Steam Press, 1883), 8–9.

5. Pratt, *Battlefield and Classroom*, 121, 220; Stowe, "The Indians at St. Augustine," 345; "A New Era for the Indians," *Hartford Daily Times*, 1 February 1879; Bear's Heart to S. A. Mather, 29 July 1878, in Samuel C. Armstrong, *Statement and Appeal in Behalf of Indian Education* (Hampton, Va.: Hampton Normal School Steam Press, 1878).

6. Richard H. Pratt, "American Indians, Chained and Unchained, Address before the Pennsylvania Commandery of the Military Order of the Loyal Legion at the Union League" (Philadelphia, Pa., 23 October 1912); Lizzie W. Champney, "The Indians at San Marco," *Independent* 30 (13 June 1878): 27–28; Richard Pratt to Phil Sheridan, 17 March 1876, Letters Received by the Office of Indian Affairs, Central Superintendency, Record Group 75, M234, Roll 68, National Archives and Records Administration; Joe F. Taylor, "The Indian Campaign on the Staked Plains, 1874–1875: Military Correspondence from the War Department, Adjutant General's Office, File 2815-1874, Conclusion," *Panhandle-Plains Historical Review* 35 (1962): 329–336; Mrs. George Gibbs, "Data About the Indians Who Came From the West," Typscript, 17 September 1932, Western Indian Prisoners at Fort Marion, Correspondence File, St. Augustine Historical Society.

7. Richard Henry Pratt to Cornelius Agnew, 23 February 1876, in "Two Letters From Captain Pratt," *El Escribano* 10 (April 1973): 29–49; Etahdleuh Doanmoe, "Anniversary Exercises at Hampton Institute," *Southern Workman* 8 (June 1879): 71–72; see also Arrell Gibson, "St. Augustine Prisoners," *Red River Valley Historical Review* 3 (1978): 259–270.

8. Henry B. Whipple, *Lights and Shadows of a Long Episcopate* (New York: Macmillan, 1902), 34; H. B. Whipple, "Mercy to Indians," *New York Daily Tribune*, 1 April 1876; Pratt, *Battlefield and Classroom*, 162–164; Herman Viola, ed., *Warrior Artists: Historic Cheyenne and Kiowa Ledger Art Drawn by Making Medicine and Zotom* (Washington, D.C.: National Geographic Society, 1998), 112–113, 122–123.

9. Amy Caruthers, "The Indian Prisoners at St. Augustine," *The Christian at Work* 11 (23 August 1877): 678–679; Broadside, Box 30, Folder 828, Richard Henry Pratt Papers, Beinecke Library.

10. Richard Pratt to Adjutant General, 6 September 1875, Box 14, Folder 493a, Richard Henry Pratt Papers, Beinecke Library; "The Indians," *The Florida Press*, 19 August 1876; Richard Pratt to James Forsyth, 18 December 1876, Box 10, Folder 341, Richard Henry Pratt Papers, Beinecke Library; J. D. Wells, "A Company of Christian Indians," in Box 28, Folder 805, Richard Henry Pratt Papers, Beinecke Library; Caruthers, "The Indian Prisoners at St. Augustine," 678–679; Burnham, "A Story from Fort San Marco," 221–223; Taylor, "The Indian Campaign," 329–330.

11. Richard Pratt to Frederick Dent, 6 January 1876, Box 14, Folder 493, Richard Henry Pratt Papers, Beinecke Library; Richard Pratt to Commissioner, 6 March 1877, Letters Received by the Office of Indian Affairs, Central Superintendency, Record Group 75, M234, Roll 69, National Archives and Records Administration; Petersen, *Plains Indian Art from Fort Marion*, 19; Whipple, *Lights and Shadows*, 34; Stowe, "The Indians at St. Augustine," 345; Pratt, *Battlefield and Classroom*, 121; see also Ruth Spack, *America's Second Tongue: American Indian Education and the Ownership of English* (Lincoln: University of Nebraska Press, 2002).

12. Richard Pratt to John Miles, 27 March 1876, Cheyenne-Arapaho Indian Prisoners Vertical File, Section X, Oklahoma Historical Society; Richard Pratt to Commissioner, 6 March 1877, Letters Received by the Office of Indian Affairs, Central Superintendency, Record Group 75, M234, Roll 69, National Archives and Records Administration; Taylor, "Indian Chiefs as Prisoners," 396; Helen Ludlow, "Incidents of Indian Life at Hampton," *Southern Workman* 8 (April 1879): 44; Spack, *America's Second Tongue*, 68; Champney, "Home Correspondence," 2 April 1878; Burnham, "A Story from Fort San Marco," 221–223; "An Indian Raid on Hampton Institute," *Southern Workman* 7 (May 1878): 36; Ludlow, "Incidents of Indian Life at Hampton," 44.

13. "Experiences of H. C. Roman Nose," *School News* 1 (January 1881), 1; Mary D. Burnham, "An Evening at San Marco," *The Gospel Messenger and Church Journal*, May 1878, 229–230; George Fox to Henry Field, 15 January 1877, Box 14, 493a, Richard Henry Pratt Papers, Beinecke Library; Harriet Beecher Stowe, "The Indians at St. Augustine, (part 2)" *Christian Union* 15 (25 April 1877): 372–373; see also Luke E. Lassiter, Clyde Ellis, and Ralph Kotay, *The Jesus Road: Kiowas, Christianity, and Indian Hymns* (Lincoln: University of Nebraska Press, 2002).

14. Alvin O. Turner, "Journey to Sainthood: David Pendleton Oakerhater's Better Way," *Chronicles of Oklahoma* 70 (Summer 1992): 116–143; Esther Baker Steele, "The Indian Prisoners at Fort Marion," *National Teachers Monthly* 3 (August 1877): 289–292; Pratt, *Battlefield and Classroom*, 180–183.

15. Richard Pratt to Adjutant General, 4 February 1877, Cheyenne-

Arapaho Indian Prisoners Vertical File, Section X, Oklahoma Historical Society; Turner, "Journey to Sainthood," 125.

16. Soaring Eagle, A Church Bulletin, Saint Augustine, 1 October 1877, Scrapbook, Box 26, Folder 799, Richard Henry Pratt Papers, Beinecke Library; Pam Oestricher, "On the White Man's Road? Acculturation and the Fort Marion Southern Plains Prisoners" (Ph.D. dissertation, Michigan State University, 1981), 64–65.

17. "Experiences of H. C. Roman Nose," *School News* 1 (December 1880): 1; "Experiences of H. C. Roman Nose (concluded)," *School News* 1 (March 1881): 1; Karen Daniels Petersen, "The Writings of Henry Roman Nose," *Chronicles of Oklahoma* 42 (Winter 1964–65): 458–478; Ellsworth Collings, "Roman Nose: Chief of the Southern Cheyenne," *Chronicles of Oklahoma* 42 (Winter 1964–65): 429–457.

18. *Eadle Keatah Toh* 1 (January 1880): 4; "An Indian Letter," *Eadle Keatah Toh* 1 (April 1880): 4; Wells, "A Company of Christian Indians."

19. Burnham, "A Story from Fort San Marco," 221–223; Richard Henry Pratt to Cornelius Agnew, 23 February 1876, in "Two Letters From Captain Pratt," *El Escribano* 10 (April 1973): 29–49; Eagle's Head to Cheyenne, 22 July 1876, Cheyenne-Arapaho Indian Prisoners Vertical File, Section X, Oklahoma Historical Society; Richard Pratt to Adjutant General, 4 February 1877, Cheyenne-Arapaho Indian Prisoners Vertical File, Section X, Oklahoma Historical Society; Steele, "The Indian Prisoners at Fort Marion," 289–292.

20. Richard Pratt to J. D. Miles, 12 July 1875, 5 April 1877, Cheyenne-Arapaho Indian Prisoners Vertical File, Section X, Oklahoma Historical Society; John Miles to Richard Pratt, 27 June 1876, Box 6, Folder 198, Richard Henry Pratt Papers, Beinecke Library; Gibson, "St. Augustine Prisoners," 259–270; Richard Pratt to Ranald Mackenzie, 30 August 1877, Box 10, Folder 341, Richard Henry Pratt Papers, Beinecke Library.

21. Petersen, *Plains Indian Art from Fort Marion*, 121–122; Pratt, *Battlefield and Classroom*, 154–155.

22. "Echoes from the Ancient City," *Daily Florida Union*, 29 March 1877; "More Echoes from the Ancient City," *Daily Florida Union*, 30 March 1877; "State Exchange Items," *Daily Florida Union*, 24 April 1877.

23. M. E. Winslow, "Taming the Savage," *New York Observer* 54 (9 March 1876): 77; see also Nancy Cott, *The Bonds of Womanhood: Woman's Sphere in New England* (New Haven, Conn.: Yale University Press, 1977).

24. "The Indians," *The Florida Press*, 19 August 1876.

25. Richard Pratt to Cornelius Agnew, 31 March 1876, in "Two Letters From Captain Pratt," *El Escribano* 10 (April 1973): 29–49; Richard Pratt to J. D. Miles, 3 January 1876, Cheyenne-Arapaho Indian Prisoners Vertical File, Section X, Oklahoma Historical Society; Pratt, *Battlefield and Classroom*, 126–127, 132.

26. Richard Pratt to John Eaton, 23 January 1883, Box 10, Folder 342, Richard Henry Pratt Papers, Beinecke Library; Pratt, "American Indians, Chained and Unchained"; Pratt, *Battlefield and Classroom*, 128–131; see also Robert A. Trennert, "From Carlisle to Phoenix: The Rise and Fall of the Indian Outing System, 1878–1930," *Pacific Historical Review* 52 (August 1983): 267–291.

27. Richard Pratt to Adjutant General, 21 March 1876, Box 14, Folder 493a, Richard Henry Pratt Papers, Beinecke Library; Richard Pratt to John Miles, 27 March 1876, Cheyenne-Arapaho Indian Prisoners Vertical File, Section X, Oklahoma Historical Society; Richard Pratt to John Eaton, 23 January 1883, Box 10, Folder 342, Richard Henry Pratt Papers, Beinecke Library; Burnham, "A Story from Fort San Marco," 221–223.

28. Richard Pratt to Philip Sheridan, 17 March 1876, Letters Received by the Office of Indian Affairs, Central Superintendency, Record Group 75, M234, Roll 68, National Archives and Records Administration; Richard Pratt to Philip Sheridan, 17 April 1876, Box 14, Folder 493a, Richard Henry Pratt Papers, Beinecke Library; Richard Pratt to J. W. Forsyth, 23 September 1876, Letters Received by the Office of Indian Affairs, Central Superintendency, Record Group 75, M234, Roll 69, National Archives and Records Administration; Richard Pratt to Commissioner, 6 March 1877, Letters Received by the Office of Indian Affairs, Central Superintendency, Record Group 75, M234, Roll 69, National Archives and Records Administration.

29. Champney, "The Indians at San Marco," 27–28.

30. Champney, "The Indians at San Marco," 27–28.

31. Richard Pratt to Phil Sheridan, 17 March 1876, Letters Re-

ceived by the Office of Indian Affairs, Central Superintendency, Record Group 75, M234, Roll 68, National Archives and Records Administration; E. D. Townsend to General John Pope, 5 April 1876, Letters Sent by the Office of the Adjutant General, Main Series, 1800–1890, Record Group 94, M565, Volume 59, Roll 46, National Archives and Records Administration; E. D. Townsend to R. H. Pratt, 27 June 1876, Letters Sent by the Office of the Adjutant General, Main Series, 1800–1890, Record Group 94, M565, Volume 59, Roll 46, National Archives and Records Administration; Taylor, "The Indian Campaign," 336–346.

32. Richard Pratt to Philip Sheridan, 1 May 1876, Box 14, Folder 493a, Richard Henry Pratt Papers, Beinecke Library; Richard Pratt to General Stark, 18 May 1876, Box 14, Folder 493a, Richard Henry Pratt Papers, Beinecke Library; Gibson, "St. Augustine Prisoners," 259–270.

33. Richard Pratt to Commissioner, 20 October 1876, Letters Received by the Office of Indian Affairs, Central Superintendency, Record Group 75, M234, Roll 67, National Archives and Records Administration; Richard Pratt to J. D. Miles, 5 April 1877, Cheyenne-Arapaho Indian Prisoners Vertical File, Section X, Oklahoma Historical Society; Richard Pratt to James Forsyth, 18 December 1876, Box 10, Folder 341, Richard Henry Pratt Papers, Beinecke Library; Stowe, "The Indians at St. Augustine," 345.

34. Richard Pratt to Adjutant General, 5 December 1876, Letters Received by the Office of Indian Affairs, Central Superintendency, Record Group 75, M234, Roll 68, National Archives and Records Administration; Richard Pratt to James Forsyth, 18 December 1876, Box 10, Folder 341, Richard Henry Pratt Papers, Beinecke Library; Richard Pratt to General, 8 April 1877, Box 10, Folder 341, Richard Henry Pratt Papers, Beinecke Library. In various reports, Pratt called the deceased "Starving Wolf" or "Shaving Wolf," though the names referred to the same person.

35. Report, 2 January 1877, Letters Received by the Office of Indian Affairs, Central Superintendency, Record Group 75, M234, Roll 69, National Archives and Records Administration; Richard Pratt to James Forsyth, 8 April 1877, Box 14, Folder 493, Richard Henry Pratt Papers, Beinecke Library; Richard Pratt to J. D. Miles, 5 April 1877, Cheyenne-Arapaho Indian Prisoners Vertical File, Section X, Oklahoma Historical Society.

36. Luis Arana and Eugenia Arana, eds., "Two Letters From Captain Pratt," *El Escribano* 10 (April 1973): 29–49; N. D. W. Miller to Richard Henry Pratt, Box 6, Folder 207, Richard Henry Pratt Papers, Beinecke Library; Pratt, *The Indian Industrial School*, 8, 36–37; Pratt, *Battlefield and Classroom*, 188–189, 326.

37. Steele, "The Indian Prisoners at Fort Marion," 289–292; J. D. Wells to Richard Pratt, 27 April 1877, 14 May 1877, Box 8, Folder 318, Richard Henry Pratt Papers, Beinecke Library; Pratt, *Battlefield and Classroom*, 180–183.

38. Burnham, "A Story from Fort San Marco," 221–223; Burnham, "An Evening at San Marco," 229–230; Turner, "Journey to Sainthood," 126–127.

39. Stowe, "The Indians at St. Augustine," 345; Stowe, "The Indians at St. Augustine, (part 2)," 372–373; Pratt, *Battlefield and Classroom*, 154–162; Susan A. Eacker, "Gender in Paradise: Harriet Beecher Stowe and Postbellum Prose on Florida," *Journal of Southern History* 64 (August 1998): 495–512.

40. Stowe, "The Indians at St. Augustine, (part 2)," 372–373.

41. Stowe, "The Indians at St. Augustine," 345; Stowe, "The Indians at St. Augustine (part 2)," 372–373.

42. Richard Pratt to James Forsyth, 8 April 1877, Box 14, Folder 493, Richard Henry Pratt Papers, Beinecke Library; Stowe, "The Indians at St. Augustine, (part 2)," 372–373.

43. Stowe, "The Indians at St. Augustine, (part 2)," 373.

44. Report, 26 June 1877, Letters Received by the Office of Indian Affairs, Central Superintendency, Record Group 75, M234, Roll 69, National Archives and Records Administration.

45. Pratt, *Battlefield and Classroom*, 130–131; Gibson, "St. Augustine Prisoners," 259–270.

46. Spencer Baird to Richard Pratt, 21 May 1877, 15 June 1877, Box 1, Folder 24, Richard Henry Pratt Papers, Beinecke Library; Pratt, *Battlefield and Classroom*, 130, 136–146; see also Curtis M. Hinsley, Jr., *Savages and Scientists: The Smithsonian Institution and the Development of American Anthropology, 1846–1910* (Washington, D.C.: Smithsonian Institution Press, 1981).

47. Spencer Baird to Commissioner of Indian Affairs, 1 June 1877, Roll 68, Letters Received by the Office of Indian Affairs, Central Super-

intendency, M234, Record Group 75, National Archives and Records Administration.

48. Rosemary Butler Hopkins, "Clark Mills: The First Native American Sculptor" (Master's Thesis, University of Maryland, 1966), 116–118; Spencer Baird to Richard Pratt, 15 June 1877, Box 1, Folder 24, Richard Henry Pratt Papers, Beinecke Library; Pratt, *Battlefield and Classroom*, 136–137; "The St. Augustine Indians in Plaster," *The Weekly Floridian*, 6 November 1877.

49. Spencer Baird, "Catalogue of Casts," in *Proceedings of the United States National Museum for 1878* (Washington, D.C.: U.S. Government Printing Office, 1878), 201; Pratt, *Battlefield and Classroom*, 137; Richard Pratt to James Forsyth, 20 August 1877, Box 10, Folder 341, Richard Henry Pratt Papers, Beinecke Library.

50. Clark Mills to Spencer Baird, 15 July 1877, in Hopkins, "Clark Mills," 227–228; "The St. Augustine Indians in Plaster," *The Weekly Floridian*, 6 November 1877; see also Hopkins, "Clark Mills," 116–118.

51. Clark Mills to Spencer Baird, 31 July 1877, in Hopkins, "Clark Mills," 229–232; Baird, "Catalogue of Casts," 201; Clark Mills to Richard Pratt, 16 December 1878, Box 6, Folder 212, Richard Henry Pratt Papers, Beinecke Library. Molds and full busts were subsequently fashioned by Joseph Palmer and were held by the Division of Ethnology until transferred in 1947 to the Division of Physical Anthropology. In 1879, Mills journeyed to Hampton Institution, Hampton, Virginia, to make life masks of forty-seven Indian children. The artist's phrenological interest spurred him in 1882 to make a life mask of Charles Guiteau, the assassin of President James Garfield; See the Smithsonian Institution, Physical Anthropology Acc. No. 6020, History of Item 30,676-739.

52. Pratt, "The Florida Indian Prisoners of 1875 to 1878"; Petersen, *Plains Indian Art from Fort Marion*, 3–93; Brent Ashabranner, *A Strange and Distant Shore: Indians of the Great Plains in Exile* (New York: Cobblehill Books, 1996), 28–39; Viola, *Warrior Artists*, 5–17; see also Jamake Highwater, *Many Smokes, Many Moons: A Chronology of American Indian History through Indian Art* (New York: J. P. Lippincott, 1978); Dorothy Dunn, ed., *1877: Plains Indian Sketch Books of Zotom and Howling Wolf* (Flagstaff, Ariz.: Northland Press, 1969); Evan M. Maurer, ed., *Visions of the People: A Pictorial History of Plains Indian Life* (Minneapolis: Minneapolis Institute of Art, 1992); Janet Ca-

therine Berlo, ed., *Plains Indian Drawings, 1865–1935: Pages from a Visual History* (New York: Harry B. Abrams, 1996).

53. When asked what the Fort Marion artists were trying "to tell" their audience, Parker McKenzie, a Kiowa historian and linguist, answered that they were "too mystifying" for him; see Parker McKenzie to Brent Ashabranner, 12 October 1994, Box 3, Folder 1, Parker McKenzie Collection, Oklahoma Historical Society.

Chapter 6

1. Richard Pratt to Adjutant General, 4 February 1877, Cheyenne-Arapaho Indian Prisoners Vertical File, Section X, Oklahoma Historical Society; Richard Pratt to Commissioner, 6 March 1877, Letters Received by the Office of Indian Affairs, Central Superintendency, Record Group 75, M234, Roll 69, National Archives and Records Administration; Joe F. Taylor, "The Indian Campaign on the Staked Plains, 1874–1875: Military Correspondence from the War Department, Adjutant General's Office, File 2815-1874, Conclusion," *Panhandle-Plains Historical Review* 35 (1962): 352–353; Arrell Gibson, "St. Augustine Prisoners," *Red River Valley Historical Review* 3 (1978): 259–270.

2. Richard Pratt to Commissioner, 6 March 1877, Letters Received by the Office of Indian Affairs, Central Superintendency, Record Group 75, M234, Roll 69, National Archives and Records Administration; Richard Pratt to J. D. Miles, 5 April 1877, Cheyenne-Arapaho Indian Prisoners Vertical File, Section X, Oklahoma Historical Society.

3. Ezra A. Hayt in *Report of the Commissioner of Indian Affairs for 1878* (Washington, D.C.: U.S. Government Printing Office, 1878), xxv–xxvi.

4. Richard Pratt to J. D. Miles, 5 April 1877, Cheyenne-Arapaho Indian Prisoners Vertical File, Section X, Oklahoma Historical Society; Richard Pratt to Frederick Dent, 7 April 1877, Box 14, Folder 493, Richard Henry Pratt Papers, Beinecke Library; Richard Pratt to James Forsyth, 8 April 1877, Box 14, Folder 493, Richard Henry Pratt Papers, Beinecke Library; Richard Pratt to General, 8 April 1877, Box 10, Folder 341, Richard Henry Pratt Papers, Beinecke Library; Richard Pratt to Anonymous, Box 9, Folder 340, Richard Henry Pratt Papers, Beinecke Library.

5. E. D. Townsend to Commander, 12 April 1877, Letters Sent by the Office of the Adjutant General, Main Series, 1800–1890, Record Group 94, M565, Volume 60, Roll 47, National Archives and Records Administration; James Haworth to William Nicholson, 4 May 1877, Letters Received by the Office of Indian Affairs, Kiowa Agency, Record Group 75, M234, Roll 382, National Archives and Records Administration; "Roaming the Prairies Wild," *Daily Florida Union*, 19 April 1877; "Returned from the Frontier," *Daily Florida Union*, 10 May 1877; "St. Augustine Press," *Weekly Floridian*, 29 May 1877.

6. Talks of the Kiowa, Comanche, and Apache Chiefs at a Council, 30 April 1877, Letters Received by the Office of Indian Affairs, Kiowa Agency, Record Group 75, M234, Roll 382, National Archives and Records Administration; James Haworth to William Nicholson, 4 May 1877, Letters Received by the Office of Indian Affairs, Kiowa Agency, Record Group 75, M234, Roll 382, National Archives and Records Administration.

7. James Haworth to Richard Pratt, 20 June 1877, Box 9, Folder 331, Richard Henry Pratt Papers, Beinecke Library.

8. John Hatch to James Haworth, 24 March 1877, Letters Received by the Office of the Adjutant General Main Series, 1871–1880, Record Group 94, M666, Roll 163, National Archives and Records Administration; William Nicholson to Commissioner, 26 June 1877, Letters Received by the Office of Indian Affairs, Central Superintendency, Record Group 75, M234, Roll 68, National Archives and Records Administration.

9. James Haworth to William Nicholson, 26 March 1877, Letters Received by the Office of Indian Affairs, Central Superintendency, Record Group 75, M234, Roll 68, National Archives and Records Administration.

10. J. K. Mizener to John Miles, 13 May 1877, Letters Received by the Office of Indian Affairs, Cheyenne and Arapaho Agency, Record Group 75, M234, Roll 122, National Archives and Records Administration; John Miles to William Nicholson, 12 May 1877, Letters Received by the Office of Indian Affairs, Cheyenne and Arapaho Agency, Record Group 75, M234, Roll 122, National Archives and Records Administration; Philip McCusker to Richard Pratt, 30 May 1877, Box 5, Folder 181,

Richard Henry Pratt Papers, Beinecke Library; Richard Pratt to J. D. Miles, 5 April 1877, Cheyenne-Arapaho Indian Prisoners Vertical File, Section X, Oklahoma Historical Society.

11. William Nicholson to Commissioner, Letters Received by the Office of Indian Affairs, Kiowa Agency, Record Group 75, M234, Roll 382, National Archives and Records Administration; S. A. Galpin to the Secretary of the Interior, 8 May 1877, Letters Received by the Office of the Adjutant General, Main Series, Record Group 94, M666, Roll 163, National Archives and Records Administration; Philip Sheridan endorsement, 18 April 1877, Box 14, Folder 493, Richard Henry Pratt Papers, Beinecke Library; Chief Clerk for William T. Sherman, 26 June 1877, Box 14, Folder 493, Richard Henry Pratt Papers, Beinecke Library.

12. Joyce Szabo, ed., *Howling Wolf and the History of Ledger Art* (Albuquerque: University of New Mexico Press, 1994), 85–121; Richard Pratt to Doctor, 19 April 1876, Box 14, Folder 493a, Richard Henry Pratt Papers, Beinecke Library; Lawrie Tatum, "Correspondence," *Friends' Review* 31 (1 June 1878): 667–668; Robert Taylor, "The Journey of Howling Wolf," *Boston Globe Magazine*, 11 April 1993, 10–17.

13. Taylor, "The Journey of Howling Wolf," 10–17.

14. Karen Daniels Petersen, ed., *Howling Wolf: A Cheyenne Warrior's Graphic Interpretation of His People* (Palo Alto, CA: American West Publishing Company, 1968), 21–30; Szabo, *Howling Wolf*, 85–121; Joyce B. Szabo, "A Case of Mistaken Identity: Plains Picture Letters, Fort Marion, and Sitting Bull," *American Indian Art Magazine* 16 (Autumn 1991): 48–55, 89; Taylor, "The Journey of Howling Wolf," 10–17.

15. Szabo, "A Case of Mistaken Identity," 48–55, 89; Petersen, *Howling Wolf*, 21–30; Szabo, *Howling Wolf*, 85–121.

16. Richard Pratt to J. D. Miles, 5 April 1877, Cheyenne-Arapaho Indian Prisoners Vertical File, Section X, Oklahoma Historical Society; Richard H. Pratt, *Battlefield and Classroom: Four Decades with the American Indian, 1867–1904*, edited by Robert Utley (New Haven, Conn.: Yale University Press, 1964), 130.

17. Richard Pratt to Mason Pratt, 10 December 1877, Box 10, Folder 341, Richard Henry Pratt Papers, Beinecke Library; Richard Pratt to Mary Pratt, 15 December 1877, Box 10, Folder 341, Richard Henry Pratt Papers, Beinecke Library; Pratt, *Battlefield and Classroom*, 126.

18. C. M. Bevan to Editor, 27 August 1877, Box 25, Folder 789, Richard Henry Pratt Papers, Beinecke Library.

19. Richard Pratt to Doctor, 5 December 1877, Box 10, Folder 341, Richard Henry Pratt Papers, Beinecke Library; Richard Pratt to Amy Caruthers, 7 December 1877, Box 10, Folder 341, Richard Henry Pratt Papers, Beinecke Library; Richard Pratt to Mason Pratt, 10 December 1877, Box 10, Folder 341, Richard Henry Pratt Papers, Beinecke Library; Richard Pratt to Mary Pratt, 15 December 1877, Box 10, Folder 341, Richard Henry Pratt Papers, Beinecke Library; Richard Pratt to Brother Caroll, 11 January 1878, Box 10, Folder 341, Richard Henry Pratt Papers, Beinecke Library.

20. *Weekly Floridian*, 23 October 1877; Richard Pratt to M. V. Sheridan, 16 October 1877, Letters Received by the Office of the Adjutant General, Main Series, Record Group 94, M666, Roll 163, National Archives and Records Administration; Karen Daniels Petersen, ed., *Plains Indian Art from Fort Marion* (Norman: University of Oklahoma Press, 1971), 52.

21. William T. Sherman to Secretary of War, 10 November 1877, Letters Sent by the Office of the Adjutant General, Main Series, Record Group 94, M565, Volume 61, Roll 48, National Archives and Records Administration; Ezra A. Hayt to Secretary of the Interior, 10 November 1877, Letters Received by the Office of the Adjutant General, Main Series, Record Group 94, M666, Roll 163, National Archives and Records Administration; A. Bell to Secretary of the Interior, 6 December 1877, Letters Received by the Office of the Adjutant General, Main Series, Record Group 94, M666, Roll 163, National Archives and Records Administration.

22. Richard Henry Pratt, "Address by Captain Pratt before the National Convention of Charities and Correction," (Denver Colo., 28 June 1892); Petersen, *Howling Wolf*, 22–23.

23. Lizzie W. Champney, "The Indians at San Marco," *Independent* 30 (13 June 1878): 27–28; Richard Pratt to Alice Pendleton, 6 January 1878, Box 10, Folder 341, Richard Henry Pratt Papers, Beinecke Library.

24. Richard Pratt to Commissioner, 23 August 1877, Letters Received by the Office of Indian Affairs, Central Superintendency, Record Group 75, M234, Roll 69, National Archives and Records Administra-

tion; Richard Pratt to Commissioner, 8 January 1878, Letters Received by the Office of Indian Affairs, Central Superintendency, Record Group 75, M234, Roll 69, National Archives and Records Administration; Pratt, *Battlefield and Classroom*, 187.

25. Richard Pratt to Alice Pendleton, 6 January 1878, Box 10, Folder 341, Richard Henry Pratt Papers, Beinecke Library; Richard Pratt, "An Indian Raid on Hampton Institute," *Southern Workman* 7 (May 1878): 36.

26. Amy Caruthers, "The Indian Prisoners at St. Augustine," *The Christian at Work* 11 (23 August 1877): 678–679; Pratt, "An Indian Raid on Hampton Institute," 36; Richard Pratt to Alice Pendleton, 6 January 1878, Box 10, Folder 341, Richard Henry Pratt Papers, Beinecke Library; Broadside, Box 30, Folder 828, Richard Henry Pratt Papers, Beinecke Library; "State News," *The Weekly Floridian*, 12 March 1878; Richard Pratt in "Indians at Hampton," *Friends' Review* 31 (11 May 1878): 613; Pratt, *Battlefield and Classroom*, 188–190.

27. Broadside, Box 30, Folder 828, Richard Henry Pratt Papers, Beinecke Library; Pratt, *Battlefield and Classroom*, 188–190.

28. Broadside, Box 30, Folder 828, Richard Henry Pratt Papers, Beinecke Library.

29. Richard Pratt to Commissioner, 6 March 1878, Box 10, Folder 341, Richard Henry Pratt Papers, Beinecke Library; Richard Pratt to Captain Atwood, 11 March 1878, Box 10, Folder 341, Richard Henry Pratt Papers, Beinecke Library; Ezra A. Hayt to Richard Pratt, 30 March 1878, Box 3, Folder 127, Richard Henry Pratt Papers, Beinecke Library; Pratt, *Battlefield and Classroom*, 190.

30. Winfield S. Hancock report, 27 March 1878, Letters Received by the Office of the Adjutant General Main Series, 1871–1880, Record Group 94, M666, Roll 164, National Archives and Records Administration; Richard Pratt to Colonel W. Mitchell, 15 March 1878, Box 10, Folder 341, Richard Henry Pratt Papers, Beinecke Library; Pratt, "An Indian Raid on Hampton Institute," 36; Pratt, *Battlefield and Classroom*, 120, 188.

31. Donal F. Lindsey, *Indians at Hampton Institute, 1877–1923* (Urbana: University of Illinois Press, 1995), 18–30; Samuel C. Armstrong, *The Indian Question* (Hampton, Va.: Hampton Normal School Steam Press, 1883), 8–9; Pratt, *Battlefield and Classroom*, 190.

32. Richard Pratt to E. A. Hayt, 27 March 1878, 23 April 1878, Letters Received by the Office of Indian Affairs, Central Superintendency, Record Group 75, M234, Roll 69, National Archives and Records Administration; Pratt, "An Indian Raid on Hampton Institute," 36; Lindsey, *Indians at Hampton Institute*, 18–30; Gibson, "St. Augustine Prisoners," 259–270.

33. Interior Department dispatch, 25 March 1878, Letters Received by the Office of the Adjutant General Main Series, 1871–1880, Record Group 94, M666, Roll 164, National Archives and Records Administration; War Department dispatch, 29 March 1878, Letters Received by the Office of the Adjutant General Main Series, 1871–1880, Record Group 94, M666, Roll 164, National Archives and Records Administration; Adjutant General dispatch, 5 April 1878, Letters Received by the Office of the Adjutant General Main Series, 1871–1880, Record Group 94, M666, Roll 164, National Archives and Records Administration.

34. Adjutant General dispatch, 8 April 1878, 10 April 1878, Letters Sent by the Office of the Adjutant General, Main Series, 1800–1890, Record Group 94, M565, Volume 61, Roll 48, National Archives and Records Administration; "Indians Rennovated," *New York Observer*, 24 April 1878; Pratt, *Battlefield and Classroom*, 191–192.

35. "The Indian Outlaws From Florida," *New York Times*, 15 April 1878.

36. "An Indian Raid on Hampton Institute," 36; Helen Ludlow, "Indian Education at Hampton and Carlisle," *Harper's New Monthly Magazine* 62 (April 1881): 659–675; Lindsey, *Indians at Hampton Institute*, 30–33.

37. James O'Beirne to Commissioner, 23 April 1878, Letters Received by the Office of Indian Affairs, Central Superintendency, Record Group 75, M234, Roll 69, National Archives and Records Administration; James O'Beirne telegrams, 14 April 1878, 16 April 1878, Letters Received by the Office of Indian Affairs, Central Superintendency, Record Group 75, M234, Roll 69, National Archives and Records Administration; "An Indian Raid on Hampton Institute," 36; Pratt, *Battlefield and Classroom*, 192; Gibson, "St. Augustine Prisoners," 259–270.

38. Amy Caruthers to Laura Gibbs, 20 June 1878, Western Indian Prisoners at Fort Marion, Miscellaneous File, St. Augustine Historical Society; "Incidents of Indian Life at Hampton," *Southern Workman* 8

(March 1879): 31–32; Petersen, ed., *Plains Indian Art from Fort Marion*, 242–243, 252–253, 258–259.

39. Mary D. Burnham, "Cheyennes, Kiowas, and Comanches," *Churchman* 38 (27 July 1878): 103; Zotom to Richard Pratt, 22 November 1878, Box 9, Folder 339, Richard Henry Pratt Papers, Beinecke Library; John B. Wicks to Richard Pratt, 14 January 1879, Box 9, Folder 328, Richard Henry Pratt Papers, Beinecke Library; "About Three of the Florida Boys," *Eadle Keatah Toh* 2 (September 1881), 2, 4; Alvin O. Turner, "Journey to Sainthood: David Pendleton Oakerhater's Better Way," *Chronicles of Oklahoma* 70 (Summer 1992): 116–143.

40. "Anniversary Day at Hampton," *Southern Workman* 7 (June 1878): 46; Samuel Armstrong, "Indians," *Southern Workman* 7 (June 1878): 44; Helen Ludlow, "Record of Indian Progress," *Southern Workman* 8 (May 1879): 55; Ludlow, "Indian Education at Hampton and Carlisle," 659–675; Helen Ludlow, *Ten Years Work for Indians at the Hampton Normal and Agricultural Institute, 1878–1888* (Hampton, Va.: Normal School Press, 1888), 9–10; Lindsey, *Indians at Hampton Institute*, 30–38; David Wallace Adams, "Education in Hues: Red and Black at Hampton Institute, 1878–1893," *South Atlantic Quarterly* 76 (Spring 1977): 159–176.

41. "Anniversary Day at Hampton," 46; Ludlow, "Indian Education at Hampton and Carlisle," 659–675; Richard Pratt to Mason Pratt, 25 May 1878, Box 18, Folder 617, Richard Henry Pratt Papers, Beinecke Library; "Indian Students at Hampton Normal," Scrapbook, 1878–1880, Box 26, Folder 799, Richard Henry Pratt Papers, Beinecke Library; Lindsey, *Indians at Hampton Institute*, 34.

42. Koba to Richard Pratt, 22 June 1879, Box 4, Folder 147, Richard Henry Pratt Papers, Beinecke Library; "Indians in Berkshire Co. Mass.," *Southern Workman* 8 (August 1879): 85; Richard Pratt, *The Indian Industrial School: Its Origin, Purposes, Progress and the Difficulties Surmounted* (Carlisle: Hamilton County Library Association, 1908), 8, 15–16; Petersen, *Plains Indian Art from Fort Marion*, 250; Lindsey, *Indians at Hampton Institute*, 33–38; Pratt, *Battlefield and Classroom*, 193–194.

43. Bear's Heart to Laura Gibbs, 6 April 1879, Western Indian Prisoners at Fort Marion, Miscellaneous File, St. Augustine Historical Society; Bear's Heart, "Indian Talk," *Southern Workman* 9 (July 1880):

77; Bear's Heart, "A Letter," *Southern Workman* 9 (December 1880): 129; Burton Supree, ed., *Bear's Heart: Scenes from the Life of a Cheyenne Artist of One Hundred Years Ago with Pictures by Himself* (Philadelphia: J.B. Lippincott, 1977), 56.

44. Ludlow, "Indian Education at Hampton and Carlisle," 659–675; Ludlow, *Ten Years Work for Indians*, 9–10; Petersen, *Plains Indian Art from Fort Marion*, 238; Richard Pratt to Mrs. Nellie Robertson Denny, 21 January 1908, Box 10, Folder 351, Richard Henry Pratt Papers, Beinecke Library; Pratt, *Battlefield and Classroom*, 195–215; Lindsey, *Indians at Hampton Institute*, 34–44.

45. Pratt, *Battlefield and Classroom*, 215–220; Evelyn C. Adams, *American Indian Education* (New York: King's Crown Press, 1946), 51–53; Louis Morton, "How the Indians Came to Carlisle," *Pennsylvania History* 29 (1962): 53–73; see also David Wallace Adams, *Education for Extinction: American Indians and the Boarding School Experience, 1875–1928* (Lawrence: University Press of Kansas, 1995).

46. Pratt, *The Indian Industrial School*, 9–10; Ludlow, "Indian Education at Hampton and Carlisle," 659–675; Ludlow, *Ten Years Work for Indians*, 9–10; Richard Henry Pratt, "American Indians, Chained and Unchained," Address before the Pennsylvania Commandery of the Military Order of the Loyal Legion at the Union League, (Philadelphia, Pa., 23 October 1912); Pratt, *Battlefield and Classroom*, 220–235; Turner, "Journey to Sainthood," 116–143.

47. Roman Nose, "From One of Our Cheyenne Boys," *Southern Workman* 9 (April 1880): 44; Samuel Armstrong, "Indian Education in the East," *Southern Workman* 9 (November 1880): 114; Ludlow, "Indian Education at Hampton and Carlisle," 659–675; Richard Pratt to Mrs. Nellie Robertson Denny, 21 January 1908, Box 10, Folder 351, Richard Henry Pratt Papers, Beinecke Library; Pratt, *The Indian Industrial School*, 8, 15–16; Pratt, *Battlefield and Classroom*, 227–267; Petersen, *Plains Indian Art from Fort Marion*, 258.

48. Roman Nose, "Roman Nose Goes to New York," *School News* 1 (September 1880): 1; Roman Nose, "Experiences of H. C. Roman Nose (continued)," *School News* 1 (January 1881), 1; Helen Ludlow to Richard Pratt, Box 5, Folder 174, Richard Henry Pratt Papers, Beinecke Library; see also Karen Daniels Petersen, "The Writings of Henry Roman Nose," *Chronicles of Oklahoma* 42 (Winter 1964–65): 458–478.

49. Tsaitkopeta to Richard Pratt, 16 December 1881, Box 8, Folder 303, Richard Henry Pratt Papers, Beinecke Library; Petersen, *Plains Indian Art from Fort Marion*, 252–253.

50. Tsaitkopeta to Richard Pratt, Box 8, Folder 303, Richard Henry Pratt Papers, Beinecke Library.

51. For a scholarly study of the vision quest, see Lee Irwin, *The Dream Seekers: Native American Visionary Traditions of the Great Plains* (Norman: University of Oklahoma Press, 1994).

Chapter 7

1. "St. Augustine Prisoners in Wichita," *Wichita Eagle*, 25 April 1878; "The Indian Reunion," *Wichita Eagle*, 2 May 1878; "Indians Return Home," *Southern Workman* 7 (June 1878): 44; John Miles to Richard Pratt, 23 May 1878, Box 6, Folder 198, Richard Henry Pratt Papers, Beinecke Library; Aulih to Etahdleuh, 26 May 1878, Box 30, Folder 820, Richard Henry Pratt Papers, Beinecke Library.

2. For the significance of language in Indian country, see Ruth Spack, *America's Second Tongue: American Indian Education and the Ownership of English* (Lincoln: University of Nebraska Press, 2002); Margaret Connell Szasz, *Education and the American Indian: The Road to Self Determination Since 1928*, 2nd ed. (Albuquerque: University of New Mexico Press, 1999).

3. *Southern Workman* 8 (February 1879): 19; P. B. Hunt to E. A. Hayt, 7 May 1878, Roll 383, Letters Received by the Office of Indian Affairs, Kiowa Agency, M234, Record Group 75, National Archives and Records Administration; Pam Oestricher, "On the White Man's Road? Acculturation and the Fort Marion Southern Plains Prisoners" (Ph.D. dissertation, Michigan State University, 1981), 262–263, 288.

4. James Mooney, *Calendar History of the Kiowa Indians, Seventeenth Annual Report of the Bureau of American Ethnology, 1895–1896*, Part 1 (Washington, D.C.: U.S. Government Printing Office, 1998; Reprinted Washington, D.C.: Smithsonian Institution Press, 1979), 328–346; Mildred Mayhill, *The Kiowas* (Norman: University of Oklahoma Press, 1962); see also Paul H. Carlson, "Indian Agriculture, Changing Subsistence Patterns, and the Environment on the Southern Great Plains," *Agricultural History* 66 (Spring 1992): 52–60.

5. P. B. Hunt to Richard Pratt, 12 February 1879, Box 4, Folder

116, Richard Henry Pratt Papers, Beinecke Library; *Southern Workman* 8 (February 1879): 19; J. W. Davidson to Assistant Adjutant General, 22 July 1878, Kiowa Agency, KA 47, Indian Archives Division, Oklahoma Historical Society; *Report of the Commissioner of Indian Affairs for 1878* (Washington, D.C.: U.S. Government Printing Office, 1878), 55–62; see also William T. Hagan, *Indian Police and Judges: Experiments in Acculturation and Control* (New Haven, Conn.: Yale University Press, 1966).

6. Philip McCusker to Richard Pratt, 11 April 1879, Box 5, Folder 181, Richard Henry Pratt Papers, Beinecke Library; P. B. Hunt to Richard Pratt, 12 February 1879, Box 4, Folder 116, Richard Henry Pratt Papers, Beinecke Library.

7. "Pathetic Letters from Indians," *Southern Workman* 8 (June 1879): 68.

8. *Southern Workman* 8 (February 1879): 19; Janet Catherine Berlo, "Wo-Haw's Notebooks: Nineteenth Century Kiowa Indian Drawings in the Collections of the Missouri Historical Society," *Gateway Heritage* 3 (February 1982): 3–13; Dana O. Jensen, "Wo-Haw: Kiowa Warrior," *Missouri Historical Society Bulletin* 7 (October 1950): 76–88; Karen Daniels Petersen, ed., *Plains Indian Art from Fort Marion* (Norman: University of Oklahoma Press, 1971), 207–214; Moira Harris, ed., *Between Two Cultures: Kiowa Art from Fort Marion* (Minneapolis: Pogo Press, 1989), 14–22.

9. *Eadle Keatah Toh* 2 (October 1881): 5, 6; *Eadle Keatah Toh* 1 (March 1881), 3; Samuel Armstrong, "Indian Education in the East," *Southern Workman* 9 (November 1880): 114; see also Petersen, *Plains Indian Art from Fort Marion*, 161–170, 248.

10. *Southern Workman* 8 (May 1879): 55–56; Petersen, *Plains Indian Art from Fort Marion*, 234; Donald J. Berthrong, *The Cheyenne and Arapaho Ordeal: Reservation and Agency Life in the Indian Territory, 1875–1907* (Norman: University of Oklahoma Press, 1976), 32–66.

11. Petersen, *Plains Indian Art from Fort Marion*, 228.

12. "Pathetic Letters from Indians," 68.

13. Lawrie Tatum, "Correspondence," *Friends' Review* 31 (1 June 1878): 667–668; John Miles to Richard Pratt, 23 May 1878, Box 6, Folder 198, Richard Henry Pratt Papers, Beinecke Library; Richard Henry Pratt, "Address by Captain Pratt before the National Convention

of Charities and Correction," (Denver, Colo., 28 June 1892); Petersen, *Plains Indian Art from Fort Marion*, 221–224; Karen Daniels Petersen, ed., *Howling Wolf: A Cheyenne Warrior's Graphic Interpretation of His People* (Palo Alto, Calif.: American West Publishing Company, 1968), 21–30; see also Joyce Szabo, ed., *Howling Wolf and the History of Ledger Art* (Albuquerque: University of New Mexico Press, 1994).

14. *Southern Workman* 8 (February 1879): 19; Charles Campbell to J. K. Misner, 16 July 1878, Letters Received by the Office of Indian Affairs, 1824–1881, Cheyenne and Arapaho Agency, Record Group 75, M234, Roll 123, National Archives and Records Administration.

15. Howling Wolf to Richard Pratt, 5 June 1879, Box 4, Folder 133, Richard Henry Pratt Papers, Beinecke Library; Petersen, *Howling Wolf*, 21–30.

16. John Miles to Richard Pratt, 26 October 1878, Box 6, Folder 198, Richard Henry Pratt Papers, Beinecke Library; "Still on the White Man's Road," *Southern Workman* 7 (December 1878): 95; "Incidents of Indian Life at Hampton," *Southern Workman* 8 (March 1879): 31–32; see also Szabo, ed., *Howling Wolf and the History of Ledger Art*.

17. "Incidents of Indian Life at Hampton," *Southern Workman* 8 (March 1879): 31–32; Marion Pratt Stevick, "Minimic," Box 22, Folder 722, Richard Henry Pratt Papers, Beinecke Library; Pratt, "Address by Captain Pratt."

18. Minimic to Richard Pratt, 26 January 1880, Box 5, Folder 188, Richard Henry Pratt Papers, Beinecke Library; Marion Pratt Stevick Essay, "Minimic," Box 22, Folder 722, Richard Henry Pratt Papers, Beinecke Library.

19. *Eadle Keatah Toh* 1 (September 1880): 3; *Eadle Keatah Toh* 1 (November 1880): 3; Petersen, *Plains Indian Art from Fort Marion*, 129–133, 244.

20. John Miles to Richard Pratt, 27 January 1882, Box 6, Folder 200, Richard Henry Pratt Papers, Beinecke Library; Burton Supree, ed., *Bear's Heart: Scenes from the Life of a Cheyenne Artist of One Hundred Years Ago with Pictures by Himself* (Philadelphia: J. B. Lippincott, 1977), 56–57.

21. *Eadle Keatah Toh* 2 (October 1881): 5, 6; John Miles to Richard Pratt, 25 February 1883, Box 6, Folder 200, Richard Henry Pratt Papers, Beinecke Library; Petersen, *Plains Indian Art from Fort Marion*, 236.

22. Roman Nose to John Miles, 3 November 1880, Cheyenne-Arapaho Indian Prisoners Vertical File, Section X, Oklahoma Historical Society; Richard Pratt to John Miles, 11 January 1881, Cheyenne-Arapaho Indian Prisoners Vertical File, Section X, Oklahoma Historical Society; John Miles to Richard Pratt, 9 March 1881, Box 6, Folder 199, Richard Henry Pratt Papers, Beinecke Library; John Miles to Richard Pratt, 28 November 1881, Box 6, Folder 199, Richard Henry Pratt Papers, Beinecke Library; Karen Daniels Petersen, "The Writings of Henry Roman Nose," *Chronicles of Oklahoma* 42 (Winter 1964–65): 458–478; Ellsworth Collings, "Roman Nose: Chief of the Southern Cheyenne," *Chronicles of Oklahoma* 42 (Winter 1964–65): 429–457.

23. Mary Burnham, "About Three of the Florida Boys," *Eadle Keatah Toh* 2 (September 1881): 2, 4; James Mooney, *The Ghost Dance Religion and Wounded Knee, Fourteenth Annual Report of the Bureau of Ethnology to the Smithsonian Institution, 1892–1893*, Part 2 (Washington, D.C.: U.S. Government Printing Office, 1896; Reprinted New York: Dover, 1973), 906–914; Alvin O. Turner, "Journey to Sainthood: David Pendleton Oakerhater's Better Way," *Chronicles of Oklahoma* 70 (Summer 1992): 116–143; Petersen, *Plains Indian Art from Fort Marion*, 178–182; see also Clyde Ellis, "We Don't Want Your Rations, We Want this Dance: Changing Use of Song and Dance on the Southern Plains," *Western Historical Quarterly* 30 (Summer 1999): 133–154.

24. *Eadle Keatah Toh* 2 (October 1881), 5, 6; Petersen, *Plains Indian Art from Fort Marion*, 180–186; see also Herman Viola, ed., *Warrior Artists: Historic Cheyenne and Kiowa Ledger Art Drawn by Making Medicine and Zotom* (Washington, D.C.: National Geographic Society, 1998); Oestricher, "On the White Man's Road," 247–291.

25. Burnham, "About Three of the Florida Boys," 2, 4; Turner, "Journey to Sainthood," 116–143; Petersen, *Plains Indian Art from Fort Marion*, 225–226.

26. Turner, "Journey to Sainthood," 132.

27. Making Medicine quoted in Turner, "Journey to Sainthood," 133.

28. Turner, "Journey to Sainthood," 116–143; John Miles to Richard Pratt, 31 May 1889, Box 6, Folder 200, Richard Henry Pratt Papers, Beinecke Library.

29. Etahdleuh, "His Two Years' Home Experience," *Morning Star*

5 (March 1885): 5; Petersen, *Plains Indian Art from Fort Marion*, 135–159; Oestricher, "On the White Man's Road," 89, 256–257.

30. Etahdleuh, "His Two Years' Home Experience," 5.

31. Mason Pratt to Richard Pratt, 8 July 1882, Box 17, Folder 579, Richard Henry Pratt Papers, Beinecke Library; Mason Pratt to Richard Pratt, 11 July 1882, Box 17, Folder 579, Richard Henry Pratt Papers, Beinecke Library; Mason Pratt's Notebook, Trip to Cheyenne and Kiowa Agencies, 1882, Box 17, Folder 579, Richard Henry Pratt Papers, Beinecke Library.

32. Mason Pratt to Anna Laura Pratt, 10 July 1882, Box 17, Folder 579, Richard Henry Pratt Papers, Beinecke Library.

33. *Eadle Keatah Toh* 2 (October 1881): 5, 6; John Miles to Richard Pratt, 16 February 1884, Box 6, Folder 200, Richard Henry Pratt Papers, Beinecke Library; L. M. W. Gibbs to Cheyenne Agency, 20 May 1885, Cheyenne-Arapaho Indian Prisoners Vertical File, Section X, Oklahoma Historical Society.

34. "Pathetic Letters from Indians," 68; Richard Pratt to John Eaton, 23 January 1883, Box 10, Folder 342, Richard Henry Pratt Papers, Beinecke Library; Richard H. Pratt, *Battlefield and Classroom: Four Decades with the American Indian, 1867–1904*, edited by Robert Utley (New Haven, Conn.: Yale University Press, 1964), 245–293; Arlene Feldmann Jauken, *The Moccasin Speaks: Living as Captive of the Dog Soldier Warriors* (Lincoln: Dageforde Publishing, 1998), 202; Joel Pfister, *Individuality Incorporated: Indians and the Multicultural Modern* (Durham: Duke University Press, 2004), 31–132.

35. "Etahdleuh Doanmoe," *Morning Star* 7 (May 1887): 8; Etahdleuh to Richard Pratt, 17 June 1886, Box 2, Folder 67, Richard Henry Pratt Papers, Beinecke Library; Petersen, *Plains Indian Art from Fort Marion*, 135–159; see also Mooney, *The Ghost Dance Religion and Wounded Knee*.

36. J. J. Methvin to Richard Pratt, 22 April 1888, Box 5, Folder 177, Richard Henry Pratt Papers, Beinecke Library; Petersen, *Plains Indian Art from Fort Marion*, 135–159.

37. *Southern Workman* 8 (February 1879): 19; Petersen, *Plains Indian Art from Fort Marion*, 111–127; Wilbur S. Nye, ed., *Bad Medicine and Good: Tales of the Kiowas* (Norman: University of Oklahoma Press, 1962), 109–110.

38. *Eadle Keatah Toh* 2 (October 1881): 5, 6; Petersen, *Howling Wolf*, 24–30; Szabo, *Howling Wolf and the History of Ledger Art*, 123–143.

39. Robert Utley in Pratt, *Battlefield and Classroom*, xiii–xix, 336; David Wallace Adams, *Education for Extinction: American Indians and the Boarding School Experience, 1875–1928* (Lawrence: University Press of Kansas, 1995), 307–333; Wilbert H. Ahern, "An Experiment Aborted: Returned Indian Students in the Indian School Service, 1881–1908," *Ethnohistory* 44 (Spring 1997): 263–304; Arrell Gibson, "St. Augustine Prisoners," *Red River Valley Historical Review* 3 (1978): 259–270; Pfister, *Individuality Incorporated*, 45.

40. Richard Henry Pratt, "American Indians, Chained and Unchained, Address before the Pennsylvania Commandery of the Military Order of the Loyal Legion at the Union League," (Philadelphia, Pa., October 23, 1912); Richard Pratt to H. M. Teller, 5 March 1906, Box 10, Folder 349, Richard Henry Pratt Papers, Beinecke Library.

41. Richard Pratt to John Miles, 18 November 1907, Box 10, Folder 350, Richard Henry Pratt Papers, Beinecke Library; Richard Pratt to Charles Himes, 26 January 1910, Box 1, PI 1-1-22, Carlisle Indian School Records, Cumberland County Historical Society; Adams, *Education for Extinction*, 321–328; Pratt, *Battlefield and Classroom*, 268–273.

42. "Incidents of Indian Life at Hampton," *Southern Workman* 8 (March 1879): 31–32; Oestricher, "On the White Man's Road," 283–284; Petersen, *Plains Indian Art from Fort Marion*, 252–253.

43. Petersen, *Plains Indian Art from Fort Marion*, 171–192; see also Omer C. Stewart, *The Peyote Religion: A History* (Norman: University of Oklahoma Press, 1987).

44. Richard Davis to Richard Pratt, 10 February 1897, Box 2, Folder 70, Richard Henry Pratt Papers, Beinecke Library; Collings, "Roman Nose" 429–457; Petersen, "The Writings of Henry Roman Nose," 458–478.

45. Petersen, *Plains Indian Art from Fort Marion*, 11, 215–220, 228–230, 234–237; E. Adamson Hoebel and Karen Daniels Petersen, eds., *A Cheyenne Sketchbook by Cohoe* (Norman: University of Oklahoma Press, 1964), 13–21; Oestricher, "On the White Man's Road," 252, 253–255, 260–261, 266; "Medicine Water," Standing Bird Family, John

Sipes Cheyenne Family Oral Histories as Transcribed by Barbara Landis, Cumberland County Historical Society; see also Brian Dippie, *The Vanishing American: White Attitudes and U.S. Indian Policy* (Middletown, Conn.: Wesleyan University Press, 1982).

46. Richard Pratt to U.S. Indian Agent, 29 October 1914, Cheyenne-Arapaho Indian Prisoners Vertical File, Section X, Oklahoma Historical Society; Robert Utley in Pratt, *Battlefield and Classroom*, xvii–xix; Adams, *Education for Extinction*, 321–328; see also Elaine Goodale Eastman, *Pratt: The Red Man's Moses* (Norman: University of Oklahoma Press, 1935).

47. Harris, *Between Two Cultures: Kiowa Art from Fort Marion*, 14–22; Petersen, *Plains Indian Art from Fort Marion*, 207–214; Benjamin Kracht, "The Kiowa Ghost Dance, 1894–1916: An Unheralded Revitalization Movement," *Ethnohistory* 39 (Winter 1992): 452–477; see also William C. Meadows, *Kiowa, Comanche, and Apache Military Societies: Enduring Veterans, 1800 to the Present* (Austin: University of Texas Press, 1999).

48. Petersen, *Howling Wolf*, 24–30; Szabo, *Howling Wolf and the History of Ledger Art*, 123–143.

49. Turner, "Journey to Sainthood," 116–143; Oestricher, "On the White Man's Road," 161, 261–262, 263–264; *Native American Celebration*, Brochure, Grace Church (Episcopal), Syracuse N.Y., 16 April 2005.

50. Petersen, *Plains Indian Art from Fort Marion*, 193–206; Frank L. Kalesnik, "Caged Tigers: Native American Prisoners in Florida, 1875–1888," (Ph.D. dissertation, Florida State University, 1992), 74–78.

51. *Eadle Keatah Toh* 2 (October 1881): 5, 6; Petersen, *Plains Indian Art from Fort Marion*, 161–170; Parker Mackenzie Notes on Kiowa POW's, Box 12, Folder 8, Parker MacKenzie Collection, Oklahoma Historical Society; Pfister, *Individuality Incorporated*, 127–131.

Epilogue

1. Frederick Hoxie, *A Final Promise: The Campaign to Assimilate the Indians, 1880–1920* (Lincoln: University of Nebraska Press, 1984); Jon Reyhner and Jeanne Eder, *American Indian Education: A History* (Norman: University of Oklahoma Press, 2004); Ruth Spack, *America's Second Tongue: American Indian Education and the Ownership of English* (Lincoln: University of Nebraska Press, 2002); For an overview of

American educational history, see David Nasaw, *Schooled to Order: A Social History of Public Schooling in the United States* (New York: Oxford University Press, 1979).

2. Diana S. Edwards, "In a World Not Their Own: Indian Prisoners at Fort Marion," *The East Florida Gazette* 16 (April 1996): 1–4; Frank L. Kalesnik, "Caged Tigers: Native American Prisoners in Florida, 1875–1888," (Ph.D. dissertation, Florida State University, 1992), 80–268; see also H. Henrietta Stockel, *Shame and Endurance: The Untold Story of the Chiricahua Apache Prisoners of War* (Tucson: University of Arizona Press, 2004).

3. James Auchiah, Notes on Indians at Fort Marion, St. Augustine Historical Society; F. Hilton Crowe, "Indian Prisoner–Students at Fort Marion," *The Regional Review* 5 (December 1940): 5–8, 30; Maggi Hall and the St. Augustine Historical Society, *Images of America: St. Augustine* (Charleston, S.C.: Arcadia, 2002), 49–72; see also James Auchiah, Box 22, Folder 719, Richard Henry Pratt Papers, Beinecke Library.

4. Mason D. Pratt to Missouri Historical Society, 20 July 1943, Box 17, Folder 572a, Richard Henry Pratt Papers, Beinecke Library; Stella M. Drum to Mason D. Pratt, 3 August 1943, Box 17, Folder 572a, Richard Henry Pratt Papers, Beinecke Library; Mason D. Pratt to Julien Yonge, 24 August 1943, Box 17, Folder 572a, Richard Henry Pratt Papers, Beinecke Library; Julien Yonge to Mason D. Pratt, 1 September 1943, Box 17, Folder 572a, Richard Henry Pratt Papers, Beinecke Library; Richard H. Pratt, *Battlefield and Classroom: Four Decades with the American Indian, 1867–1904*, edited by Robert Utley (New Haven, Conn.: Yale University Press, 1964).

5. Joan F. Denton, "Kiowa Murals," *Southwest Art* 17 (July 1987): 68–75; see also Arthur Silberman, "The Art of Fort Marion," *Native Peoples* 5 (Summer 1993): 32–39; Evan M. Maurer, ed., *Visions of the People: A Pictorial History of Plains Indian Life* (Minneapolis: Minneapolis Institute of Art, 1992).

6. "Bitter Memories at Castillo for Indians," *St. Augustine Record*, 27 February 1993; see also Western Indian Prisoners at Fort Marion, Miscellaneous File, St. Augustine Historical Society.

Bibliography

Archives

Beinecke Rare Book and Manuscript Library. New Haven, Conn.
   Wahnee Clark Papers
   George Fox Papers
   Richard Henry Pratt Papers
Cumberland County Historical Society. Carlisle, Pa.
   Carlisle Indian School Records
   John Sipes Cheyenne Family Oral Histories as Transcribed by
      Barbara Landis
Fort Sill National Historic Landmark. Fort Sill, Okla.
   Museum Collection
Hampton University. University Archives. Hampton, Va.
   Native American Collection
Kiowa Nation Cultural Museum. Anadarko, Okla.
   Mural Exhibition.
Missouri Historical Society. St. Louis, Mo.
   Wohaw Ledger Art
National Archives. Washington, D.C.
   Records of the Office of the Adjutant General
   Records of the Office of Indian Affairs
Oklahoma Historical Society. Oklahoma City, Okla.
   Indian Archives Division Files
   Parker MacKenzie Collection
Smithsonian Institution. Washington, D.C.
   Anthropological Archives

St. Augustine Historical Society. St. Augustine, Fla.
  James Auchiah Notes on Indians at Fort Marion
  Indian Prisoner Files
  Western Indian Prisoners at Fort Marion Files

Articles

Adams, David Wallace. "Education in Hues: Red and Black at Hampton Institute, 1878–1893." *South Atlantic Quarterly* 76 (Spring 1977): 159–176.

Ahern, Wilbert H. "An Experiment Aborted: Returned Indian Students in the Indian School Service, 1881–1908." *Ethnohistory* 44 (Spring 1997): 263–304.

Anthes, William. "The Indian's White Man." *Journal of the West* 40 (December 2001): 26–33.

Aquila, Richard. "Plains Indian War Medicine." *Journal of the West* 13 (April 1974): 19–43.

Arana, Luis R. and Eugenia B. Arana, eds. "Two Letters from Captain Pratt." *El Escribano* 10 (April 1973): 29–49.

Berlo, Janet Catherine. "Portraits of Dispossession in Plains Indian and Inuit Graphic Arts." *Art Journal* 49 (Summer 1990): 133–140.

———. "Wo-Haw's Notebooks: Nineteenth Century Kiowa Indian Drawings in the Collections of the Missouri Historical Society." *Gateway Heritage* 3 (February 1982): 3–13.

Burnham, Mary D. "Cheyennes, Kiowas, and Comanches." *Churchman* 38 (27 July 1878): 103.

———. "An Evening at San Marco," *The Gospel Messenger and Church Journal* (May 1878): 229–230.

———. "A Story from Fort San Marco," *The Gospel Messenger and Church Journal* (April 1878): 221–223.

Butler, G. "A Day Among the Kiowas and Comanches." *Catholic World* 23 (September 1876): 837–848.

Calloway, Colin G. "The Intertribal Balance of Powers on the Great

Plains, 1760–1850." *Journal of American Studies* 16 (April 1982): 25–47.

Carlson, Paul H. "Indian Agriculture, Changing Subsistence Patterns, and the Environment on the Southern Great Plains." *Agricultural History* 66 (Spring 1992): 52–60.

Caruthers, (Amy) Mrs. Horace. "The Indian Prisoners at St. Augustine." *The Christian at Work* 11 (23 August 1877): 678–679.

Champney, J. Wells. "Home Correspondence." *Weekly Transcript* (London). 2 April 1878.

———. "Indian School at Fort Marion." *Harper's Weekly* 22 (11 May 1878): 373, 375.

Champney, Lizzie W. "The Indians at San Marco." *Independent* 30 (13 June 1878): 27–28.

Collings, Ellsworth. "Roman Nose: Chief of the Southern Cheyenne." *Chronicles of Oklahoma* 42 (Winter 1964–65): 429–457.

Crowe, F. Hilton. "Indian Prisoner-Students at Fort Marion." *The Regional Review* 5 (December 1940): 5–8, 30.

Denton, Joan F. "Kiowa Murals." *Southwest Art* 17 (July 1987): 68–75.

Eacker, Susan A. "Gender in Paradise: Harriet Beecher Stowe and Postbellum Prose on Florida." *Journal of Southern History* 64 (August 1998): 495–512.

Edmunds, R. David. "Native Americans, New Voices: American Indian History, 1895–1995." *American Historical Review* 100 (June 1995): 717–740.

Edwards, Diana S. "In a World Not Their Own: Indian Prisoners at Fort Marion." *The East Florida Gazette* 16 (April 1996): 1–4.

Ellis, Clyde. "We Don't Want Your Rations, We Want this Dance: The Changing Use of Song and Dance on the Southern Plains." *Western Historical Quarterly* 30 (Summer 1999): 133–154.

Fear-Segal, Jacqueline. "Nineteenth-Century Indian Education: Universalism Versus Evolutionism." *Journal of American Studies* 33 (August 1999): 323–341.

———. "Use the Club of White Man's Wisdom in Defense of Our

Customs: White Schools and Native Agendas." *American Studies International* 40 (October 2002): 6–32.

Flores, Dan. "Bison Ecology and Bison Diplomacy: The Southern Plains from 1800 to 1850." *Journal of American History* 78 (September 1991): 465–485.

Gage, Duane. "Black Kettle: A Noble Savage?" *Chronicles of Oklahoma* 45 (1967): 244–251.

Gibson, Arrell Morgan. "St. Augustine Prisoners." *Red River Valley Historical Review* 3 (1978): 259–270.

Greene, Candace S. "Artists in Blue: The Indian Scouts of Fort Reno and Fort Supply." *American Indian Art Magazine* 18 (Winter 1992): 50–57.

Harmon, Alexandra. "When Is an Indian Not an Indian? The Friends of the Indians and the Problem of Indian Identity." *Journal of Ethnic Studies* 18 (Summer 1990): 95–123.

Hoxie, Frederick E. "Thinking Like an Indian: Exploring American Indian Views of American History." *Reviews in American History* 29 (March 2001): 1–14.

Hultgren, Mary. "American Indian Collections of the Hampton University Museum." *American Indian Art Magazine* 13 (Winter 1987): 32–39.

Jensen, Dana O. "Wo-Haw: Kiowa Warrior." *Missouri Historical Society Bulletin* 7 (October 1950): 76–88.

Kaestle, Carl F. "Ideology and American Educational History." *History of Education Quarterly* 22 (Summer 1982): 123–137.

Kalesnik, Frank L. "Caged Tigers: Native American Prisoners in Florida, 1875–1888." *Journal of America's Military Past* 28 (Spring 2001): 60–76.

Keller, Robert H. "American Indian Education: An Historical Context." *Journal of the West* 13 (April 1974): 75–82.

Kracht, Benjamin. "The Kiowa Ghost Dance, 1894–1916: An Unheralded Revitalization Movement." *Ethnohistory* 39 (Winter 1992): 452–477.

————. "Kiowa Powwows: Continuity in Ritual Practice." *American Indian Quarterly* 18 (Summer 1994): 321–348.

Leckie, William H. "The Red River War of 1874–1875." *Panhandle-Plains Historical Review* 29 (1956): 78–100.

Littlefield, Alice. "The BIA Boarding School: Theories of Resistance and Social Reproduction." *Humanity and Society* 13 (Winter 1989): 428–441.

Lomawaima, K. Tsianina. "Domesticity in the Federal Indian Schools: The Power of Authority over Mind and Body." *American Ethnologist* 20 (May 1993): 1–14.

Ludlow, Helen. "Indian Education at Hampton and Carlisle." *Harper's New Monthly Magazine* 62 (April 1881): 659–675.

Makofsky, Abraham. "Experience of Native Americans at a Black College: Indian Students at Hampton Institute, 1878–1923." *Journal of Ethnic Studies* 17 (Fall 1989): 31–46.

McBeth, Sally J. "Indian Boarding Schools and Ethnic Identity: An Example from the Southern Plains Tribes of Oklahoma." *Plains Anthropologist* 28 (Spring 1983): 119–128.

Medicine, Beatrice. "The Anthropologist as the Indian's Image Maker." *Indian Historian* 4 (Spring 1971): 27–29.

Miles, Nelson A. "The Indian Problem." *North American Review* 128 (March 1879): 304–314.

Mitchell, Michael Dan. "Acculturation Problems Among the Plains Tribes." *Chronicles of Oklahoma* 44 (Fall 1966): 281–289.

Morgan, Lewis Henry. "The Indian Question." *Nation* 29 (November 1878): 332–333.

Morton, Louis. "How the Indians Came to Carlisle." *Pennsylvania History* 29 (1962): 53–73.

Nash, Philleo. "The Education Mission of the Bureau of Indian Affairs." *Journal of American Indian Education* 3 (January 1964): 1–4.

Native American Celebration. Brochure. Grace Church (Episcopal). Syracuse, N.Y. 16 April 2005.

Pennington, William D. "Government Policy and Indian Farming on the Cheyenne and Arapaho Reservation: 1869–1880." *Chronicles of Oklahoma* 57 (Summer 1979): 171–189.

Petersen, Karen Daniels. "Cheyenne Soldier Societies." *Plains Anthropologist* 9 (August 1964): 146–172.

———. "The Writings of Henry Roman Nose." *Chronicles of Oklahoma* 42 (Winter 1964–65): 458–478.

Pratt, Richard Henry. "Indians at Hampton." *Friends' Review* 31 (11 May 1878): 613.

Quimby, George I. "Plains Art from a Florida Prison." *Chicago Natural History Museum Bulletin* 36 (October 1965): 1–4.

Rodee, Howard. "The Stylistic Development of Plains Indian Painting and Its Relationship to Ledger Drawings." *Plains Anthropologist* 10 (November 1965): 218–232.

Silberman, Arthur. "The Art of Fort Marion." *Native Peoples* 5 (Summer 1993): 32–39.

Sipes, John. "Ft. Marion POW Descendants Planning Activities for Spring." *Watonga Republican*. 22 January 2003.

Steele, Aubrey L. "Lawrie Tatum's Indian Policy." *Chronicles of Oklahoma* 22 (Spring 1944): 83–98.

Steele, Esther Baker. "The Indian Prisoners at Fort Marion." *National Teachers Monthly* 3 (August 1877): 289–292.

Stefon, Frederick J. "Richard Henry Pratt and His Indians." *Journal of Ethnic Studies* 15 (Summer 1987): 86–112.

Stowe, Harriet Beecher. "The Indians at St. Augustine." *Christian Union* 15 (18 April 1877): 345.

———. "The Indians at St. Augustine." *Christian Union* 15 (25 April 1877): 372–373.

Szabo, Joyce B. "A Case of Mistaken Identity: Plains Picture Letters, Fort Marion, and Sitting Bull." *American Indian Art Magazine* 16 (Autumn 1991): 48–55, 89.

———. "Chief Killer and a New Reality: Narration and Description in

Fort Marion Art." *American Indian Art Magazine* 19 (Spring 1994): 50–57.

———. "Mapped Battles and Visual Narratives: The Arrest and Killing of Sitting Bull." *American Indian Art Magazine* 21 (Autumn 1996): 64–75.

———. "Medicine Lodge Treaty Remembered." *American Indian Art Magazine* 14 (Autumn 1989): 52–59, 87.

———. "Shields and Lodges, Warriors and Chiefs: Kiowa Drawings as Historic Records." *Ethnohistory* 41 (Spring 1994): 1–24.

Taylor, Frank H. "Indian Chiefs as Prisoners." *Daily Graphic* 16 (26 April 1878): 396.

Taylor, Joe F. "The Indian Campaign on the Staked Plains, 1874–1875: Military Correspondence from the War Department, Adjutant General's Office, File 2815-1874." *Panhandle-Plains Historical Review* 34 (1961): 1–216.

———. "The Indian Campaign on the Staked Plains, 1874–1875: Military Correspondence from the War Department, Adjutant General's Office, File 2815-1874, Conclusion." *Panhandle-Plains Historical Review* 35 (1962): 215–368.

Taylor, Robert. "The Journey of Howling Wolf." *Boston Globe Magazine*, 11 April 1993, 10–17.

Townsend, E. R. "Aboriginal Junketing." *Daily Graphic* 10 (6 January 1876): 519.

———. "A City of the South." *Daily Graphic* 10 (30 March 1876): 239.

Trennert, Robert A. "From Carlisle to Phoenix: The Rise and Fall of the Indian Outing System, 1878–1930." *Pacific Historical Review* 52 (August 1983): 267–291.

Turner, Alvin O. "Journey to Sainthood: David Pendleton Oakerhater's Better Way." *Chronicles of Oklahoma* 70 (Summer 1992): 116–143.

Winslow, M. E. "Taming the Savage." *New York Observer* 54 (9 March 1876): 77.

Zwink, T. Ashley. "On the White Man's Road: Lawrie Tatum and the Formative Years of the Kiowa Agency, 1869–1873." *Chronicles of Oklahoma* 56 (Winter 1978–79): 431–441.

Books, Memoirs, and Pictographic Collections

Adams, David Wallace. *Education for Extinction: American Indians and the Boarding School Experience, 1875–1928*. Lawrence: University Press of Kansas, 1995.

Adams, Evelyn C. *American Indian Education*. New York: King's Crown Press, 1946.

Afton, Jean, Andrew E. Masich, David Fridtjof Halaas, Richard N. Ellis, eds. *Cheyenne Dog Soldiers: A Ledgerbook History of Coups and Combats*. Boulder: University Press of Colorado, 1997.

Anderson, Charles, ed. *The Centennial Edition of the Works of Sidney Lanier*. Baltimore: Johns Hopkins University Press, 1945.

Andrist, Ralph K. *The Long Death: The Last Days of the Plains Indians*. New York: Collier Books, 1964.

Armstrong, Samuel C. *The Indian Question*. Hampton, Va.: Hampton Normal School Steam Press, 1883.

———. *Statement and Appeal in Behalf of Indian Education*. Hampton, Va.: Hampton Normal School Steam Press, 1878.

Ashabranner, Brent. *A Strange and Distant Shore: Indians of the Great Plains in Exile*. New York: Cobblehill Books, 1996.

Battey, Thomas C. *The Life and Adventures of a Quaker Among the Indians*. Boston: Lee and Shepard, 1875. Reprint Norman: University of Oklahoma Press, 1968.

Bederman, Gail. *Manliness and Civilization: A Cultural History of Gender and Race in the United States, 1800–1917*. Chicago: University of Chicago Press, 1996.

Berkhofer, Robert F. *The White Man's Indian: Images of the American Indian from Columbus to the Present*. New York: Alfred A. Knopf, 1978.

Berlo, Janet Catherine, ed. *Plains Indian Drawings, 1865–1935: Pages from a Visual History.* New York: Harry B. Abrams, 1996.

Berry, Brewton. *The Education of the American Indian: A Survey of the Literature.* Washington, D.C.: Government Printing Office, 1968.

Berthrong, Donald J. *The Cheyenne and Arapaho Ordeal: Reservation and Agency Life in the Indian Territory, 1875–1907.* Norman: University of Oklahoma Press, 1976.

———. *The Southern Cheyennes.* Norman: University of Oklahoma Press, 1963.

Bordewich, Fergus M. *Killing the White Man's Indian: Reinventing Native Americans at the end of the Twentieth Century.* New York: Anchor Books, 1996.

Boyd, Maurice, ed. *Kiowa Voices, Ceremonial Dance, Ritual, and Song.* 2 vols. Fort Worth: Texas Christian University Press, 1981.

Brooks, James F. *Captives and Cousins: Slavery, Kinship, and Community in the Southwest Borderlands.* Chapel Hill: University of North Carolina Press, 2002.

Brown, Dee. *Bury My Heart at Wounded Knee.* New York: Holt, Rinehart and Winston, 1970.

Calloway, Colin, ed. *Our Hearts Fell to the Ground: Plains Indian Views of How the West Was Lost.* New York: St. Martin's Press, 1996.

Carlson, Paul H. *The Plains Indians.* College Station: Texas A&M University Press, 1998.

Chalfant, William Y. *Cheyennes at Dark Water Creek: The Last Fight of the Red River War.* Norman: University of Oklahoma Press, 1997.

Child, Brenda. *Boarding School Seasons: American Indian Families, 1900–1940.* Lincoln: University of Nebraska Press, 1998.

Churchill, Ward. *Kill the Indian, Save the Man: The Genocidal Impact of American Indian Residential Schools in Perspective.* San Francisco: City Lights Books, 2005.

Cohen, William. *At Freedom's Edge: Black Mobility and the Southern White Quest for Racial Control, 1861–1915*. Baton Rouge: Louisiana State University Press, 1991.

Coleman, Michael. *American Indian Children at School, 1850–1930*. Jackson: University Press of Mississippi, 1993.

Corwin, Hugh, ed. *The Kiowa Indians: Their History and Life Stories*. Lawton, Okla.: privately published, 1958.

Cott, Nancy. *The Bonds of Womanhood: Woman's Sphere in New England*. New Haven, Conn.: Yale University Press, 1977.

Crawford, Isabel. *Kiowa, The History of a Blanket Indian Mission*. New York: Fleming H. Revell, 1915.

Davison, Kenneth E. *The Presidency of Rutherford B. Hayes*. Westport, Conn.: Greenwood Press, 1972.

Debo, Angie. *A History of the Indians of the United States*. Norman: University of Oklahoma Press, 1970.

Dejong, D. H. *Promises of the Past: A History of Indian Education in the United States*. Golden, Colo.: North American Press, 1993.

Deloria, Philip. *Playing Indian*. New Haven, Conn.: Yale University Press, 1999.

Deloria, Philip J. and Neal Salisbury, eds. *A Companion to American Indian History*. Malden, Mass.: Blackwell, 2002.

Deloria, Vine and Daniel Wildcat. *Power and Place: Indian Education in America*. Golden, Colo.: Fulcrum Press, 2001.

Dewhurst, William W. *The History of Saint Augustine, Florida*. New York: G. P. Putnam's Sons, 1885.

Dippie, Brian. *The Vanishing American: White Attitudes and U.S. Indian Policy*. Middletown, Conn.: Wesleyan University Press, 1982.

Donnelley, Robert G., ed. *Transforming Images: The Art of Silver Horn and His Successors*. Chicago: University of Chicago Press, 2001.

Dowd, Gregory Evans. *A Spirited Resistance: The North American*

Indian Struggle for Unity, 1745–1815. Baltimore: Johns Hopkins University Press, 1993.

Drinnon, Richard. *Facing West: The Metaphysics of Indian Hating and Empire Building*. Minneapolis: University of Minnesota Press, 1980.

Dunlay, Thomas. *Wolves for the Blue Soldiers: Indian Scouts and Auxiliaries with the United States Army, 1860–1890*. Lincoln: University of Nebraska Press, 1982.

Dunn, Dorothy. *American Indian Painting of the Southwest and Plains Areas*. Albuquerque: University of New Mexico Press, 1968.

Dunn, Dorothy, ed. *1877: Plains Indian Sketch Books of Zo-tom and Howling Wolf*. Flagstaff, Ariz.: Northland Press, 1969.

Eastman, Elaine Goodale. *Pratt: The Red Man's Moses*. Norman: University of Oklahoma Press, 1935.

Ellis, Clyde. *A Dancing People: Powwow Culture on the Southern Plains*. Lawrence: University Press of Kansas, 2003.

———. *To Change Them Forever: Indian Education at the Rainy Mountain Boarding School, 1893–1920*. Norman: University of Oklahoma Press, 1996.

Engs, Robert Francis. *Educating the Disfranchised and Disinherited: Samuel Chapman Armstrong and Hampton Institute, 1839–1893*. Knoxville: University of Tennessee Press, 1999.

Ewers, John, ed. *Murals in the Round: Painted Tipis of the Kiowa and Kiowa Apache Indians*. Washington, D.C.: Smithsonian Institution Press, 1978.

Fixico, Donald, ed. *Rethinking American Indian History*. Albuquerque: University of New Mexico Press, 1997.

Foucault, Michel. *Discipline and Punish: The Birth of the Prison*. Translated by Alan Sheridan. New York: Vintage, 1979.

Fritz, Henry E. *The Movement for Indian Assimilation, 1860–1890*. Philadelphia: University of Pennsylvania Press, 1963.

Fuchs, Estelle and Robert Havighurst. *To Live on this Earth: American Indian Education*. Garden City, N.Y.: Anchor Books, 1973.

Gibson, Arrell Morgan. *The American Indian: Prehistory to the Present*. Lexington, Mass.: DC Heath, 1980.

Graber, Kay, ed. *Sister to the Sioux: The Memoirs of Elaine Goodale Eastman, 1885–1891*. Lincoln: University of Nebraska Press, 1978.

Greene, Candace, ed. *Silver Horn: Master Illustrator of the Kiowas*. Norman: University of Oklahoma Press, 2002.

Greene, Jerome A. *Washita: The U.S. Army and the Southern Cheyenne, 1867–1869*. Norman: University of Oklahoma Press, 2004.

Hagan, William T. *Indian Police and Judges: Experiments in Acculturation and Control*. New Haven, Conn.: Yale University Press, 1966.

———. *Quanah Parker, Comanche Chief*. Norman: University of Oklahoma Press, 1993.

Haley, James L. *The Buffalo War: The History of the Red River Uprising of 1874*. Garden City, N.Y.: Doubleday, 1976. Reprint, Austin: State House Press, 1998.

Hall, Maggi, and the St. Augustine Historical Society. *Images of America: St. Augustine*. Charleston, S.C.: Arcadia, 2002.

Harris, Moira, ed. *Between Two Cultures: Kiowa Art from Fort Marion*. Minneapolis: Pogo Press, 1989.

Harrod, Howard L. *The Animals Came Dancing: Native American Sacred Ecology and Animal Kinship*. Tucson: University of Arizona Press, 2000.

———. *Renewing the World: Plains Indian Religion and Morality*. Tucson: University of Arizona Press, 1987.

Highwater, Jamake. *Many Smokes, Many Moons: A Chronology of American Indian History through Indian Art*. New York: J. P. Lippincott, 1978.

Hinsley, Jr., Curtis M. *Savages and Scientists: The Smithsonian Insti-*

tution and the Development of American Anthropology, 1846–1910. Washington, D.C.: Smithsonian Institution Press, 1981.

Hoebel, E. Adamson and Karen Daniels Petersen, eds. *A Cheyenne Sketchbook by Cohoe*. Norman: University of Oklahoma Press, 1964.

Hoig, Stan. *The Kiowas and the Legend of Kicking Bird*. Boulder: University Press of Colorado, 2000.

———. *The Sand Creek Massacre*. Norman: University of Oklahoma Press, 1977.

———. *Tribal Wars of the Southern Plains*. Norman: University of Oklahoma Press, 1993.

Holder, Preston. *The Hoe and Horse on the Plains: A Study of Cultural Development among North American Indians*. Lincoln: University of Nebraska Press, 1970.

Hoxie, Frederick. *A Final Promise: The Campaign to Assimilate the Indians, 1880–1920*. Lincoln: University of Nebraska Press, 1984.

Huff, Delores J. *To Live Heroically: Institutional Racism and American Indian Education*. Albany: State University of New York Press, 1997.

Hughes, J. Patrick. *Fort Leavenworth: Gateway to the West*. Topeka: Kansas State Historical Society, 2000.

Hultgren, Mary Lou and Paulette Fairbanks Molin. *To Lead and to Serve: American Indian Education at Hampton Institute, 1878–1923*. Virginia Beach: The Virginia Foundation for the Humanities and Public Policy, 1989.

Hutton, Paul Andrew. *Phil Sheridan and His Army*. Lincoln: University of Nebraska Press, 1985.

Irwin, Lee. *The Dream Seekers: Native American Visionary Traditions of the Great Plains*. Norman: University of Oklahoma Press, 1994.

Isenberg, Andrew. *Destruction of the Bison*. Cambridge: Cambridge University Press, 2000.

Jauken, Arlene Feldmann. *The Moccasin Speaks: Living as Captive of the Dog Soldier Warriors*. Lincoln: Dageforde Publishing, 1998.

Kasson, Joy S. *Buffalo Bill's Wild West: Celebrity, Memory, and Popular History*. New York: Hill and Wang, 2000.

Kavanagh, Thomas W. *Comanche Political History: An Ethnohistorical Approach, 1706–1875*. Lincoln: University of Nebraska Press, 1996.

Kehoe, Alice. *The Ghost Dance: Ethnohistory and Revitalization*. Fort Worth: Holt, Rinehart, and Winston, 1989.

Keller, Robert H. *American Protestantism and United States Indian Policy, 1869–1882*. Lincoln: University of Nebraska Press, 1983.

Klein, Kerwin Lee. *Frontiers of Historical Imagination: Narrating the European Conquest of Native America, 1890–1990*. Berkeley: University of California Press, 1997.

Kroeker, Marvin E. *Comanches and Mennonites on the Oklahoma Plains : A. J. and Magdalena Becker and the Post Oak Mission*. Winnipeg, MB: Kindred Productions, 1997.

Lanier, Sidney. *Florida: Its Scenery, Climate, History*. A facsimile of the 1875 edition with introduction and index by Jerrell H. Shofner. Gainesville: University of Florida Press, 1973.

Lassiter, Luke E., Clyde Ellis, and Ralph Kotay. *The Jesus Road: Kiowas, Christianity, and Indian Hymns*. Lincoln: University of Nebraska Press, 2002.

Leckie, William. *Military Conquest of the Southern Plains*. Norman: University of Oklahoma Press, 1963.

Libhart, Miles, ed. *Contemporary Southern Plains Indian Painting, An Exhibition Organized by the Indian Arts and Crafts Board of the United States Department of the Interior*. Anadarko, Okla.: Oklahoma Indian Arts and Crafts Cooperative, 1972.

Lindsey, Donal F. *Indians at Hampton Institute, 1877–1923*. Urbana: University of Illinois Press, 1995.

Lomawaima, K. Tsianina. *They Called It Prairie Light: The Story of Chilocco Indian School*. Lincoln: University of Nebraska Press, 1994.

Ludlow, Helen, ed. *Ten Years' Work for Indians at the Hampton Normal and Agricultural Institute, 1878–1888*. Hampton, Va.: Normal School Press, 1888.

Mann, Henrietta. *Cheyenne-Arapaho Education, 1871–1982*. Boulder: University Press of Colorado, 1997.

Mardock, Robert Winston. *The Reformers and the American Indian*. Columbia: University of Missouri Press, 1971.

Marriott, Alice. *Kiowa Years: A Study in Culture Impact*. New York: MacMillan, 1968.

———. *The Ten Grandmothers*. University of Oklahoma Press, 1945.

Martin, Joel W. *The Land Looks After Us: A History of Native American Religion*. New York: Oxford University Press, 1999.

Maurer, Evan M. *The Native American Heritage: A Survey of North American Indian Art*. Chicago: Art Institute of Chicago, 1977.

Maurer, Evan M., ed. *Visions of the People: A Pictorial History of Plains Indian Life*. Minneapolis: Minneapolis Institute of Art, 1992.

Mayhall, Mildred. *The Kiowas*. Norman: University of Oklahoma Press, 1962.

McBeth, Sally J. *Ethnic Identity and the Boarding School Experience of West-Central Oklahoma American Indians*. Washington, D.C.: University Press of America, 1983.

McCoy, Ronald, ed. *Kiowa Memories, Images From Indian Territory*. Santa Fe, N. Mex.: Morning Star Galley, 1987.

McMaster, Gerald and Clifford E. Trafzer, eds. *Native Universe: Voices of Indian America*. Washington, D.C.: National Museum of the American Indian, 2004.

McNickle, D'Arcy. *Native American Tribalism: Indian Survivals and Renewals*. New York: Oxford University Press, 1973.

———. *They Came Here First: The Epic of the American Indian*. New

York: Harper & Row, 1949. Reprint, New York: Octagon Books, 1975.

Meadows, William C. *Kiowa, Comanche, and Apache Military Societies: Enduring Veterans, 1800 to the Present*. Austin: University of Texas Press, 1999.

Miles, Nelson A. *Personal Recollections and Observations*. Chicago: Werner Co., 1896.

Momaday, N. Scott. *The Way to Rainy Mountain*. Albuquerque: University of New Mexico Press, 1969.

Monnett, John H. *Massacre at Cheyenne Hole: Lieutenant Austin Henely and the Sappa Creek Controversy*. Boulder: University Press of Colorado, 1999.

Moore, John. *The Cheyenne Nation: A Social and Demographic History*. Lincoln: University of Nebraska Press, 1987.

Moses, L. G. *Wild West Shows and the Images of American Indians, 1883–1933*. Albuquerque: University of New Mexico Press, 1999.

Nabokov, Peter. *A Forest of Time: American Indian Ways of History*. Cambridge: Cambridge University Press, 2002.

Nasaw, David. *Schooled to Order: A Social History of Public Schooling in the United States*. New York: Oxford University Press, 1979.

Nye, Wilbur S. *Carbine and Lance: The Story of Old Fort Sill*. Norman: University of Oklahoma Press, 1937.

Nye, Wilbur S., ed. *Bad Medicine and Good: Tales of the Kiowas*. Norman: University of Oklahoma Press, 1962.

Parsons, Elsie, ed. *Kiowa Tales*. New York: American Folklore Society, 1929.

Petersen, Karen Daniels, ed. *Howling Wolf: A Cheyenne Warrior's Graphic Interpretation of His People*. Palo Alto, CA: American West Publishing Company, 1968.

———. *Plains Indian Art from Fort Marion*. Norman: University of Oklahoma Press, 1971.

Pfister, Joel. *Individuality Incorporated: Indians and the Multicultural Modern.* Durham, N.C.: Duke University Press, 2004.

Pratt, Richard, H. *Battlefield and Classroom: Four Decades with the American Indian, 1867–1904.* Edited by Robert Utley. New Haven, Conn.: Yale University Press, 1964.

———. *The Indian Industrial School: Its Origin, Purposes, Progress and the Difficulties Surmounted.* Carlisle, Pa.: Hamilton Library Association, 1908.

Priest, Loring B. *Uncle Sam's Stepchildren: The Reformation of United States Indian Policy, 1865–1887.* New Brunswick, N.J.: Rutgers University Press, 1942.

Prucha, Francis Paul. *American Indian Policy in Crisis: Christian Reformers and the Indian, 1865–1900.* Norman: University of Oklahoma Press, 1976.

———. *The Great Father: The United States Government and the American Indians.* 2 vols. Lincoln: University of Nebraska Press, 1984.

Prucha, Francis Paul, ed. *Americanizing the American Indian: Writings by 'Friends of the Indian,' 1865–1900.* Cambridge, Mass.: Harvard University Press, 1973.

Reyhner, Jon and Jeanne Eder. *American Indian Education: A History.* Norman: University of Oklahoma Press, 2004.

Rickey, Don. *Forty Miles a Day on Beans and Hay: The Enlisted Soldier Fighting the Indian Wars.* Norman: University of Oklahoma Press, 1963.

Robinson, Charles M. *The Indian Trial: The Complete Story of the Warren Train Massacre and the Fall of the Kiowa Nation.* Spokane, Wash.: Arthur H. Clark, 1997.

Rothman, David. *The Discovery of the Asylum: Social Order and Disorder in the New Republic.* Boston: Little, Brown, 1971.

Shaffer, Marguerite S. *See America First: Tourism and National Identity, 1880–1940.* Washington, D.C.: Smithsonian Institution Press, 2001.

Silberman, Arthur, ed. *Making Medicine: Ledger Drawing Art from Fort Marion*. Oklahoma City: Center of the American Indian, 1984.

Smith, Sherry. *The View From Officers' Row: Army Perceptions of Western Indians*. Tucson: University of Arizona Press, 1990.

Spack, Ruth. *America's Second Tongue: American Indian Education and the Ownership of English*. Lincoln: University of Nebraska Press, 2002.

Stewart, Omer C. *The Peyote Religion: A History*. Norman: University of Oklahoma Press, 1987.

Stockel, H. Henrietta. *Shame and Endurance: The Untold Story of the Chiricahua Apache Prisoners of War*. Tucson: University of Arizona Press, 2004.

Supree, Burton, ed. *Bear's Heart: Scenes from the Life of a Cheyenne Artist of One Hundred Years Ago with Pictures by Himself*. Philadelphia: J. B. Lippincott, 1977.

Szabo, Joyce, ed. *Howling Wolf and the History of Ledger Art*. Albuquerque: University of New Mexico Press, 1994.

Szasz, Margaret Connell, ed. *Between Indian and White Worlds: The Cultural Broker*. Norman: University of Oklahoma Press, 1994.

———. *Education and the American Indian: The Road to Self Determination Since 1928*. 2nd edition. Albuquerque: University of New Mexico Press, 1999.

Tate, Michael L. *The Frontier Army and the Settlement of the West*. Norman: University of Oklahoma Press, 1999.

Tatum, Lawrie. *Our Red Brothers and the Peace Policy of President Ulysses S. Grant*. John Winston Co., 1899. Reprint, Lincoln: University of Nebraska Press, 1970.

Thornton, Russell. *We Shall Live Again: The 1870 and 1890 Ghost Dance Movements as Demographic Revitalization*. Cambridge: Cambridge University Press, 1986.

Trafzer, Clifford. *As Long as the Grass Shall Grow and Rivers Flow: A History of Native Americans*. New York: Harcourt, 2000.

Utley, Robert M. *Frontier Regulars: The United States Army and the Indian, 1866–1891.* New York: Macmillan, 1973.

——. *The Indian Frontier of the American West, 1846–1890.* Albuquerque: University of New Mexico Press, 1984.

Vanderwerth, W. C., ed. *Indian Oratory.* Norman: University of Oklahoma Press, 1971.

Viola, Herman, ed. *Warrior Artists: Historic Cheyenne and Kiowa Ledger Art Drawn by Making Medicine and Zotom.* Washington, D.C.: National Geographic Society, 1998.

Wade, Edwin L., ed. *The Arts of the North American Indian, Native Traditions in Evolution.* Tulsa, Okla.: Philbrook Art Center, 1986.

Wade, Edwin L. and Rennard Strickland. *Magic Images, Contemporary Native American Art.* Norman: University of Oklahoma Press, 1981.

Wallace, Ernest. *Ranald S. MacKenzie on the Texas Frontier.* College Station: Texas A&M University Press, 1993.

Wallace, Ernest and E. Adamson Hoebel. *The Comanches: The Lords of the South Plains.* Norman: University of Oklahoma Press, 1952.

Waterbury, Jean Parker, ed. *The Oldest City: St. Augustine Saga of Survival.* St. Augustine, Fla.: St. Augustine Historical Society, 1983.

Watkins, Laurel J. *A Grammar of Kiowa.* Lincoln: University of Nebraska Press, 1984.

West, Elliott. *The Contested Plains: Indians, Goldseekers, and the Rush to Colorado.* Lawrence: University Press of Kansas, 1998.

Whipple, Henry B. *Lights and Shadows of a Long Episcopate.* New York: Macmillan, 1902.

Witmer, Linda F. *The Indian Industrial School: Carlisle, Pennsylvania, 1879–1918.* Camp Hill, Pa.: Plank's Suburban Press, 1993.

Wong, Hertha Dawn. *Sending My Heart Back Across the Years: Tradition and Innovation in Native American Autobiography.* Norman: University of Oklahoma Press, 1989.

Wooster, Robert. *The Military and United States Indian Policy, 1865–1903*. New Haven, Conn.: Yale University Press, 1988.

———. *Nelson A. Miles and the Twilight of the Frontier Army*. Lincoln: University of Nebraska Press, 1996.

Government Publications

Mooney, James. *Calendar History of the Kiowa Indians, Seventeenth Annual Report of the Bureau of American Ethnology, 1895–1896*, Part 1. Washington, D.C.: U.S. Government Printing Office, 1898. Reprint, Washington, D.C.: Smithsonian Institution Press, 1979.

———. *The Ghost Dance Religion and Wounded Knee, Fourteenth Annual Report of the Bureau of Ethnology to the Smithsonian Institution, 1892–1893*, Part 2. Washington, D.C.: U.S. Government Printing Office, 1896. Reprint, New York: Dover, 1973.

National Parks Service. *Castillo de San Marcos: A Guide to Castillo de San Marcos National Monument Florida*. Handbook 149. U.S. Department of the Interior. Washington, D.C.: U.S. Government Printing Office, n.d.

Proceedings of the United States National Museum for 1878 Washington, D.C.: U.S. Government Printing Office, 1878.

Report of the Commissioner of Indian Affairs for 1875. Washington, D.C.: U.S. Government Printing Office, 1875.

Report of the Commissioner of Indian Affairs for 1876. Washington, D.C.: U.S. Government Printing Office, 1876.

Report of the Commissioner of Indian Affairs for 1877. Washington, D.C.: U.S. Government Printing Office, 1877.

Report of the Commissioner of Indian Affairs for 1878. Washington, D.C.: U.S. Government Printing Office, 1878.

Record of Engagements with Hostile Indians Within the Military Division of the Missouri from 1868 to 1882. Washington, D.C.: U.S. Government Printing Office, 1882.

Newspapers

Daily Florida Union
Daily Louisville Commercial
Eadle Keatah Toh (Carlisle)
Florida Sun
Florida Weekly Press
Frank Leslie's Illustrated Newspaper
Friends' Review
Indianapolis Journal
Indianapolis Sentinel
Kansas City Times
Leavenworth Daily Commercial
Louisville Courier-Journal
Morning News (Savannah)
New York Daily Tribune
New York Observer
New York Times
School News (Carlisle)
Southern Workman (Hampton)
St. Augustine Press
St. Augustine Record
St. Louis Daily Globe
St. Louis Daily Times
St. Louis Republican
Tarrytown Argus
Tri-Weekly Florida Union
Weekly Floridian
Wichita Eagle

Theses and Dissertations

Andrews, Richard Allen. "Years of Frustration: William T. Sherman, the Army, and Reform, 1869–1883." PhD diss., Northwestern University, 1968.

Greene, Candace S. "Women, Bison, and Coup: A Structural Analysis of Cheyenne Pictographic Art." PhD diss., University of Oklahoma, 1985.

Gilcreast, Everett A. "Richard Henry Pratt and American Indian Policy, 1877–1906: A Study of the Assimilation Movement." PhD diss., Yale University, 1967.

Hamley, Jeffrey Louis. "Cultural Genocide in the Classroom: A History of the Federal Boarding School Movement in American Indian Education, 1875–1920." PhD diss., Harvard University, 1994.

Hopkins, Rosemary Butler. "Clark Mills: The First Native American Sculptor." Master's thesis, University of Maryland, 1966.

Kalesnik, Frank L. "Caged Tigers: Native American Prisoners in Florida, 1875–1888." PhD diss., Florida State University, 1992.

Kracht, Benjamin R. "Kiowa Religion: An Ethnohistorical Analysis of Ritual Symbolism, 1832–1937." PhD diss., Southern Methodist University, 1989.

Mann, Henrietta. "Cheyenne-Arapaho Education, 1871–1982." PhD diss., University of New Mexico, 1982.

McBurney, Charles R. "A Study in Religious Education among the Comanche, Apache, and Kiowa Indians of Southwestern Oklahoma." Master's thesis, University of Kansas, 1948.

Moore, Ida C. "Schools and Education among the Kiowa and Comanche Indians, 1870–1940." Master's thesis, University of Oklahoma, 1940.

Muir, Margaret Rosten. "Indian Education at Hampton Institute and Federal Indian Policy: Solution to the Indian Problem." Master's thesis, Brown University, 1970.

Oestreicher, Pam. "On the White Man's Road? Acculturation and the Fort Marion Southern Plains Prisoners." PhD diss., Michigan State University, 1981.

Szabo, Joyce. "Ledger Art in Transition: Late Nineteenth and Early Twentieth Century Drawing and Painting on the Plains, with an

Analysis of the Work of Howling Wolf." PhD diss., University of New Mexico, 1983.

Waltman, Henry G. "The Interior Department, War Department, and Indian Policy, 1865–1887." PhD diss., University of Nebraska, 1962.

Wild, George P. "History of Education of the Plains Indians of Southwestern Oklahoma since the Civil War." PhD diss., University of Oklahoma, 1941.

Wilson, Terry Paul. "Panaceas for Progress: Efforts to Educate the Southern Cheyennes and Arapahoes, 1870–1908." Master's thesis, University of Oklahoma, 1965.

Index

Davidson, John W., 21, 26, 38, 176
Davis, Edmund J., 20
Davis, N. H., 125
Delano, Columbus, 27, 62
Dent, Frederick T., 78–79, 99, 103, 150
Dick, 42, 59
Dog soldiers, 13, 21–24, 28, 39, 70, 184, 190
Double Vision (Tozance), 40, 58, 63, 98
Dry Wood (Wyako), 99–100
Dunleavy, Sergeant, 150–151

Eagle's Head (Minimic), 39, 46–47, 55, 60, 74, 77–78, 87, 93, 99, 114, 123, 154, 157–58, 180–81, 190
Eaton, John, 121, 170
Edmunds, George F., 125
Edwards, K. D., 202
Eighth Cavalry, 23
Eleventh Cavalry, 41
Eleventh Infantry, 23, 156
Emmet, Robert, 50
Emory, C. D., 38
Episcopalian Church, 7, 121, 164, 167, 183–84, 193, 196
Ethnic cleansing, 4, 26

Faribault, Minn., 163
Fifth Infantry, 21–24, 52, 167
First Artillery, 58–59, 70, 79
Fort Cobb, 14
Fort Coffee, 4
Fort Concho, 20, 38
Fort Dodge, 21
Fort Laramie Treaty, 12
Fort Leavenworth, 4, 24–29, 41, 45–48
Fort Marion, 5–9, 28, 56–174, 176–80, 182, 186, 188, 199–203
Fort Reno, 18, 40, 153, 180

Fortress Monroe, 166
Fort Richardson, 19
Fort Sill, 6, 18, 20–29, 33–48, 67, 73, 150, 152, 154, 164, 174, 176, 195
Fort Snelling, 24
Fort Wallace, 85
Fort Wise Treaty of 1861, 12
Fourth Cavalry, 15, 20, 23, 41
Fox, George, 51, 60, 62, 75, 80, 98–100, 120
Fragrance (Quanah), 17, 30

German family, 22, 24, 28–32, 39, 85
Geronimo, 200
Ghost Dance, 189, 194–95
Gibbs, Julia, 108
Gibbs, Laura, 108, 187
Giving His Sister to Another Man (Madawith), 127
Good Talk (Tounkeuh), 58, 163, 177
Gourd Clan, 193
Grace Church (Syracuse, N.Y.), 167, 196
Grant, Ulysses S., 19, 20, 24, 27, 38, 67, 78, 118
Gravatt, J. J., 167
Gray Beard, 24, 46, 47, 54–55

Hail Stone (Owussait), 22, 85, 87, 163, 187
Haley, James L., 5
Hamilton, John, 62–63, 65, 68, 78
Hampton Institute, 7, 163, 164–68, 170–72, 176–77, 180–81, 195, 196
Hancock, Winfield S., 162, 171
Hatch, John P., 152
Haworth, James M., 25–26, 29–30, 43, 48, 67, 73, 151–53

CPSIA information can be obtained
at www.ICGtesting.com
Printed in the USA
FFOW03n1526120917
39881FF